To Save China, To Save Ourselves:
The Chinese Hand Laundry Alliance of New York

In the series
Asian American History and Culture,
edited by Sucheng Chan

Renqiu Yu

To Save China, To Save Ourselves

The Chinese Hand Laundry Alliance of New York

Temple University Press
Philadelphia

Temple University Press, Philadelphia 19122
Published 1992
Printed in the United States of America

The paper used in this publication meets the minimum requirements
of American National Standard for Information Sciences—
Permanence of Paper for Printed Library Materials, ANSI Z39.48-
1984

Library of Congress Cataloging-in-Publication Data
Yu, Renqiu, 1955–
    To save China, to save ourselves : the Chinese Hand Laundry
Alliance of New York / Renqiu Yu.
        p. cm. — (Asian American history and culture)
    Includes bibliographical references and index.
    ISBN 0-87722-996-1 (alk. paper)
    1. Chinese Hand Laundry Alliance of New York—History.
2. Laundry industry—New York (N.Y.)—History. 3. Chinese
Americans in business—New York (N.Y.)—History. I. Title.
II. Series: Asian American history and culture series.
HD9999.L383U639 1992
338.4′76481′097471—dc20   92-9205

"Laundry Song" by Wen I-to, p. v, from *Twentieth Century Chinese Poetry* by Kai-Yu Hsu. Copyright © 1963 by Kai-Yu Hsu. Used by permission of Doubleday, a division of Bantam Doubleday Dell Publishing Group, Inc.

Laundry Song (1923)

By Wen I-to

(One piece, two pieces, three pieces,)
Washing must be clean.
(Four pieces, five pieces, six pieces,)
Ironing must be smooth.

I can wash handkerchiefs wet with sad tears;
I can wash shirts soiled in sinful crimes.
The grease of greed, the dirt of desire . . .
And all the filthy things at your house,
Give them to me to wash, give them to me.

Brass stinks so; blood smells evil.
Dirty things you have to wash.
Once washed, they will again be soiled.
How can you, men of patience, ignore them!
Wash them (for the Americans), wash them!

You say the laundry business is too base.
Only Chinamen are willing to stoop so low?
It was your preacher who once told me:
Christ's father used to be a carpenter.
Do you believe it? Don't you believe it?

There isn't much you can do with soap and water.
Washing clothes truly can't compare with building warships.
I, too, say what great prospect lies in this—
Washing the others' sweat with your own blood and sweat?
(But) do you want to do it? Do you want it?

Year in year out a drop of homesick tears;
Midnight, in the depth of night, a laundry lamp . . .
Menial or not, you need not bother,
Just see what is not clean, what is not smooth,
And ask the Chinaman, ask the Chinaman.

I can wash handkerchiefs wet with sad tears,
I can wash shirts soiled in sinful crimes.
The grease of greed, the dirt of desire . . .
And all the filthy things at your house,
Give them to me—I'll wash them, give them to me!

Contents

Acknowledgments

I am especially grateful to the two dozen elderly Chinese laundrymen I interviewed, some of them several times each, for sharing their experiences with me and for giving me access to their documents, newspaper clippings, and pictures. I want to express my deep gratitude to Professor Marilyn B. Young, Professor David Reimers, and Mrs. Naomi B. Levine for their constant encouragement and unfailing support from the very inception of the research for my dissertation until the completion of this book. I am also indebted to Professors Thomas Bender, Patricia Bonomi, Vincent Carroso, Warren Dean, A. Tom Grunfeld, Molly Nolan, Carl Prince, and other members of the History Department at New York University, for their support, advice, and encouragement.

Special thanks are owed my friend John Kuo Wei Tchen, who introduced me to New York City and to the history of New York's Chinese community. Actually, it was Jack who suggested this subject to me, and his support and help were indispensable during the study. I wish to express my profound appreciation to Professor Sucheng Chan and Kim Vivier, whose superb editing made the publication of this book possible.

I am greatly indebted to Him Mark Lai, of the Chinese Historical Society of America; Wei Chi Poon, of the Asian American Studies Library, University of California, Berkeley; and An Chen, of the C. V. Starr East Asian Library, Columbia University, not only for helping me find many valuable documents but also for providing this help in a timely manner. I would like to thank Fay Chew, Charles Lai, Mei-li Lin, Mary Ting Yi Lui, Judith Wingsiu Luk, and Dorothy Rony—the staff members of the New York Chinatown History Museum (formerly the New York Chinatown History Project)—who were helpful whenever I showed up to explore their archives. I also thank Phyllis Deutsch, Harriet Jackson, Lynn Johnson, Annelise Orleck, Claire Potter, Nancy Robertson, and Suzanne Wasserman—my cheerful friends of the dissertation writing group at NYU—for reading the manuscript and for their insightful and constructive comments. I am truly grateful to Kalin Wang, whose help was indispensable in beating my deadlines. And I thank the State University of New York at Purchase for giving me support, both material and intellectual.

I alone am responsible for any shortcomings and errors that remain.

Chinese Names and Transliteration

Chinese names are given in the Chinese order: family name (surname) followed by given name, such as Chen Ke, Tan Lian'ai. The pinyin system is used in transliterations, with the following exceptions: (1) the names of well-known figures, such as Sun Yat-sen, Chiang Kai-shek, and Mao Tse-tung, for which widely accepted transliterations are commonly used; and (2) the Westernized names of a few Chinese Americans that have been used in English-language documents and newspapers, such as Eugene Moy and Thomas Tang. The English titles of Chinese-language newspapers—the *China Daily News*, *The Chinese Nationalist Daily*, and *The Chinese Vanguard*—are original.

To Save China, To Save Ourselves:
The Chinese Hand Laundry Alliance of New York

Introduction

This book documents and analyzes the experiences of a group of Chinese laundrymen and their reflections on these experiences. It focuses on the Chinese Hand Laundry Alliance of New York (CHLA), founded in 1933 and still in existence today. In recent years, more and more scholars have examined and presented the voices of people who have been ignored in past historical writings.[1] I chose the CHLA for my study because the organization had published some pamphlets and newsletters as well as a newspaper, the *China Daily News* (*CDN*). In addition to reading *CDN* page by page from its founding in 1940 to 1958, I conducted more than fifty oral history interviews with veteran CHLA members. On Sundays, while enjoying *dim sum* and green tea in Chinese restaurants, these old-timers, now in their sixties or seventies, told me their life stories, their hardships, and their struggles against discrimination and exploitation, as well as anecdotes about and gossip in the Chinese community of New York. Though these interviews helped me to understand better the CHLA and New York's Chinese community, I did not rely totally on them. Frequently, I used them to verify the information I gathered from old newspapers and other historical documents. But I tried to record these laundrymen's own reflections on their lives, and I cite many of their opinions in this study out of respect for their interpretations of their experiences and the belief that their voices should be integrated into historical writings. Like other scholars, I found that the immigrant press is a rich source for historical studies and that ordinary people are often articulate.[2] As Ronald Takaki puts it, the voices of those people who have previously been ignored "contain particular expressions and phrases with their own meanings and nuances, the cuttings from the cloth of languages."[3]

Many books in Chinese American history present only general information. Perhaps because of a scarcity of historical materials, the Chinese Americans in these books are almost always faceless and nameless.[4] Focusing on one organization and using information from old documents and oral history interviews, I present biographical sketches of some figures who were active in New York's Chinese community half a century ago. For a variety of reasons, many of my interviewees did not want to reveal their identities. Thus, those who have returned to China or died appear here under their real names, while those who are alive in New York remain anonymous. All quotations from the Chinese press and the oral history interviews are my translations from Chinese into English.

The Chinese laundryman is hardly a new subject. Most studies of the Chinese in the United States generally recognize that the hand laundry business was one of the most significant occupations among Chinese Americans for a century. Paul Siu's *The Chinese Laundryman: A Study of Social Isolation,*[5] a Ph.D. dissertation completed in 1953 and finally published in 1987, is the best book on the subject. Son of a laundryman and himself a Chinese laundry supply agent for two years, Siu was a native Taishanese who had numerous relatives and friends among Chicago's Chinese laundrymen; his "insider's" descriptions of Chinese laundrymen's lives have become invaluable sources for studying Chinese Americans in the United States.

One of Siu's important contributions is the concept of the "sojourner," an immigrant who does not take root. Because of the various restrictions imposed on them, he says, "the Chinese immigrants were driven to make a choice, and they founded the laundry as a form of accommodation to the situation. But, since its establishment [in the 1850s] the laundry has served to isolate the laundryman and, therefore, has created a type of personality which is directly contrary to the expectation of assimilation." Rather than become assimilated, the Chinese laundryman remained a sojourner, who, as Siu puts it, "clings to the culture of his own ethnic group as in contrast to the bicultural complex of the marginal man." A sojourner is "a stranger who spends many years of his lifetime in a foreign country without being assimilated by it."[6] The sojourner thesis assumes that exclusion and discrimination in the host society determined the Chinese laundrymen's sojourner mentality. Siu also assumes, though he does not explicitly state it, that culture is virtually static, unchanging or changing very little. Thus the laundrymen's sojourning behavior persisted in an immigrant society; according to Siu's analysis, the dream of returning to China as wealthy "Guests from Gold Mountain" lasted for more than a hundred years. As John Tchen argues, Siu presents the Chinese laundry-man's experience as a *variant* of the immigrant experience, rather than as a "deviant" type that does not fit the assimilation pattern of European immigrants.[7] The laundry, meanwhile, was an institution within an immigrant economy that both protected and isolated the Chinese.

Though significant and sophisticated, Paul Siu's approach has its limitations. The evidence I have uncovered adds some different dimensions to the laundrymen's experiences and is the basis for the new interpretations I offer in this study. I was very impressed by the CHLA members' own reflections on their experience in their campaign "to save China, to save ourselves." To the CHLA members, helping China resist Japan's invasion was the most important thing in their lives in the 1930s and 1940s, and that campaign also influenced their efforts to change the power structure in the Chinese community, their emotional ties with the homeland, their perception of the host society, and their self-image in American society. My interviewees proudly recalled their patriotic activities in the 1930s—donating money to China and campaigning to win American sympathy and support for China's struggle against Japan. Siu does not discuss this aspect of the Chinese experience.

The CHLA members, who were just as socially isolated as the laundry-men in Siu's study, did not passively accept the conditions that enforced their isolation. Rather, they made persistent efforts to change that situation and to improve their status in American society. At first they organized themselves to fight the city government's discriminatory policies, and later they linked their struggle for survival and basic dignity in American society to the national salvation movement in China.

While Siu's understanding of the Chinese laundrymen's isolated situation and their sojourner mentality was largely conditioned by the persistent exclusionary and discriminatory policies of the host society is an important insight into the Chinese laundrymen's experience, it also narrows his view. He fails to take into consideration how changes in the homeland affected the Chinese laundrymen's sojourner mentality. My study suggests that changes in U.S. policies regarding the Chinese in the United States, in the political and social conditions in China, and in Sino-American relations all had an impact on Chinese immigrants, but reactions to these changes varied considerably among individuals. Rather than treat the Chinese immigrants as a homogeneous group whose members all behaved in the same way, I emphasize the concrete conditions they faced and how different individuals responded to such changes. These historical factors sometimes strengthened and at other times modified the sojourner's homeland orientation, even though a sojourning mentality may have been the dominant tendency among first-generation Chinese in the United States.

In sociological studies of the Chinese in the United States, sweeping generalizations based on abstract assumptions are often used in place of careful analyses of historical evidence. While describing the Chinese laundryman as a sojourner who "clings to the culture of his own ethnic group," Paul Siu does not define that "culture." Indeed, such terms as "Chinese culture" or "Chinese tradition," which are complex and multidimensional, resist definition. While the dominant Confucian tradition emphasized authority, loyalty, and total obedience, numerous peasant uprisings in Chinese history represented an opposite tradition of struggling against repression and exploitation. The latter was as deeply rooted in Chinese society as was orthodox Confucianism. Moreover, in the twentieth century, foreign incursions led to the rise of nationalism and antitraditional sentiments. After the May Fourth Movement of 1919, anti-Confucianism itself became an integral part of the multiple traditions of twentieth-century China. In other words, seen in a proper historical context, "Chinese culture" is neither static nor singular; it defies a simplistic definition and requires careful analysis.

Rose Hum Lee, an acknowledged authority on Chinese Americans, recognizes this problem. Adopting Siu's sojourner thesis as an analytical framework for her work, she correctly points out that the Chinese in the United States were a heterogeneous group, and she attempts to identify the aspects of Chinese tradition that had been brought over and retained.[8] Though Lee urges scholars to study "Chinese civilization" carefully, however, she herself provides answers based on general impressions rather than solid empirical studies.[9]

Based on the CHLA's experiences in fighting the elite-dominated organizations in New York's Chinese community, I examine the conditions under which some outdated traits of Chinese tradition were retained in the United States. The patriarchal and authoritarian rule embodied in the power structure of the Chinese immigrant community in the late nineteenth and early twentieth centuries, for example, had been rejected by reform-minded Chinese in China itself but survived in the United States, a society upholding democratic principles in conflict with authoritarian values. I argue that while Chinese immigrants generally shared a common culture, certain individuals in the twentieth century were strongly influenced by revolutionary ideology, or at least the revolutionary terminology that had developed in China, and by particular American democratic ideas. Their efforts to improve their political and economic status in American society as well as to affect China's politics and Sino-American relations represent a different type of behavior. I further argue that conditions in the host society were determining factors in perpetuating authoritarian rule within the Chinese immigrant community, and that for first-generation Chinese immigrants, breaking the authoritarian rule in their own community was a first step in their efforts to integrate themselves into the larger society. Since the CHLA failed to change the power structure in the Chinese immigrant community, I also discuss factors in both the larger society and in the Chinese community that blocked and paralyzed those efforts.

Among the works dealing with New York's Chinese community, Peter Kwong's *Chinatown, New York*[10] is a groundbreaking study. Using a national approach to analyze the politics of and labor movement in New York's Chinatown between 1930 and 1950, Kwong suggests that Chinatowns in the United States have not been immune to changes in the larger society and that "the history of New York's Chinatown is one of ongoing class conflict between organizations representing the merchant elite and those serving the working class."[11] The so-called national approach, according to Kwong, assumes that there is a close correspondence between an ethnic group's treatment in the United States and the international standing of that group's homeland. While Siu reveals the sad and helpless isolation of the Chinese laundrymen, Kwong indicates that the U.S. government–sanctioned exclusionary policy did not guarantee any excluded ethnic group total immunity from the influences of the larger society. Nevertheless, in this exploratory work, Kwong discusses more scenes than actors and gives few solid details. We learn more about the historical background than the Chinese Americans themselves.[12] In contrast, I make a special effort to present the Chinese laundrymen's own perspectives and to place them at center stage.

Chapter One traces the early history of the Chinese hand laundries in New York City, discusses the larger social environment in which the laundrymen lived, and analyzes the internal structure of the Chinese community and the relationship between the laundrymen and traditional community organizations. It suggests that while the clan/family associations provided some basic services and protection for the Chinese in a hostile environment, such associations also had a patriarchal and authoritarian structure inherited from China, dominated by wealthy and conservative figures. Because Chinese immigrants were forced to fall back on their ethnic community, institutionalized racism helped to perpetuate the most repressive Chinese traditions on American soil; it also allowed the dominant elite to exploit ordinary Chinese.

Chapter Two describes in detail the beginnings of the CHLA and discusses its significance in the context of Chinese American history. It examines the background of the Chinese laundrymen who founded the organization and describes the CHLA's victory in a legal battle against a discriminatory city ordinance. That success helped the organization establish itself in the Chinese community.

Chapter Three discusses the CHLA's efforts to make itself a democratic organization and the complex relationship between the laundrymen and the Chinese American left in the 1930s. It suggests that although the CHLA did not accept the left's Marxist ideology, it was influenced by the revolutionary ideas developed in China. Its members communicated with the left through a shared political language.

Chapters Four and Five focus on the CHLA's "to save China, to save ourselves" campaign and its "people's diplomacy" movement in the 1930s and 1940s. Chapter Four examines the idea of "to save China, to save ourselves" in detail and discusses the role of the CHLA in establishing the New York Overseas Chinese United Front to support China's resistance against Japan's invasion. The experiences of the Chinese in New York indicate that a new kind of nationalism had developed among overseas Chinese by the 1930s and 1940s: overseas Chinese began to see themselves more as participants in saving China and in building a democratic new China than as passive monetary donors. One section of this chapter documents the founding of the CHLA's newspaper, the *China Daily News*.

Chapter Five shows that the slogan "to save China, to save ourselves" clearly related Chinese Americans' nationalistic campaigns to their struggle for survival in American society and explores the meaning and accomplishments of the CHLA's "people's diplomacy." It argues that the CHLA tried to present a new image of the Chinese to the American public. This chapter also reveals that the people's diplomacy movement expanded the scope of the Chinese laundrymen's concerns. They began to relate their experiences to those of African Americans and called for solidarity with African Americans in a common struggle for equality. Meanwhile, the group identity of the CHLA members was enhanced. The final section in this chapter discusses the CHLA's appeal and its response to the repeal of all the Chinese exclusion acts in 1943.[13]

Chapter Six deals with a complex struggle between the hand laundrymen and the Chinese power laundry owners in the late 1940s. This chapter examines in detail the class relations and class struggle between the hand laundries and the power laundries within the Chinese laundry business; the function and application of the concept of ethnic solidarity in the Chinese community; the interplay of internal class struggle and external racial discrimination and its impact on Chinese Americans; and why the CHLA, a self-styled "progressive" organization that tried to integrate itself into the larger society, rejected the white labor unions.

Chapter Seven analyzes the nature of the CHLA's criticism of the Kuomintang (Chinese Nationalist) government in the 1940s, the factors that affected the CHLA members' plans whether to return to China or to settle in the United States, the various forms of Federal Bureau of Investigation harassment and persecution that CHLA members endured in the 1950s, and how these events led to a change in the CHLA's conception of American democracy and a strengthening of its emotional attachment to the People's Republic of China. The theoretical implications of this study for Chinese American history are presented in the Conclusion.

Chapter One

Chinese Laundrymen in New York City

Chinese Laundrymen and New York's Chinatown

Historians are still trying to answer the questions of who were the first Chinese to live in New York and how New York's Chinatown started.[1] More research is needed to determine whether the sailors or cigar vendors listed in the 1855 New York municipal census were the first group of Chinese settlers in the city of New York. The available materials tell us only that when the New York Chinese community began to take shape in the 1870s, the majority of the Chinese inhabitants in New York City were laundrymen. Here I use the term "community" instead of "Chinatown," because although Chinatown was the headquarters for Chinese of all sorts, the laundrymen lived not in Chinatown itself but in their hand laundry shops, which were "scattered over an area of about thirty miles in all directions from that center [Chinatown]."[2] According to an 1888 article, there were about ten thousand Chinese living in metropolitan New York, "probably a little over two thousand" Chinese "laundries in the city of New York alone, some eight hundred or nine hundred in Brooklyn, and about one hundred and fifty in Jersey City. . . . Each laundry has from one to five men working in it, and they all make money."[3] The thirteenth census of the United States of 1910 counted 4,614 Chinese (3,904 foreign-born) in New York City, and suggested that a majority of them was engaged in the laundry business. In this census, 8,573 male and 103 female "Indian, Chinese, Japanese, and all other [nonwhite and non-black]" were classified as "laundresses and laundrymen" in the country as a whole. In New York alone, 3,175 such males and 45 such females were found in the categories of "launderers," "laundry operatives," and "laundry owners, officials, and managers." Most of them can be assumed to be Chinese since the Chinese population (4,614) constituted 77 percent of the total number (6,012) of these people who were put into the category (there were 1,037 Japanese and 343 Indians).[4] Although we shall never find accurate statistics of the Chinese in general and Chinese laundrymen in particular from the late 1880s to the 1930s, most observers of New York's Chinese community recorded seven thousand to eight thousand Chinese laundrymen in New York City.[5]

Though people generally acknowledge that the hand laundry business was one of the most important economic "lifelines" of the Chinese community in the United States, no one is absolutely certain of its origin. A widely accepted version of the story is that the Chinese hand laundry started in San Francisco. It is believed that Wah Lee, an unsuccessful gold miner, was the first Chinese to open a "wash-house establishment" in San Francisco in the spring of 1851.[6] But scholars cannot elaborate on the story because of a paucity of historical materials.

As in the case of San Francisco, a similar lack of materials makes it difficult to reconstruct the story of the early Chinese hand laundry in New York City. According to some records, a decision to use Chinese laborers to replace the militant Irish female workers in the Passaic Steam Laundry led to the spread of Chinese hand laundry shops in the metropolitan area. In the early 1870s James B. Harvey, owner of the Passaic Steam Laundry, which had been established in 1856 on the east bank of the Passaic River, in Belleville, New Jersey, shipped one hundred fifty Chinese from San Francisco to replace his plant's Irish female workers, whose frequent strikes disrupted business. To Harvey's dismay, the Chinese turned out to be just as independent and militant as the Irish women: "After a time, as the Chinese laundry workers learned how white employees gained financial advantage by striking, there was a series of walkouts and labor disputes."[7] "The Chinese even went to strike, and [were] beginning to become more and more like their white neighbors."[8]

Following Harvey's example, other plant owners on the East Coast began to talk of shipping gangs of Chinese workers to their plants. "One shipment was sent to a shoe factory in North Adams, Mass., but plans for others fell through" because the surprising lack of docility on the part of the Chinese at the Belleville plant made other plant owners lose their enthusiasm. Many Chinese left the Belleville laundry plant a few years after they got there, and all Chinese were discharged in 1885. "Some came to Newark, some drifted to New York. Having been trained as laundry workers, it was natural that most of them turned to this trade for a living."⁹ This group of Chinese has been regarded as the pioneers of the Chinese laundrymen in the New York area. Wong Chin Foo observed that these Chinese wrote to their cousins, and "their cousins and other relatives came so rapidly that in a few years nearly every street and avenue in New York became filled with Chinese laundries, and the flaming red signs of Wah Sing, One Lung, and Goon Hi Fa Toy dangled gloriously in great numbers."¹⁰ By 1879 the number of Chinese hand laundries in New York City was large enough to alarm the white power laundry owners. The first issue of their trade journal discussed the "menace" of this Chinese competition in the industry in a long editorial.¹¹

The Chinese chose to engage in the hand laundry business because they were excluded from most desirable occupations, and many rapidly expanding cities needed their cheap labor to fill the least desirable unskilled jobs. As Wong Chin Foo observed in 1888:

> They [the Chinese] become laundrymen here simply because there is no other occupation by which they can make money as surely and quickly. The prejudice against the race has much to do with it. They are fine cooks, neat and faithful servants, and above all, very skillful mechanics at any trade they have a mind to try. In the Western States, they are used in as many different positions as any other foreigners, and the laundry business is occupied only by those who fail to find other employment.
>
> But here in New York as yet there is no other alternative. Many an able-minded man as well as skillful mechanic who came to America to better his condition may be found wielding the polishing-irons in a New York Chinese laundry.¹²

To open a hand laundry shop did not require substantial capital or skill. In the 1880s it took "from seventy-five dollars to two hundred dollars to start one of these Chinese wash-houses," as "the main expenditure in a Chinese laundry is a stove and a trough for washing, and partitions for dry-room and sleeping apartment, and a sign."¹³ In the nineteenth-century hand laundry the laundrymen did the washing, ironing, and folding. After the 1920s most hand laundrymen, Chinese or non-Chinese, in New York City did not do the washing themselves. In 1950 a hand laundry was defined as "a small establishment that receives bachelor and family bundles, sends them out to be washed and extracted by a wholesale power laundry, and then does the finishing itself."¹⁴ To get the two hundred dollars to start a hand laundry, the Chinese often turned to a "whey" (*hui*), defined by sociologist Paul Siu as "a sort of collective loan fund administered by a small group of persons usually affiliated with the clan or with a store in Chinatown."[15] Wong Chin Foo described how a "whey" functioned in the nineteenth century:

> Suppose I have an established laundry, and want to borrow two hundred dollars at a certain percent premium, but I cannot find any one Chinaman who is able to loan me the amount. I put up a notice in Mott Street that upon such and such a day I wish to make a "whey" of twenty men, who all are supposed to be situated like myself, each wanting to borrow two hundred dollars. When we twenty borrowers all come together, we each put down ten dollars. Then each one secretly writes upon a slip of paper the amount of interest he is willing to give to get the two hundred dollars. These slips are carefully sealed and thrown into a bowl. At a given time they are opened, and to the highest bidder goes the two hundred dollars, less the interest, which is invariably deducted immediately from the principal. Frequently as high as four dollars is offered for the use of ten dollars for a single month. In such cases each of the nineteen other borrowers gives to the lucky one only six dollars apiece for the ten dollars apiece which they make him pay next month. Then the next highest bidder gets the two hundred dollars, less the interest he offered, and so on, until the entire twenty, at twenty different times, have obtained the use of this two hundred dollars; but the one that comes the last, having offered the least interest of them all, reaps the harvest of the "whey." This method is adopted by most Chinese laundrymen, in New York and other large cities, to open new laundries.[16]

A hand laundry started by a capital of one hundred dollars or so was usually small, owned by one person. Before the 1940s most Chinese hand laundries in the metropolitan New York area were one-man businesses. After the repeal of the Chinese exclusion acts and relaxation of the restriction on Chinese immigration in the 1940s, some Chinese women came to join their husbands. Subsequently, many hand laundries were operated by families, but the size of the typical hand laundry remained pretty much the same, though the volume of its business may have increased.[17] Some hand laundries were owned and conducted by two proprietors who contributed equal shares of the capital. The two partners were usually "cousins"—immigrants from the same clan or village. "They work together, eat together, and sleep together, and at the end of the year divide the earnings equally."[18]

At the turn of the century the Chinese hand laundry's charge for laundering shirts was 10 cents apiece; for handkerchiefs, 2 cents each; for cuffs and collars, also 2 cents each; and so on.[19] Comparatively, these prices were not lower than those of other ethnic laundries, as Helen F. Clark observed: "Today it is evident to all who have studied the question that there is no such thing as 'Chinese cheap labor.' Chinese laundries charge higher rates than domestic laundries. Chinese laundrymen command higher prices than laundresses of other nationalities. A Chinese earns ordinarily from eight to fifteen dollars a week and his board and lodging. The white or colored laundress makes from four to ten dollars a week, without board or lodging."[20] Louis Beck's record supports this observation: "An ordinary laundry, owned by two men and employing no outside help, will earn, as an average, about $1,000 a year, or say $500 for each proprietor."[21]

From its inception, the New York Chinese community relied on the hand laundry business, the "economic lifeline" of the community, as the Chinese themselves called it. Wong Chin Foo described this symbiotic relationship in 1888: "There are now over thirty Chinese grocery stores in the city and most of these are in Mott Street, or in that vicinity of Mott Street called 'Chinatown.' . . . These stores import all their good[s] from China direct[ly], and they depend entirely upon the laundrymen for support."[22] Ten years later Helen Clark offered a similar observation:

> The population of Chinatown on Sundays is about four or five thousand, on week-days very much less. The difference may be accounted for by the fact that on Sunday the Chinese from all parts of New York and Brooklyn, and from Long Island, New Jersey, and Connecticut towns, flock to Chinatown to visit their friends and to do business. Since the American Sunday does not permit laundry work on that day, the laundrymen seize upon it as a general recreation day, and go to Chinatown by hundreds. This, therefore, is the great business day of that region, and all the stores are open and every employee is constantly occupied.
>
> Here the laundrymen buy all their dry groceries, their clothing, and their laundry supplies.[23]

In addition to economic relations, the Chinese laundrymen also maintained close social relations with Chinatown.

Chinese Laundrymen and Chinatown Organizations

Among the social organizations established in the Chinese community, *gongsi fang* (*fong*) was one of the oldest and remained a major institution well into the 1940s. In Chinese, *gongsi* means "company" or "corporation;" *fang* means "house," "(a) branch of (a) clan," or "family." Why the Chinese chose this term as the name of the organization is not clear.

As early as 1874, when New York's Chinese community was in its inception, artist Winslow Homer of *Harper's Weekly* found two "clubs" in

New York's Chinatown, whose functions were "to aid members in distress, and to extend a helping hand to young Chinese who might come as strangers to the City."[24] One of the two clubs, Poolon Kun Cee, located at 34 Mott Street, had fifty members who paid membership dues, and it provided eleven beds for twenty-two people in "three dark and badly ventilated" rooms. The other club was found at 12 Baxter Street, no name given, with a smaller membership. According to historian John Tchen,

> these early mutual aid societies were clearly remarkable, multipurpose spaces. . . . They presented a collective level of organization, not an individual entrepreneurial effort. Brought together by some shared background or interest, the members used dues to pay for the rent. Within their facility, a complex of overlapping activities were contained, ranging from festivities to burial, temporary lodging to gaming, self-government to social welfare, smoking and eating to producing consumer goods. The two organizations encompassed the work, sleep, play, and spiritual needs of Chinese New Yorkers in a communal setting run by an elected and rotating committee. In such spaces affectional bonds were developed and reestablished, memories were made and celebrated, and the Chinatown of the future was incubated.[25]

These fang were very important in the life of the Chinese immigrants. Because the Chinese exclusion acts banned the U.S. entry of Chinese laborers and their wives, the majority of the Chinese in the United States were male laborers without a normal family life. To them the fang served as a substitute family, a credit union, a clinic, and health insurance. Since social conditions did not change much for the Chinese until the repeal of the exclusion acts in 1943, these fang thus demonstrated a longevity in meeting the needs of the Chinese. In the 1930s, more than half a century after the Chinese community was built in New York City, the fang still played a significant role. Two Chinese laundrymen who lived in New York City in the 1930s and 1940s recalled: "Some laundrymen joined with their fellow countrymen to rent an apartment in Chinatown, which became a place where they got together on Sundays and where they could stay when they became unemployed. . . . On Sundays they sometimes put money together, bought some food, then while eating they talked and talked until very late."[26]

A Chinese laundryman who was a generation younger remembered:

> The fang was the organization that consisted of people with the same surnames. However, if a member had a good friend who had a different surname but wanted to join the fang, that's O.K., as long as he paid the

membership fee. How much was the fee? Well, it depends. Each month it would be figured out how much money was needed for the rent, for the telephone bill, gas, electricity, and so on. If you have forty members, the total amount would be equally divided into forty shares. Pay your share, then you maintain your membership. Why did so many people join the fang? Well, as a laundryman, the worst thing you could worry about was being sick or being kicked out of your place because you could not pay that month's rent. Where else can you go? The fang apartment will provide you a temporary place to stay. Every fang rented an apartment in Chinatown. On weekends that's the place friends and relatives would meet and talk to each other.[27]

During the Great Depression of the 1930s the fang was the primary mutual-aid organization, providing food and shelter for many unemployed Chinese laundrymen and restaurant workers and saving many lives.[28] As described in the next chapter, the fang also became an important factor in the formation of New York Chinese laundrymen's own organization.

Another type of social organization in Chinatown was the family/clan association. In China the family was a basic social unit. The people bearing the same surname constituted a zu (clan), a large family. In South China it was not uncommon for all inhabitants in a village to belong to the same zu. In villages where several zu lived together, usually one big zu dominated local affairs. The eldest persons in the wealthiest families held the power and ruled their zu according to traditional ideas and customs.

Chinese immigrants in the United States founded many family/clan organizations. Such a group sometimes tried to unite its members for the sake of building a commercial monopoly in a certain business. Then, with economic power as well as large membership, it would become powerful in a given Chinese community. In New York, large clan organizations had a long history: the Ng's Association, Lee's Family Association, and Loong Kung Kung Saw (comprising of those surnamed Liu, Guan, and Zhang) were founded in 1887; Wing Chun Tong of the Chan's Family Association and Sam Yip Gung Saw, in 1900; and Shao Lum Gung Saw and Wong Kong Har Tong, in 1911.[29] The main difference between the gongsi fang and the family/clan associations seemed to be that a gongsi fang was a loosely organized mutual-aid association built on a principle of equality by Chinese immigrant laborers, while wealthy merchants assumed the leadership of the family/clan associations, in which the poor members did not have much power.[30] Usually, a gongsi fang was smaller than the family/clan organization. Furthermore, gongsi fang disappeared in the 1940s when the removal of legal restrictions allowed Chinese Americans to establish families, but family/clan organizations continue to exist today.

Poorer Chinese had even less power in the *hui guan,* or district association. The origin of hui guan dates back to the Ming dynasty (1368–1644). There were three types. The first was a club, founded in Beijing, the nation's capital, to meet the needs of government officials from the same district or province who needed a place to get together, chat, and entertain each other. The second, called shi guan (hotel for examination candidates), furnished room and board for candidates from each province who came to the capital to take the imperial civil service examinations. The third was similar to a businessmen's association, consisting of merchants from the same locality. The first two types of hui guan were established mainly in the capital, although after the sixteenth century they could be found in some provincial capitals or large cities as well. Their activities were simple and repetitive. They had less influence than the third type, the hui guan of businessmen.[31]

The main goal and function of the businessmen's hui guan was to protect the interests of its members in a strange place. It also provided food and lodging for visitors from the same districts. The overwhelming majority of hui guan had a temple where members came together to offer sacrifices to their native deity. The temple and sacrificial rites played an important role in evoking the native feelings and friendship of its members and promoting and strengthening unity among them. The funds of the hui guan came from contributions of the general members. Naturally, the richest merchants, who contributed most, usually held the most powerful positions in the association.[32]

Generally speaking, hui guan engaged in six kinds of activities. First, they settled disputes among members, between members and local merchants, and between themselves and other hui guan. As "foreigners" in other provinces, individuals would suffer in competition with local merchants or the organized merchants of other hui guan. (Some hui guan were trade associations that intended to monopolize a certain type of business, which often led to other hui guan's envy and competition.) Second, hui guan interred the deceased in a cemetery founded by members' donations and later sent the bones of the deceased to their home villages. Third, hui guan provided medicine and medical treatment for the members, a necessary function because there were few doctors in traditional China. Fourth, they established schools for members' children. Fifth, they took care of the poor, the sick, and orphans. Finally, they held dinner parties and performances of dramas in their local dialects, providing recreation for the members. Most of these were charitable activities.[33]

Soon after the Chinese immigrants came to the United States, they established hui guan to protect themselves. Some of the immigrants may have been members of hui guan in China and so were familiar with them. Thus hui guan became the most acceptable organizational form for the early Chinese immigrants who found themselves in California under frontier conditions. As early as 1849 a Kong Chow Hui Guan was founded in San Francisco.[34]

By the late nineteenth century many hui guan, or district organizations of the same nature but with other names (such as *gongsuo*), had been founded in the New York Chinese community. The New York Ning Yang Hui Guan (Ning Yong Association), the most powerful hui guan in New York, organized by immigrants from Taishan (Toishan; or Xinning [Sunning] before 1910), was established in 1890.[35] An examination of the functions of the Chinese hui guan in the United States suggests that they bore clear vestiges of businessmen's hui guan in China: they provided temples for the performance of sacrificial rites; shipped the bones of deceased members back to China and purchased ground for cemeteries in the United States; provided medical services for the sick; took care of the aged and the poor; and established Chinese schools to teach Chinese children the rudiments of Chinese history, language, and philosophy.[36]

Though these hui guan on American soil inherited many traditions from China, they should not be seen as a replica of China's social organizations.[37] Even if the name *hui guan* (or, for that matter, *gongsuo, tongxianghui, zhongqinhui*, etc.) and the hierarchical structure were kept, fundamental differences distinguished the Chinese district associations in America from those in China. First of all, those in China were citizens' groups in their own country, while those in America were immigrants' organizations in a foreign land. The latter functioned as mutual-aid groups to serve the needs of the immigrants in a new environment. Thus, although hui guan offered the same services in China as in the United States, the contexts in which they operated were different. For example, hui guan provided medical services for their members; in China, they did so because of a lack of readily available medical services outside the organization; in California, it was because in the 1860s and 1870s Chinese immigrants were barred from the county hospitals.[38]

The most important characteristic differentiating the Chinese American hui guan from those in China was the development of a new institution: a single organization that united all hui guan in a given city, the

Chinese Consolidated Benevolent Association (CCBA). The San Francisco CCBA, founded in the 1860s as a loose federation of all Chinese organizations in that city, was urged by the Chinese consul general, Huang Zunxian, to strengthen itself in the early 1880s to lead the fight against the anti-Chinese movement that resulted in the passage of the Chinese Exclusion Act.[39] The New York CCBA was founded in 1883,[40] though there are no records of its struggle against the exclusion acts and other anti-Chinese legislation.[41]

In China there was no such united organization as the CCBA. The need to form a CCBA to serve as a representative of the entire Chinese community arose *after* the Chinese immigrants arrived in the United States, especially when anti-Chinese sentiments and agitation reached their peak in the 1880s. Individual hui guan alone could not assume the responsibility to protest such hostility because anti-Chinese agitation and legislation were directed not against a particular group of Chinese but against all of them. Moreover, before the Chinese government set up its first consulate in San Francisco in 1878, the CCBA acted as the spokesperson of the Imperial Qing government in its relations with the Chinese in the United States.[42]

Both individual hui guan and the CCBA, though established to meet the needs of Chinese immigrants, were authoritarian in nature. The officials of the New York CCBA, for example, were not elected by the membership but were chosen by the merchant elite from the two largest hui guan: the Ning Yang Hui Guan (consisting of immigrants from Taishan, dominated by merchants) and the Lian Cheng (Lun Sing) Gong Suo (consisting of all non-Taishan immigrants in New York City). According to the CCBA bylaws, its four officers—president, Chinese secretary, English secretary, and office boy—were to be elected alternately by the Ning Yang Hui Guan and the Lian Cheng Gong Suo. For instance, if the president and the Chinese secretary were elected by the Ning Yang Hui Guan, the English secretary and the office boy had to be chosen by the Lian Cheng Gong Suo, and vice versa.[43] There were seven permanent members of the CCBA Standing Committee: representatives from the Ning Yang Hui Guan, Lian Cheng Gong Suo, Chinese Chamber of Commerce, On Leong Association, Hip Sing Association, Mei Chi Party, and Eastern American Branch of the Kuomintang after its founding in China. These organizations had the right "to propose and vote for resolutions" and "to help the president handle all affairs."[44]

Those who were chosen to serve as president of the CCBA before the 1930s were usually Chinese scholars who had earned a degree in the pre-

1905 era by passing the traditional civil service examinations. They enjoyed some prestige in the community. Yee Wing Yan (Yu Xingjian), for example, was born in Taishan in 1861, earned a *juren* degree (equivalent to an M.A.) in China, and served as president of the San Francisco CCBA in 1904. He returned to China for several years and came back to the United States in 1916 to become president of the New York CCBA.[45] Such Confucian scholars were hardly efficient administrators in a community as complex as the Chinatowns in the United States; therefore, the wealthy merchants actually controlled the CCBA, the self-styled "highest authority" in the Chinese community.[46]

While the rank-and-file Chinese immigrants had no right to vote, they were required by the CCBA bylaws to pay a variety of fees to support the association's existence. Every Chinese living in the greater New York area (including New Jersey and Connecticut) was automatically a member, whether he or she wanted to join it or not. A member was required to pay a "foundation fee" of three dollars and an annual membership fee of one dollar, plus a so-called port duty of three dollars before leaving for China. In addition, each laundryman had to pay an extra annual laundry-shop fee of two dollars. Moreover, the CCBA bylaws required all Chinese business transactions to be conducted at the association's headquarters at 16 Mott Street for a fee of five dollars each. This was a unique regulation practiced only in New York.[47] Through its regulation of business transactions, the official positions in the CCBA became profitable, since the Chinese hand laundries changed hands quite often.[48] The account books of the CCBA were kept secret, thus giving rise to considerable suspicion of corruption and embezzlement.[49]

The elite-controlled CCBA enjoyed a reputation as the internal government that took care of everything in the Chinese community, acting as a spokesperson for the Chinese immigrants, protecting the common interests of all Chinese, and settling disputes among the Chinese organizations. In reality it could not do all these things. On a day-to-day basis it was the gongsi fang and the smaller clan organizations that helped the Chinese immigrants solve problems they encountered.

The CCBA, more than any other Chinese immigrant organization, was an American product. Its power stemmed partly from a historical situation created by anti-Chinese sentiment and legislation such as the Chinese exclusion acts and partly from its connections with the Chinese government. In that context, the CCBA was originally created to defend the civil and legal rights of Chinese immigrants. But this elite-dominated organization became alienated from its membership with the passage of time and developed into a repressive institution whose existence and function to a large degree depended on the larger society's ignorance of the Chinese community on the one hand and the Chinese community's ignorance as well as fear of the larger community on the other hand. It was not based on democratic principles, and its officials often abused and exploited the ordinary Chinese immigrants. Moreover, it was more concerned with controlling the community than with providing its constituencies basic protection. Thus in the 1930s, as we will see in the following chapters, a group of Chinese laundrymen rose up to challenge its authority.

Under the Shadow of Exclusion

The Chinese were welcomed when they first arrived in California. In 1852 the governor of California, John McDougal, praised them as "one of the most worthy of our newly adopted citizens."[50] Although many Chinese returned to China after working in the United States for a period of time, some intended to stay permanently, and a few had become U.S. citizens before the 1878 *In Re Ah Yup* decision and 1882 Chinese Exclusion Act deprived all Chinese of the right to be naturalized. According to John Tchen, in 1868 at least ten Chinese had acquired U.S. citizenship in Manhattan.[51] Even after the Chinese Exclusion Act was passed in 1882, some Chinese immigrants still cherished the idea of becoming U.S. citizens, as one missionary observed in 1897:

> I know of a certainty the high value which many of these Chinamen put upon American citizenship. At one time, a number of years ago, it was possible for a man to swear to his intention to become a citizen, and until the constitutional amendment [the Chinese Exclusion Act] was passed which forbade any State to naturalize them, many judges issued such papers. I well remember many instances in which Chinese have preserved these useless papers as their greatest treasures, and have showed them to me with pride, and their eyes glistened with joy while they told me how they would sometime be citizens of this great American country. Poor fellows, how little they realized the utter worthlessness of those bits of well-loved paper![52]

Although some Chinese immigrants wanted to settle permanently in the United States (or the Gold Mountain, as they called it), once they came in large numbers beginning in the 1850s, hostility against them arose among white Americans. From 1850 on, the California legislature passed a series of measures—such as the Foreign Miners Tax of 1850, the 1854 statute that prohibited the Chinese from testifying for or against whites in court, the 1858 legislation that barred Chinese from entering the state, the 1862 "police tax" that levied a monthly capitation tax on "Mongolians," and an 1870 ordinance that prohibited persons from walking on streets while balancing poles with baskets hanging at each end on their shoulders (apparently aimed at Chinese who delivered clean laundry in this way)—to discourage Chinese immigration and to limit the rights of Chinese immigrants. Although most of these discriminatory bills were later declared unconstitutional by the U.S. Supreme Court, they were passed in an atmosphere unmistakably anti-Chinese and cumulatively laid the foundation for anti-Chinese institutional racism.[53]

The Chinese Exclusion Act of 1882 had a profound impact on the Chinese in the United States. Chinese were singled out as the only ethnic group to be excluded from this country on racial grounds. The most significant provisions of the act were that it suspended the entry of Chinese laborers, both skilled and unskilled, for ten years (it was extended for another ten years in 1892 and indefinitely in 1904) and ruled that "hereafter no State Court or Court of the United States shall admit Chinese to citizenship."[54] Because of this act, many Chinese returned to China, and those who remained were excluded from the mainstream of American society.

After the passage of the Chinese Exclusion Act, not only Chinese laborers but also their wives were denied the right to enter the United States. The U.S. Circuit Court for California in two 1884 decisions ruled that a Chinese wife had the same legal status as her immigrant husband and consequently could not be admitted into the United States.[55] Thus the majority of the Chinese immigrants who were laborers could not legally bring their wives to join them in this country. The result was a great imbalance in the sex ratio in the Chinese American community, which became known as a bachelor society. In New York State the ratio of Chinese males fifteen years of age to Chinese females of the same age group was 3,961 to 100 in 1910, 1,562 to 100 in 1920, 1,402 to 100 in 1930, and 896 to 100 in 1940.[56]

It should be emphasized that most members of this bachelor society were laundrymen and other laborers. According to a study by Shepard Schwartz, of the 254 Chinese marriages registered in New York City in the period 1931 to 1938, 41 (16.1 percent) Chinese grooms were "laundry workers and owners;" 77 (30.3 percent) were "restaurant workers and owners." Since the study put both "workers" and "owners" in the same category, it can be assumed that the portion of bona fide laborers in the group was even smaller. Meanwhile, Chinese merchants, in addition to enjoying legal permission to bring in their foreign-born wives, had more chances to get married in the United States, as shown in their disproportionate representation (112 of the total of 254, or 44 percent) in the above-mentioned study.[57]

In addition to the Chinese exclusion acts, other legal barriers prevented the Chinese from building families in the United States. Some U.S. laws specifically discouraged marriage between Chinese male immigrants and women (both Chinese and non-Chinese) who were American citizens. During the exclusion period fourteen states—Arizona, California, Georgia, Idaho, Mississippi, Missouri, Montana, Nebraska, Nevada, Oregon, South Dakota, Utah, Virginia, and Wyoming—specifically outlawed marriages between whites and Chinese or "Mongolians."[58] (New York did not have a law banning interracial marriages, and some occurred between Chinese male laborers and white as well as black women.)[59] Moreover, a federal law passed in 1922 specified that a woman who married a Chinese alien would automatically lose her U.S. citizenship.[60] Under these restrictions, it was very difficult for Chinese males to form families in the United States: interracial marriage was almost impossible, and marriage with an American-born Chinese woman was difficult.

These legal restrictions may have contributed to the fact that most of the Chinese immigrants in the United States before the 1950s were unattached males, although many were married with wives in China.[61] Anti-Chinese agitators justified the exclusion by accusing the Chinese of being "unassimilable aliens" who were not civilized enough to appreciate family life and higher living standards.[62] Thanks to a series of U.S. Supreme Court decisions, however, the door to Chinese immigration was not completely shut. In 1898, in the case of *United States v. Wong Kim Ark*, the Court ruled that a person born of Chinese parents in the United States was an American citizen by birth and was eligible for reentry to this country after a trip abroad.[63] Then, in the case of Ng Doo Wing in 1915 and the cases of Lee Dong Mo, Tom Toy Tin, Leung Wah Jam, and Wong Foo in 1916, the Court decided that the foreign-born children of the Chinese who were American citizens were entitled to American citizenship. These decisions were important: in the years 1920 to 1949, 66,039 Chinese entered this country as "aliens," while 71,040 were admitted as "foreign-born citizens."[64]

Many of the foreign-born citizens were actually so-called paper sons— individuals who had bought documents from Chinese who had acquired U.S. citizenship. A Chinese returning from a trip to China usually reported to the immigration authorities that he and his wife had produced a child, in most cases a son, during his stay at home, while in actuality no child may have been born. Then he could sell the legal papers at a high price to those who were eager to come to America. In the first half of the twentieth century many Chinese came to the United States under "paper names," and it is believed to have been a common practice.[65] The following story gives a sense of the illegal practice and the burden that a paper son or an illegal immigrant, such as Chen Ke, carried:

> I was born in 1902 to a peasant family in the village of Zhongli, Taishan, Guangdong. My family had no land, no property, dependent on toiling a small piece of land rented from a landlord. I got married when I was twenty, and soon we had children. . . . I had to support a family of six; it's very difficult.
>
> In 1924, my elder brother in Boston borrowed $1,000 from a loan shark and bought me a "paper of the merchant son." . . . This should be a safe way. However, because my elder brother did not bribe the interpreter of the Boston Customs Service, he took his revenge as soon as I landed [in the U.S.]. He reported that I had fake documents. As a result I was detained for half a year, and later deported back to China.[66]

Having failed to enter as a paper son, Chen tried another way to smuggle himself into the United States:

> In 1928, I went to Hong Kong with several fellow villagers to pay a *jingshan zhuang* [underground organization that smuggled people into the U.S.] to go to America. . . . [But we failed.] Then we went to Shanghai, each paid 600 Hong Kong dollars to a Chinese sailor, who introduced us to work in his ship [sailing for the U.S.]. . . . Three months later, we arrived in Boston. . . . The next day the ship sailed to New York. The Captain permitted no one to leave the ship because he was told that a few days before some sailors from other ships had escaped. We said we had to buy Chinese food, then the Captain allowed only two to leave the ship. The two went to inform the local Chinese "receiving station" [which sent a boat to pick us up that night]. . . . We were brought to New York City and locked in a small room, where we took out the letter from the Hong Kong *jingshan zhuang*. It said: "Enclosed are six ginseng; please charge each a fee of $2,200 upon seeing them." But the local agent charged us each three more hundred. By this time my elder brother had died. I contacted my cousin in New York, who borrowed the money from a loan shark to pay for my release. So, upon arriving in America I had a debt of $2,500 plus interest, and 600 Hong Kong dollars.
>
> . . . At that time America was hit by the Great Depression. I first worked in a Chinese restaurant, then helped my cousin in his hand laundry shop. He

had three helping hands already, and I did not want to add to his burden and a few months later I left.

... After I left my cousin, I met a fellow countryman who together with a partner had just bought a laundry shop with a $4,000 loan. A few days earlier, his partner had died suddenly. He asked me to cooperate with him and share the loan. But soon he left without saying goodbye. Then I alone had to pay the $4,000 loan. All together, I owed others a total of $6,500. ... It took me more than twenty years to pay back all the money.[67]

Under the Chinese exclusion acts, the status of many Chinese immigrants was ambiguous and they lived in constant fear. Those who entered the United States illegally were often subjected to intimidation and exploitation. Two former laundrymen recalled:

Under the restrictions of the Chinese Exclusion Act and other anti-Chinese acts and ordinances, the Chinese hand laundry workers suffered greatly. They were subjected to the oppression and exploitation of the authorities and their "running dogs" [lackeys]. These are the most common cases:

The government officials and their running dogs came up to extort money. The officials from the city government—from the Department of Buildings, Department of Sanitation, Department of Labor, and Department of Fire—could come to a hand laundry shop at any time, and they would be very fussy about everything. Then the laundrymen would have to bribe them. If you did not bribe them, they could easily find an excuse to issue you a summons. To avoid the trouble of going to court, the laundrymen had to swallow the insults and put up with the racket. The policemen also came often to squeeze money the same way.

There were a few scums among overseas Chinese, who went to English school for a few years, but never did anything good for overseas Chinese. Rather, they stood on the side of the American government, became its running dogs, and would frame up overseas Chinese. We overseas Chinese called these scums *chufan ren* [interpreters]. These scums would come to hand laundries frequently to check documents—residency certificate, passport, or other "papers"—and they tried to find problems in the documents and make them excuses for "borrowing" money from the laundrymen. If they were not satisfied, they would collude with the Immigration officials to arrest and deport the laundrymen [who failed to bribe them].

[Moreover,] the laundrymen had to face the racketeering of the local white hoodlums and despots any minute. They brought their laundry to you. After you cleaned the dirty clothes, they came to pick it up and paid nothing. Sometimes they would give you some clothes of poor quality, and when they came to pick them up they would claim those were not the original clothes. They'd say that you damaged or misplaced or lost their clothes and insist on compensation. If you argued with them, you might have to go to court. Then you might have to spend a lot of money on hiring a lawyer and an interpreter, probably much more than the compensation the hoodlums demanded. Plus, you had to close your laundry shop and spend time in court. Since the racial discrimination against Chinese in the United States was so deep, there was no hope for poor Chinese to win against hoodlums in the court. So, [in most cases] the Chinese laundrymen were forced to submit to humiliations and pay the compensation.[68]

The Chinese exclusion acts and other discriminatory laws put the Chinese laborers in a very disadvantageous position in the job market. In the case of Chinese hand laundries, from the 1870s onward they faced the threat of white owners of laundry plants, who were determined to use their financial power and the exclusion acts to eliminate their Chinese competitors. As described earlier, in the very first issue of a trade journal published by large laundry plant owners in 1879, a long editorial was "devoted to the menace of the 'Heathen Chinee,' a competitor 'at once dangerous and illegitimate.'" The editorial claimed that "just so soon as they are reinforced by a sufficient number of their countrymen to fully occupy the field, laundry prices among their kind will fall to one-fourth of what they now are, and still the Mongolian will continue to grow rich." After the passage of the Chinese Exclusion Act in 1882, every year at their conventions these large laundry owners demanded stricter enforcement of the act to limit Chinese immigration. In 1914 a resolution to ask the president of the United States to tighten enforcement of the act was considered too moderate: "We want to get rid of a lot of those that are already here," one of the large laundry plant owners emphasized.[69]

The Laundryman's Life

Living in a strange land generally hostile to his presence, the Chinese laundryman faced an especially big problem: the language barrier. The following story vividly describes the frustration of Chinese laundrymen who did not know English:

> It's so difficult to survive in this country without knowledge of English. Let me tell you a story. The newcomers first came to Chinatown, then went to different places to work in laundry shops. They did not know any English and they dared not to ask anybody. So their friends or relatives taught them how to get to Chinatown. They gave a newcomer a box of matches and told him to take one match out of the box when he passed a stop. After taking out a certain number of matches, it's Chinatown and get off. Save those

matches, they also told him. On the way home, put one match into the box after each stop. After those matches were all put back into the box, you get off. Oh, it's very difficult to make a living in a foreign land.[70]

The extremely limited ability of most Chinese laundrymen to speak English contributed to multiple problems. The laundryman could not communicate well with his English-speaking customers. When he had legal troubles with his customers or the authorities, he not only had no legal means to protect himself but also had no way to explain himself. Even how and where to keep his money became a problem:

[To save money for a trip home,] you needed more than a thousand dollars at least. It took about twenty years to save that much money, or at least ten or eight years. How to keep the money was another headache. There were thieves all around in American society, and most Chinese hand laundries [in New York] were operated by a single man, with little defense. If he was found having a thousand dollar cash in his shop, he could be robbed or killed. Many of them were illiterate and could not even read numbers and sign their names [in English]; and they could understand only a couple of English words, so they dared not go to deposit their money in the bank. Besides, they had no time to go to the bank, since they could only rest on Sundays, and all banks were closed on Sundays. . . . Most hid their money in old clothes, or under the floor or in the wall. . . . Some died before they saved enough money to make the China trip, and the money they hid under the floor or in the wall awaited others to find and use. There was a story: one Chinese rented an old laundry shop and when he cleaned it, he was thrilled to find a bag of money under the floor. After a while, he was hit by the thought that the former owner of the laundry shop had worked for his whole life but brought not a penny home, and ended up being buried in a foreign land. Reflecting on that fact, he felt sorrowful.[71]

The Chinese laundryman felt the pain of knowing no English and must have sensed the need to learn it, but as Paul Siu observes, "he has, in fact, no time, no chance, and no facility for learning."[72] Indeed, if a Chinese immigrant had to throw himself into working in a hand laundry as soon as he entered the United States, and like Chen Ke was under tremendous pressure to work hard to pay back his debt, how could he find time to study English? Therefore, few first-generation Chinese immigrants acquired a workable knowledge of English.

Being excluded from other occupations and without English language skills, the laundrymen worked long hours to make a living. It seems that from the nineteenth century on, the Chinese laundrymen in the United States worked more than fifteen hours a day. One observer recorded in

1897: "The Chinaman works from eight o'clock in the morning until one or two o'clock at night. Sometimes he washes, sometimes he starches, sometimes he irons; but he is always at it, not tireless, but persevering in spite of weariness and exhaustion. Other laborers clamor for a working-day of eight hours. The Chinaman patiently works seventeen."[73]

The Chinese laundrymen's long working day not only was a basic fact of life but also was passed on to the succeeding generations as a legend. A Chinese laundryman who inherited his father's laundry shop in the 1950s said in 1988: "The old generation worked very hard. They often had to work fifteen to eighteen hours a day. They were so busy that they did not even find time to eat. I heard that some of them used a string to hang a piece of bread from the ceiling, in front of them, and had a bite when they had time to do so. A lot of them suffered leg pains."[74]

The leg pain mentioned by this laundryman is varix (varicosity), a condition endured by many Chinese laundrymen because they had to stand long hours to iron shirts. One laundryman recalled that he had to put adhesive tape on his legs in order to continue his work, "otherwise I cannot work."[75] In addition to varix, many laundrymen suffered back pain, "the whole body pain," and other sorts of health problems.[76] Two former laundrymen explained why they had to work such long hours: "The laundryman's work was very tough. The job received in the first three days of the week must be done before Saturday. If one got a lot of wash, one had to work day and night. . . . Only on Sundays could [one] close the shop and take a rest. . . . But if [one] received a lot of work and could not finish it before Saturday, one would have to apologize to the customers . . . and stay at the shop to finish the job on Sunday."[77]

Most Chinese laundrymen lived in their tiny hand laundry shops, where the poor conditions were detrimental to their health. In the laundry shop the air was not clean, the floor was wet, and during the summer the temperature was unbearable. The laundrymen worked for such long hours that they usually had no time or energy to keep their living quarters clean. Moreover, they lacked adequate sleep and they had to cope with problems common to poor neighborhoods as well as bad sanitation conditions. One laundryman recalled: "The living condition was terrible. We slept in the laundry shop. I went to bed around two o'clock and got up at six. Sometimes I would wake up during the night because I was disturbed by bugs, fleas or something. I felt my hands and arms hurt, then I slapped on my arms. Boy! I had ten or more of those awful bugs in my hands! Then I went back to sleep. During the day all those bugs were gone. I never saw any of them in the daytime."[78]

Working so hard and making little money, the Chinese laundrymen tried to save every penny they made. Some were so frugal that they even spent as little money as possible on food, as this story suggests:

> The laundrymen lived very frugally. They lived—ate and slept—in the laundry shop. On Sundays, they went to Chinatown to visit relatives and friends and to buy food for the next week. . . . Their food was very simple— they ate *furu* [fermented bean curd], *douchi* [fermented soybeans], *xianyu* [salted dry fish], *xianchai* [pickled vegetable] and so on. They seldom had fresh vegetables because they did not have time to buy them. . . . Some were so frugal that they did not eat more than one *furu* for one meal. One story goes like this: one day, when a Chinese fellow saw an old Chinese laundryman eating two *furu*, he was surprised and asked the old laundryman: "Uncle, is today special? You are eating two *furu*!" The old laundryman replied: "Don't ask! I just got a letter from home, and learned that my son was a good-for-nothing—he did not take care of the family. I am so vexed. Why should I save all the money [through not eating]?"[79]

The old laundryman in this story may be an extreme example of the frugal type, though Leong Gor Yun also suggested in his book *Chinatown Inside Out* (1936) that "many a Chinese will . . . save money on necessary food."[80] If every Chinese laundryman had been as frugal as the old laundryman described above, however, the grocery stores and restaurants in Chinatown would have had no business, for they depended to a large degree on the laundrymen's patronage. Thus it is hard to accept this story. In fact, according to Wong Chin Foo's observation, in the 1880s "nearly all the Chinese in New York are 'high livers' in diet. The poorest laundryman will have chicken or duck at least once a week."[81] A few descriptions of the diets of Chicago's Chinese laundrymen in Paul Siu's study also indicate that the Chinese did have meat, vegetables, and a variety of food on Saturdays and on some festive occasions.[82]

The inconsistency in these stories suggests that some Chinese laundrymen choose to remember and tell the stories of their lives in a selective way, as most people do. The story of the frugal old laundryman was told by two former laundrymen to a group of Chinese college students in 1979, and the storytellers seemed inclined to emphasize the hardships that the laundrymen suffered in the United States. What they implicitly meant was that it was the frugal ones who were able to save money to go home, while the others were afflicted by the social evils that plagued Chinatowns—gambling, opium addiction, and prostitution—and as a result they lost money and could not return to China.[83]

Of course, different Chinese laundrymen may have had different experiences in the United States, and it is not surprising that they would reflect on their experiences in diverse ways. But it is interesting to note that for almost a century the Chinese laundrymen consistently conveyed a false notion of their livelihood in America to their relatives in China so as to perpetuate the myth of the Gold Mountain in their villages. A Chinese laundryman who returned home with a certain amount of money would proudly tell his relatives and friends that his fortune came from his *yishangguan* in the United States. In Chinese, *yishangguan* is a vague term, often interpreted as "a clothing store," which is quite different from *xiyiguan*, the accurate translation of "a hand laundry shop." In many villages in Taishan, the county in Guangdong (Kwangtung) Province that contributed a majority of the nineteenth- and early twentieth-century Chinese immigrants to the United States, the term *yishangguan,* or *yiguan* for short, was widely used. It could mean either "a clothing store" or a business that had something to do with clothing. Therefore, the fact that these Chinese men were washing and ironing soiled clothing to make a living was distorted, and through the misnomer *yishangguan*, these laundrymen projected themselves and were perceived by their fellow villagers as merchants. Even in 1979, when my colleagues and I did field research in Taishan, many relatives of Chinese Americans still did not have a clear idea of what a yishangguan actually was, and the myth that many Chinese Americans were successful merchants of "clothing business" persisted.[84]

To understand the phenomenon of the perpetuation of the yishang-guan myth, one has to examine it in its proper historical context. First of all, to Chinese laundrymen who endured so many miseries, the return trip to their home village seemed to be the only moment of joy in their lives. It is understandable that they would show some vanity and boast a little bit in front of their relatives and friends. If they made no effort to demythologize yishangguan, or kept silent about it, that is also understandable. Since they had to endure insults, discrimination, and humiliation in the United States, why should they, during a short stay in the village, the only time in their lives when they were showered with admiration and envy, talk about their hardships and low status? Also, if another former villager had come back the previous year as a successful merchant of a "clothing business," why should a laundryman reveal his true occupation (which might suggest failure "to make it in the Gold Mountain") and thus disgrace himself and his family?

Therefore, the adoption of the vague term *yishangguan* and the perpetuation of its myth in Guangdong's community of returned overseas Chinese can be seen as one of the ways that the humble Chinese laundrymen protected their self-esteem. It can be related to their habit of dressing up on Sundays. Old pictures show that the Chinese laundrymen in New York in the 1930s and 1940s always dressed in a suit and tie. When asked why they did so, an old-timer explained:

> Yes, in those years, on Sundays, when we came to Chinatown, we always dressed up, wearing a tie. Why? You see, generally speaking, Chinese were looked down on by whites. Then if you went out dressing poorly, they looked down on you even more. So, not only on Sundays, but whenever we went out, we always dressed up and tried to behave decently. Of course, a suit would cost you money. But a lot of old "uncles laundry" bought only one suit. That one suit was with them for their lives. I myself had several suits [he proudly smiled].[85]

Second, poor economic conditions and the lack of opportunities in China's rural areas also helped to maintain the yishangguan myth. From the early nineteenth century until the 1940s, economic conditions in Guangdong's rural areas did not improve, and constant civil wars and disturbances destroyed many peasants' livelihood. An average Chinese peasant could not dream of making several thousand dollars in his lifetime, no matter how hard he worked. In most cases, mere survival was the priority. While the village remained as poor as ever, those who were lucky enough to have gone to the United States always sent and brought money home. The villagers were simply entranced by the fact that so-and-so brought thousands of American dollars home by doing "clothing business" in the United States, and they had no strong interest or incentive to investigate the nature of that business.

Therefore, even the Chinese laundrymen's intimate relatives may not have realized how poor the living and working conditions were in a Chinese laundry shop. The sons of the Chinese laundrymen who came to the United States sometimes under the pressure of their fathers, who believed that the situation in the village was hopeless, were usually shocked by their first glimpse of the hand laundry shop. Some expressed the feeling that if they had known the real situation of the Chinese laundrymen in the United States, they would rather have stayed home, as the following two stories indicate. The first story is from a man who came to the United States in 1939.

> I have been here about two months. No, I don't like it here. In China, people were talking about going to the "Flowery Flag" [America], and I was dreaming, too, about coming over. Now I am here. What I see in this coun-

try is just like this: working day and night. I thought my brother had a big store. But all of us Chinese are just laborers. I have to work so hard in order to earn a small sum of money. If I had only realized the hard work I must do, I would rather stay home. I would rather stay in the village, feeling content to be a farmer.[86]

The second story is from a man who came in 1940.

Oh, tell me how difficult the life was! You guess how much I earned a week? At the beginning, I earned only four dollars a week! Four dollars a week! For that four dollars, I had to work sixteen to twenty hours a day. So I complained to my father: "I told you that I didn't want to come, but you insisted that I must come. Earning four dollars a week, when the hell can I return to China?" I wished I'd stayed home.[87]

The shock of realizing how different the reality of the hand laundry shop in the United States was from the yishangguan myth in Guangdong's villages must have produced a certain amount of tension in the minds of the Chinese laundrymen. Nevertheless, once they came to this country, they had to face reality. Did they simply put up with that reality or did they try to change it? We may never know how the Chinese laundrymen of the nineteenth and early twentieth centuries reflected on their lives, but in the following pages I discuss a group of Chinese laundrymen in New York in the 1930s. Their own reflections illustrate their experiences and their status in American society, as well as their efforts to change their conditions.

Chapter Two

The Emergence of the CHLA

Uncle Laundry Stands Up

For many years the Chinese laundrymen in New York City had no common organization to protect their interests. According to Louis Beck, in *New York's Chinatown* (1898), there were two Chinese laundrymen's guilds in metropolitan New York in the nineteenth century, the Chop Sing Hong and the Sing Me Hong. (In Chinese, *hong* means "guild.") "The former embraces those employed in the Boroughs of Manhattan and The Bronx and Jersey City only, and the latter those working in the Borough of Brooklyn and Hoboken." These two hong fixed service prices, defined each hand laundry shop's "district" and prevented encroachment, and supervised the selling and purchasing transactions of the laundry shops. In exercising their power, the hong cooperated closely with the highest authority in Chinatown: the CCBA. In fact, the CCBA's headquarters and the Sing Me Hong's were at the same location, 16 Mott Street.[1] This is the only available brief account of the two hong, and we do not know when and why they ceased to exist. In any event, by the early 1930s these two hong were gone, and Chinese laundrymen in New York City had no organization of their own. In the words of a contemporary Chinese journalist, "If you were looking for the least organized class of workers before 1933, you could find no better example than the Chinese laundrymen."[2]

Without a common organization, Chinese laundrymen often depended on the CCBA and the district and family/clan associations for protection. But these organizations at times failed to protect them. This was especially true during the Great Depression, when the Chinese hand laundry business suffered as increasing unemployment led to a decline in demand for their services. In order to survive, many Chinese laundrymen had to extend their working hours and to lower service charges time and again. In addition, a systematic campaign was directed against the Chinese hand laundries in New York City. Some large white laundry companies, hoping to drive the Chinese out of business, displayed insulting cartoons of a filthy Chinese laundryman spitting on a white shirt. The Chinese hand laundries turned to the CCBA for help, but the CCBA demanded that each laundryman pay one dollar before it would consider any legal action, and then did nothing to change the situation.[3]

In 1933 a real crisis exacerbated the hardships of the Chinese hand laundrymen and at the same time created the conditions for them to organize themselves. In March the Council of Aldermen of the City of New York proposed an ordinance to charge a license fee of twenty-five dollars per year on all public laundries plus a security bond of one thousand dollars. In addition, the proposed ordinance required U.S. citizenship for operating public laundries.[4] This was designed to discriminate against small laundries (Chinese as well as non-Chinese) and would have forced most of the Chinese hand laundries out of existence since they apparently could not afford the exorbitant fees and the majority of the Chinese laundrymen did not have U.S. citizenship. Chinese newspapers in New York City—first *The Chinese Journal*, an independent paper, and later others[5]—reported on the ordinance and the entire community was shocked. As an economic lifeline of the community, Chinese hand laundries concerned everyone in Chinatown. Most people realized that the proposed ordinance would be a fatal blow to the laundries but differed in how to cope with the crisis.

The CCBA, the self-proclaimed authority in the Chinese community, offered its conventional solution to this problem. On April 16 the CCBA called a mass meeting of Chinese laundrymen in the auditorium of the Chinese School. Chen Shutang, the English Language Secretary of the CCBA, presided over the meeting. He opened the discussion of the situation by informing the audience that the CCBA was going to hire lawyers to deal with the case. As usual, the CCBA proposed that each self-employed hand laundryman donate one dollar and those shops with two or more partners donate two dollars so that the CCBA could hire a lawyer. Although *The Chinese Nationalist Daily*, the newspaper of the Kuomintang (KMT; the Chinese Nationalist Party), reported the next day that the proposal was passed "unanimously" at the meeting, Zhu Xia, editor of *The Chinese Journal*, who attended the meeting, contended that it was actually "passed" with a single seconder. Zhu also observed that many laundrymen were very disappointed and began to seek alternatives to the solution provided by the CCBA.[6]

Zhu Xia was an important figure in the Chinese laundrymen's fight against the CCBA and the city's discriminatory ordinance. A young man, Zhu had been educated in the United States and China and had a good command of both English and Chinese. The newspaper he worked for, *The Chinese Journal*, published in Chinese and maintained a neutral stand in the partisan conflicts among the Chinese newspapers. Because *The Chinese Journal* frequently reported on various events and regulations concerning the hand laundry business, many Chinese laundrymen subscribed to the paper. As a resident of Chinatown with numerous relatives and friends working in laundries, Zhu had an intimate knowledge of the trade and the laundrymen's feelings. He went to the CCBA meeting and spoke on their behalf. He questioned the capability of the CCBA to deal with the proposed ordinance and urged the laundrymen to establish their own organization to defend their interests. Although Zhu was interrupted several times by the CCBA's English Language Secretary, some laundrymen also stood up and spoke against the CCBA. They were cut off, too. Faced with the challenge from the laundrymen and their sympathizers, the CCBA's English Language Secretary called in some *tong* (secret society) gunmen to maintain order and one protester was carried out.[7]

The fact that several hundred laundrymen attended the CCBA mass meeting suggests that they came with a hope that the highest authority in the community would figure out a solution for their problem. But they were irritated by the CCBA officials' refusal to listen to the voices of ordinary laundrymen and their arrogant attitude toward opinions different from their own. Above all, the CCBA failed to present an effective solution to the ordinance crisis. The procedures and the results of the meeting showed the laundrymen that the CCBA was more concerned about its own prestige and power than their hardship. With this realization the laundrymen cast away any remaining illusions about the CCBA's efforts to protect them. Therefore, when some politically and socially more active laundrymen proposed to found an organization of their own, the response was overwhelmingly enthusiastic.

The seriousness of the problem caused some members of the elite in the community to reconsider the laundrymen's demand. On April 17 and 18 *The Chinese Nationalist Daily*, which usually represented the interests of the merchant elite, published two articles about the situation. Recognizing that the hand laundry business was a key economic activity in the

Chinese immigrant community, the articles confirmed that the proposed ordinance not only would be a blow to the hand laundries but also was a potential threat to the whole community's livelihood. The writers of the articles agreed that at this moment there was a need to organize a laundrymen's organization to deal with the crisis. They insisted, however, that such an organization should be led and directed by the CCBA and that the CCBA should "assume all the responsibilities" in dealing with the ordinance.[8]

Such advice was meaningless to the desperate laundrymen. If they were to build their own organization, why would they need the leadership of the CCBA? The laundrymen were determined to establish an independent organization. After a few days of discussions, exchange of ideas, and contacts among themselves, the laundrymen decided to hold their own meeting on Sunday, April 23, 1933, to discuss the situation and to found their own organization.[9]

Leaders of the CCBA became angry when they heard the news. The laundrymen's intention was a clear challenge to the association's prestige in the community. For decades the CCBA had been the supreme authority, and the most important mechanism it had for maintaining its dominant position was to act as the formal representative of the whole community in dealing with the larger society. It simply could not tolerate any action that would bypass it. Consequently, the association hurried to disseminate an official note in the unusual form of *chang hong* (literally, "long red," referring to long red paper posters) in Chinatown's streets, threatening that any laundryman who dared to attend the organizational meeting would "be held responsible for all consequences."[10]

Ignoring these "long reds," more than one thousand Chinese laundrymen came to Chinatown and poured into the basement of the Catholic Church on Mott Street that Sunday afternoon.[11] The preparatory committee reported to the audience the events that had led up to the meeting. Then a resolution was unanimously passed to establish a laundrymen's independent organization: The New York Chinese Hand Laundry Alliance (CHLA; Niuyue Huaqiao Yiguan Lianhehui). Seventeen people were elected as members of a temporary executive committee, which was charged to draft a constitution, rent office space, and recruit members.[12]

The meeting also issued a declaration that reflected the extent to which some people in the Chinese community, suffering from the depression and the growth of institutional racism, had learned a language and mode of analysis that challenged every aspect of the traditional ruling order in Chinatown. It is worth quoting at length here:

> Ever since China's fence of insulation was broken by European and American capitalist-imperialism, the Chinese socioeconomic basis was fundamentally shaken. The rural economy was bankrupt, and urban industries shut down one after another. Unable to make a living [in China], we were forced to part from our families, to leave our hometown, and to go overseas to seek petty profits. But we do not have large amounts of capital to invest in commerce, therefore most of us in this country are engaging in the hand laundry business. So, this trade became the lifeline of the Chinese community, and our wives and children back home depend on it too.
>
> Recently the New York City Council of Aldermen proposed a discriminatory ordinance against hand laundries. If the ordinance is unfortunately passed and becomes effective on July 1, tens of thousands of Chinese laundrymen would be stranded in this country, and our wives and children back home would be starved to death. . . . That's why we have to fight against it with every effort.
>
> However, we Chinese laundrymen in New York City never had a formal organization of our own. The organization that existed in the past exploited us in disguised names. It failed to protect our interests and, worse, it damaged our business. This has been proven by our experiences in the past. Therefore we have to organize a formal organization that truly represents our own interests in this campaign to fight the discriminatory ordinance. Without such an organization, there is no hope to abolish the discriminatory ordinance. The CCBA and the organizations under its control cannot represent our case to the City government. They are but taking this chance selfishly to serve their interests.
>
> Based on these reasons, we set up the preparatory committee of the New York Chinese Hand Laundry Alliance, expecting to establish as early as possible an organization that truly represents the interests of the Chinese hand laundries. [With such an organization] we can not only unite ourselves to fight the City government collectively so as to abolish the discriminatory ordinance, but also prevent such discrimination from occurring again in the future. Moreover, our own organization will be able to solve the problem of the rapid decline of service charges as a result of competition among hand laundries. Collective efforts will make the service charges rise again. In short, to establish a collective organization is indeed an urgent task for us.

—Two Hundred Fifty-four Hand Laundrymen[13]

The hand laundrymen's militant tone against the CCBA was unusual. Never before had any ordinary Chinese organization done such a thing to the CCBA. The CHLA became the first grassroots organization to challenge the CCBA's dominance in the New York Chinese community. It was not an isolated case. The economic crisis triggered by the depression intensified the internal conflicts within the Chinese community, and the traditional means that the CCBA had been using to control the community and to solve problems became ineffective. Furthermore, for several years a new political force—the Chinese left—had been working hard to expose the corruption and incompetence of the CCBA and to raise the political consciousness of Chinese Americans in New York City.

The Leftist Influence in Chinatown

Early left-wing activities in Chinese communities in the United States were mainly inspired by the Chinese nationalist revolution led by Sun Yat-sen. In the 1910s and 1920s left-wing Chinese in America consequently talked more about China than about the Chinese community in the United States. These leftists, most of them China-born, organized study groups to discuss Chinese political affairs, published newspapers and magazines to publicize their beliefs, and attempted to arouse the political awareness of the Chinese in the United States and mobilize them to support China's anti-imperialist struggle. By the early 1920s some Chinese leftists had become Marxists and joined the Kuomintang in the hope of building an independent and powerful China free from imperialist domination.[14]

This China-centered tendency strongly influenced the development of leftist organizations in Chinese American communities. Political changes in China had tremendous repercussions among Chinese leftists in the United States. In 1927 the split between the Kuomintang and the Chinese Communist Party (CCP) in China divided Chinese American communities into different groups, each supporting its chosen political party in China. Those who continued to support the KMT led by Chiang Kai-shek became the right wing in Chinese American communities, though (as in China) among themselves various factions fought one another vigorously.[15] The leftists, indignant about the KMT's "betrayal of the revolution," withdrew from the KMT and founded a left-wing organization, the Zhongguo Gong-Nong Geming Datongmeng (Grand Revolutionary Alliance of Chinese Workers and Peasants) (ACWP). The ACWP was first established in San Francisco; in 1928 a branch was set up in Philadelphia.[16] Few of this organization's activities have been documented, but its very name suggests its focus on China: to unite workers and peasants against the rule of the Kuomintang.

In 1930, in response to the increasing threat of a Japanese invasion of China and in protest against Chiang Kai-shek's policy of nonresistance, the Philadelphia branch of the ACWP changed its name to Meizhou Hua-qiao Fandi Datongmeng (the Chinese Anti-Imperialist Alliance of America) and soon moved both its headquarters and its organ, *Xianfeng Bao* (*The Chinese Vanguard*, founded in 1928), to New York City.[17]

The Chinese Anti-Imperialist Alliance of America (CAIA) developed a close relationship with the Communist Party of the United States of America (CPUSA) and attempted to educate and organize the Chinese people in the United States against the KMT and the traditional order in Chinese American communities. *The Chinese Vanguard*, a radical Marxist weekly, became its primary means to reach and educate ordinary Chinese Americans. Nevertheless, neither the CAIA's propaganda nor its organizational efforts produced tangible results. The reasons for this failure, in addition to the harassments of the KMT and the CCBA, lay in its dogmatic Marxist class-struggle approach to Chinatown's problems and its lack of understanding of the everyday hardships endured by common Chinese Americans. As the CAIA later had to acknowledge, its abstract and theoretical rhetoric simply did not appeal to the Chinese community.[18]

Although the CAIA's efforts did not stimulate class struggle in Chinatown as its founders had hoped, some Chinese Americans, through reading *The Chinese Vanguard*, were attracted to the group's ideas. Since the KMT and the CCBA banned the newspaper from Chinatown newsstands, CAIA members were forced to distribute the paper themselves. They brought copies to sell to Chinese hand laundries and sometimes just gave the paper to Chinese laundrymen for free.[19] This practice helped the Chinese laundrymen to develop a political awareness and to think about alternative ways to deal with their problems. One Chinese American who later became a leftist activist recalled how he was "enlightened" by *The Chinese Vanguard*: "There were several Chinese-language newspapers in New York City in the 1930s, such as *Shang Bao* [*The Chinese Journal*], *Guomin Ribao* [*The National Daily*], and there was a left-wing newspaper, too—*Xianfeng Bao* [*The Chinese Vanguard*], a semimonthly. I hadn't found a job yet, so a lot of times I stayed home reading newspapers, and I found that *Xianfeng Bao* suited me fine. Through reading the newspaper, I began to understand some hows and whys, my mind became progressive, and gradually, I approached the people of *Xianfeng Bao*."[20]

The Chinese left-wing elements were fortunate at least in one respect: they had a reasonably large literate audience. Most of the Chinese living in the United States before the 1950s were from about a dozen counties in Guangdong Province in southern China. In these so-called overseas Chinese communities (*qiaoxiang*), education was highly valued. Ever since the late nineteenth century, Chinese Americans had donated a great deal of money to build schools in their hometowns with the hope that their educated descendants could live a more decent life. As a result, many elementary schools flourished in these communities, and most of the male children there received some education. For example, in Taishan County, which contributed almost half the Chinese emigrants to the United States, it is estimated that about 90 percent of the adult males were more or less literate by 1910.[21]

After 1882 Chinese allowed to enter the United States had to have relatives there, and consequently, emigrants came mainly from the overseas Chinese communities in Guangdong. Most of these emigrants did not get a chance to learn English before or even after they came to the United States, but a majority of them could read Chinese-language newspapers, which became a basic source of information, a major means of community connection in American Chinatowns, and an important tool for the control of the community by the traditional establishments. Thus the Chinese leftists, after they split with the KMT, also used newspapers as their primary weapon against the traditional powers and as a way to reach the grass roots.

It is difficult to determine the extent of *The Chinese Vanguard*'s circulation. But it is clear that the paper had constant financial problems. Its editors and reporters, and most members of the CAIA, were unemployed.[22] The survival of the paper partly depended on the donations of the "advanced elements" in the Chinese community and, very likely, on the support of the CPUSA.[23] Because of its financial problems, the paper was published only biweekly until October 1934, when it became a weekly.

As part of its efforts to educate Chinese Americans and to raise their political consciousness, *The Chinese Vanguard* engaged in a ceaseless war against the representative of the traditionally dominant groups in the Chinese immigrant community: the CCBA. The paper devoted extensive coverage to exposing the CCBA's corruption and its "various deceptive means" to exploit the "poor laboring overseas Chinese." Whenever the CCBA planned to launch a donation drive, *The Chinese Vanguard* commented on its purposes and means in detail, pointing out possible deceptions and warning the Chinese community not to be manipulated by the seemingly appealing patriotism or the idea of ethnic solidarity. In February 1933, for example, the CCBA called a mass meeting that passed a resolution to raise money in the community to send to Chinese troops bravely resisting the invading Japanese in northeastern China. The next day the CCBA sent a notice to various organizations urging them to collect the donations and to give them to the "supreme authority," which would send the money to China. *The Chinese Vanguard* immediately raised questions about the notice. In an article on the front page, the paper pointed out that the CCBA failed to specify how the money would be sent and to whom it should be sent—to the brave Chinese soldiers or to Chiang Kai-shek's government, which was carrying out a nonresistance policy? Moreover, the paper reminded its readers of how the Chicago CCBA had embezzled the anti-Japanese donations it had collected not so long ago and urged the Chinese organizations to "democratically elect" responsible persons to handle the donation movement and to send money to the anti-Japanese Chinese troops directly. Finally, the paper asked the whole community to oversee the procedures of the CCBA's "monthly donation drive," "to make sure that every penny will reach the truly anti-Japanese troops."[24]

As a biweekly, *The Chinese Vanguard* did not play as influential a role as the liberal daily, *The Chinese Journal*, in promoting the establishment of the CHLA. Nevertheless, *The Chinese Vanguard*'s constant efforts to cultivate political consciousness among laboring Chinese Americans and its continuous radical attacks against the CCBA seemed to exert a subtle influence on many laundrymen's perception of the organization. Naturally, when the CHLA confronted the CCBA, it enlisted and accepted the help of the Chinese left.

The Alliance

The people who founded the CHLA were a diverse group. Although most Chinese immigrants who came to New York City in the first half of the twentieth century ended up in the hand laundry business, their backgrounds in China differed greatly in terms of economic status, educational attainment, and personal experience. The key figure who did the most organizational work in the first months and became the first president of the CHLA was Lei Zhuofeng.[25] A native Taishanese, Lei came to the United States as the son of a U.S. citizen and learned English in public school. Because he had a good command of both English and Chinese, a rare talent among Chinese laundrymen, he emerged as a leader and was quickly recognized as such by other Chinese laundrymen.

Lei brilliantly organized the April 23 meeting that successfully discussed and passed the constitution of the CHLA. So many laundrymen wanted to join the CHLA that a long line was formed in front of the registration desk.[26] As stated in its constitution, the purposes of the organization were to "maintain friendly relations [among the members], concentrate our strength, internally keep unity and defend the interests of the members, outwardly resist and try to abolish any discriminatory acts against the Chinese hand laundries." The qualification for membership was simple: "Any Chinese engaging in hand laundry trade, regardless of political persuasion and sex, can apply to join the Alliance as a member."[27]

The first election of the CHLA was done by mail.[28] On May 5 about three hundred members oversaw the procedure for checking the results of the mail ballot. Fifty individuals were elected as the first officials of the organization. Among them, thirty-five constituted the Executive Committee, while fifteen became members of a Supervisory Committee. The next day the first meeting of the elected committee members worked out divisions of responsibility. The Executive Committee had ten sections: External Affairs, Secretary, Organization, Finance, Investigation, Recruitment, Introduction, Examination, Treasury, and Propaganda. Each section had three committee members, with one being the section head. At the meeting Lei Zhuofeng, Zhu Huagun, Li Xinmei, Zhao Shizhi, and Li Zuofen were elected to form a five-man Standing Committee, which was responsible for the daily functioning of the organization.[29]

The elected committee members had various backgrounds in China. Zhu Huagun and Li Xinmei were former country schoolteachers, others were "college or high school graduates, minor military officers, a semiprofessional politician, [and] an ex-reporter on a country paper."[30] These people were mainly selected from the 254 laundrymen who had signed the Declaration of April 23.[31] They seemed to be more active, more educated, and more capable of articulating their opinions than ordinary laundrymen. On May 7 all the elected committee members were sworn in and the first formal membership meeting was held.[32]

One of the issues discussed at the membership meeting was how to find and hire capable lawyers to challenge the proposed city ordinance. The responsibility was delegated to Lei Zhuofeng. Another issue was how to recruit new members. All the committee members were to visit Chinese hand laundries in different areas and to persuade their owners and workers to join the newly founded organization.[33] In fact, six of the initial ten sections of the CHLA Executive Committee seem to have been set up to recruit new members: Organization, Investigation, Recruitment, Introduction, Examination, and Propaganda.

As a grassroots organization that emerged from the womb of Chinatown where the district/clan/family institutions, as well as clannish perceptions and ideas, were strong and influential, the CHLA successfully used some traditional Chinese means to recruit members and to consolidate itself. To recruit new members, the alliance fully exploited old relationships among clan members and town/village fellows, between teachers and students, and so on. The 254 hand laundries that initiated the idea of the CHLA were linked through Lei Zhuofeng, who had widespread connections in the community. Lei's closest ally, Zhu Xia, editor of *The Chinese Journal*, also had many acquaintances among Chinese laundrymen. Zhu helped organize the CHLA by promoting the idea in his paper and by encouraging his hand laundry friends to join. After the May 7 meeting, committee members first solicited their friends and relatives. Then, with the help of active members, recruiting activities were extended to the gongsi fang, where members of the laboring class met frequently.

The gongsi fang, a unique product of a bachelor society, as described in Chapter One, was different from other Chinese clan/family organizations. A fang served as a substitute family for the Chinese bachelors who had no family in the United States. In many cases, especially during the Great Depression, the hand laundrymen had closer relations with the gongsi fang than with the district/family organizations. The gongsi fang was a primary target not only for the CHLA's early organizational efforts but for its later patriotic activities as well. The CHLA's connections with the gongsi fang both reflected and defined the nature of the alliance as a grassroots organization.

The recruitment efforts proved successful. Within a month of its founding, the CHLA had more than two thousand members.[34] The laundrymen's enthusiasm for the new organization was overwhelming because it promised to challenge the proposed city ordinance and to provide all the basic services that a Chinese laundryman needed badly in a foreign and frequently hostile environment. The most important of these services was legal assistance to help the laundrymen deal with different departments of the city government and to defend them in court if necessary.[35] The CHLA's promise to protect the interests of the Chinese hand laundries through united actions, and its seemingly capable leaders, offered a ray of hope and were probably the main reasons that the alliance won tremendous popular support. Its very existence and development were determined by the laundrymen's response to their environment and their willingness to unite. Its strategy for fighting against racial discrimination, political oppression, and economic exploitation, in turn, to a great extent was shaped by its grassroots nature. How well it reached its proclaimed goals was thus dependent on concrete political, social, and economic conditions as well as the suitability of its strategy.

The Test

Just a dozen days after it was formally organized, the CHLA met its most significant test. On May 23 the alliance sent its two representatives, Lei Zhuofeng and Zhu Xia, and its lawyer, William M. Chadbourne, to the public hearing on the laundry ordinance held by the Public Welfare Committee of the Council of Aldermen. After the chairman of the committee read and explained the ordinance, the representatives of the white owners of power laundries spoke in favor of the ordinance and urged the committee to pass it. Chadbourne then stood up to oppose the ordinance and explained the hardship and financial difficulties of Chinese hand laundries. He pointed out that the diligent Chinese laundrymen provided services to and were welcomed by the residents of New York City. The proposed ordinance was clearly designed to discriminate against the Chinese hand laundries and was not accordant with the principle of justice. The chairman declared that the city government had no intention to discriminate against the Chinese hand laundries. Chadbourne replied that Clause IV of the proposed ordinance that required U.S. citizenship before one could apply for a laundry operation license was obviously discriminatory against the Chinese, since under the existing naturalization laws Chinese could not be naturalized. If the ordinance was passed, Chadbourne maintained, most of the Chinese hand laundries would be forced to close down. He argued that to make thousands of Chinese lose their jobs while the number of unemployed was increasing would seriously affect social stability and was not in the interest of American society. Finally, he explained that the average Chinese hand laundry, which earned so little, was by no means able to pay the extortionate license fee (twenty-five dollars) and the security bond (one thousand dollars).[36]

After the hearing the Public Welfare Committee passed the laundry ordinance but made some significant modifications in it. The license fee was reduced to ten dollars and the security bond to one hundred dollars. The U.S. citizenship clause was kept, but an amendment was attached that exempted "Orientals" from this requirement.[37] These modifications were perceived by the CHLA members and by the Chinese community at large as a major victory. The bankruptcy of thousands of Chinese hand laundries had been averted. Above all, this success, for the first time in the history of the New York Chinese community, clearly demonstrated to the laundrymen the effectiveness of their own collective action. In the following years this "Victory of May" and other successes in the fight against discriminatory legislation or actions became the basis of the CHLA's unity, a factor always emphasized by the alliance as the prerequisite for any successful struggle. Throughout its history the Victory of May was glorified in every CHLA anniversary celebration and served as a stimulus to inspire its members' morale in their endless battles for survival and improvements in the quality of their lives. But the victory also intensified the CCBA's animosity toward the laundrymen's alliance. The subsequent conflicts between the two Chinese organizations became more complex than the CHLA's fight against the city government's laundry ordinance.

However impressive the Victory of May, in terms of tactics and aims the CHLA had in fact behaved much as the CCBA would have done. What remains important, therefore, is the fact that these laundrymen explicitly rejected CCBA representation and chose instead to organize themselves. What was at issue, then, was the leadership and the very structure of the Chinese community. Within this context, the Victory of May, on the one hand, appeared to be a victory of the Chinese community as a whole over the proposed ordinance; on the other, it signaled that a new force had emerged to challenge the CCBA's time-honored role as the sole representative of the Chinese community in dealing with the larger society. An examination of the complicated conflicts between the CHLA and the CCBA after the Victory of May sheds light on the inner structure of the Chinese community and enhances our understanding of how institutional racism functioned in and affected the Chinese community and how ordinary Chinese responded to it.

The actions that the CCBA took to undermine the CHLA can be divided into two categories. The first were conventional means of social control: blackmail, intimidation, and bribery. The second was to use the

means created by institutional racism: secret reports to immigration officials about the "illegal" status of CHLA members and collusion with city
authorities to sabotage the CHLA's struggle against discriminatory laws.

To kill the CHLA in its infancy, the CCBA claimed that the CHLA had
been set up by a group of "opportunistic elements" to meet "their own
selfish desires," and warned Chinese laundrymen not "to be fooled" by
these "scums of the Chinese."[38] The Victory of May, however, enhanced
the laundrymen's confidence in the CHLA, and as a result, its membership expanded greatly. The CCBA then decided to use more effective
means of intimidation. It bribed the heads of the tongs and asked them to
order their members to withdraw from the CHLA. The On Leong Tong
called a membership meeting and ordered its members to withdraw from
the CHLA.[39] Consequently, some dropped out. Fearing retaliation by the
tongs, quite a few individuals put personal notices in the KMT newspaper, *The Chinese Nationalist Daily*, announcing their withdrawals from
the CHLA.[40]

Nevertheless, what could have been a decisive blow to the CHLA
proved to be a failure. The CCBA could not successfully mobilize all the
tongs in a united effort to destroy the CHLA because the tongs at the
time were busy fighting one another. In late May a "tong war" between
On Leong and Hip Sing, which started in Boston's Chinatown and
spread to New York's Chinatown, preoccupied the heads of both tongs.
Also, some tong leaders obviously did not share the CCBA's perception
of the CHLA as a potential threat to the traditional power structure.
They even played with the idea of enlisting the CHLA on their side to
fight their enemies.[41] As a result, tong leaders split over the issue of how
to deal with the CHLA. For example, Li Jiemin of the On Leong Tong ordered his tong's members to withdraw from the CHLA, but Li Shence,
another leader in the same tong, disapproved of the action. Similarly, the
Hip Sing Tong's Wu Yingguang wanted to take action to force Hip Sing
members to drop out of the CHLA but was opposed by the tong's head,
Mai De.[42]

While colluding with the tongs to undermine the membership of the
CHLA, the CCBA launched an offensive campaign against the CHLA's
ally, *The Chinese Journal*, and its editor, Zhu Xia. *The Chinese Journal*,
an independent paper, was a commercial venture owned by a publishing
company, Barrow Mussey.[43] It played a key role in the formation of the
CHLA because Zhu Xia, a liberal journalist who had been critical of the
CCBA leadership for years, published many editorials and reports promoting the cause of the laundrymen's alliance. As the largest Chinese

daily newspaper in New York City at that time (with a circulation of about five thousand),[44] *The Chinese Journal* served as the link between the founders of the CHLA and the Chinese hand laundries. While urging the Chinese hand laundrymen to organize themselves, Zhu Xia in his editorials denounced the CCBA as a corrupt and inefficient organization on which the laundrymen should not rely. Furthermore, Zhu published reports that exposed the autocratic nature of the CCBA. Therefore, the CCBA regarded him as a trouble-maker and looked for excuses to punish him and his paper.

In June the CCBA found the excuses it needed. In a report that described the success of the CHLA over the laundry ordinance, *The Chinese Journal* had ridiculed the CCBA by pointing out that the self-proclaimed supreme power of Chinatown had not even sent a representative to the public hearing on the ordinance. The CCBA was greatly irritated. On June 13 it dispatched a group of "hatchetmen" to the office building of *The Chinese Journal*; they shouted "Boycott!" in front of the paper's office and ran all over Chinatown snatching copies of the paper from the newsstands. According to *The Chinese Vanguard*, these hatchetmen were paid from five to thirty dollars by the CCBA.[45] In the following days the CCBA's hatchetmen continued to harass local newspaper vendors who sold *The Chinese Journal*, and one vendor was beaten up because he refused to pull the paper off his stand.[46] Advertisers who bought space in the paper were intimidated. Meanwhile, the KMT newspaper attacked *The Chinese Journal* in a series of articles and accused it and Zhu Xia of agitation against the CCBA.[47] Nevertheless, because of the widespread support of CHLA members and their sympathizers in the Chinese community, *The Chinese Journal* survived the CCBA's attack and boycott and served as the mouthpiece of the CHLA in the alliance's first years. Zhu Xia remained a close friend of the CHLA for many years.

Having failed to destroy the CHLA by its conventional methods of social control, the CCBA tried to subjugate the CHLA by resorting to the means created by the existing institutional racism. As discussed in Chapter One, Chinese Americans invented the CCBA in their struggle to defend themselves in a hostile society. The Chinese Exclusion Act and many similar discriminatory legislation made most Chinese Americans vulnerable to numerous legal problems. This situation created and perpetuated a fear, a psychological as well as material insecurity, among Chinese Americans, and it also made social and class relations within the Chinese community more complicated. Historically, the CCBA did play a positive role in dealing with the legal problems of its constituency and in alleviating their fears. Since from the beginning only wealthy merchants could assume official positions in the CCBA, however, it never became a genuinely representative institution for the Chinese community as a whole, though it made every effort to maintain that image inside and outside the community. Although it was designed to settle disputes among the Chinese, the CCBA in most cases acted primarily in the interests of the wealthy merchants. Even if a case involved the entire community, ordinary Chinese Americans were not allowed to express their opinions, nor were they told the details of how a case would be handled. They were simply required to contribute to the legal costs, and the amount of each individual's or unit's donation was usually set arbitrarily by the CCBA. The CCBA leaders argued that negotiations must be kept secret and that inappropriate actions (such as public demonstrations) would cause "international disputes" between China and the United States that would further damage the interests of Chinese Americans.[48] In turn, the CCBA's manipulations of the fears of ordinary Chinese Americans and its connections with the authorities, both results of existing institutional racism, became a significant part of its power basis. Operated in this context, when it perceived a threat to its power, the CCBA was never reluctant to employ all the means at its disposal to defend itself and to destroy its opponents in the Chinese community, as revealed by the two bouts of fighting between the CCBA and the CHLA after the Victory of May.

After its efforts to undermine the membership of the CHLA failed, the CCBA targeted the CHLA leadership. Lei Zhuofeng, the first president and the chief diplomat of the CHLA, was selected as the first object of attack. In August the CCBA bribed a CHLA member, Liang Mei, to accuse Lei Zhuofeng of making secret reports to the immigration authorities exposing the former's illegal status. Liang filed a grievance with the CCBA claiming that because he had failed to pay his CHLA membership fee, Lei had threatened to punish him. Later, Liang said, he was questioned by immigration officials and was given a deportation order. The CCBA immediately held a secret meeting to "examine" the case and discuss how to deal with Lei and the CHLA.[49] The details of the meeting were not made public. Probably as a result of the meeting, Liang Mei soon put a "personal note" in *The Chinese Nationalist Daily* denouncing Lei as a traitor to the Chinese.[50]

The CCBA seemed to believe that this slander would work to destroy Lei Zhuofeng and the CHLA. At that time members of the Chinese community were plagued by the fear of being deported by the Immigration and Naturalization Service (INS), which, in cooperation with other government agencies, was conducting a large-scale campaign to check papers and deport illegal aliens who were presumably involved in the tong wars that were spreading in all Chinese communities on the East Coast.[51] Any Chinese who cooperated with immigration officials to expose the illegal status of his countrymen was regarded as a traitor and became the common enemy of the Chinese community. If Lei had indeed intimidated the CHLA members and forced them to pay the membership fee by threatening to expose them to the INS, the CHLA and its leaders would undoubtedly have been condemned by the entire community.

Lei and the CHLA immediately responded to Liang Mei's allegation as it was manipulated by the CCBA. First, the CHLA held a membership meeting and made the case public. Second, the CHLA put a public statement in *The Chinese Journal* stating that Lei was not in charge of receiving membership fees, so Liang Mei's accusation was false. Finally, Lei took legal steps to defend himself and the CHLA. He sued Liang Mei and *The Chinese Nationalist Daily* in local court for slander and demanded compensation.[52] In October Lei and the CHLA won the case.[53]

If the Liang Mei case revealed that the CCBA was willing to use unethical means to destroy the newly formed CHLA, another case was even more telling. Just a few weeks after the Victory of May, the city license bureau issued a new regulation requiring all small laundry operators to submit to fingerprinting when applying for a license.[54] The intention was to expose the illegal status of some Chinese laundrymen. One white laundry trade union checked with the commissioner of the license bureau about why such a regulation was necessary. The commissioner made no explanation but showed a "long letter" he had received from the CCBA in which the CCBA claimed that the CHLA was an organization established by "bad elements" and should not be trusted.[55] It was implied that the bureau had issued the fingerprinting regulation to check out the "bad elements."

The purpose of the CCBA's scheme was twofold. First, its secret report to the license bureau aimed to discredit the legitimacy of the CHLA. As *The Chinese Vanguard* put it, the CCBA "attempted to borrow the bloody hands of the city government to kill the CHLA."[56] The CCBA hoped that the CHLA would be crippled by the harassments from the authorities so that the CCBA could resume its power over the laundrymen. Second, the fingerprinting requirement gave the CCBA a chance to amend its image, which had been badly damaged by the CHLA's Victory of May. Therefore, it is not surprising to note that, after the CHLA's legal fight against the fingerprinting regulation failed in early July, the

CCBA went so far as to celebrate the "fair judgment of the court" in a public notice.[57] It announced that it would hire "prominent lawyers" to look into the case and use "political maneuvering" to abolish the regulation.[58] As it had usually done earlier, the CCBA arbitrarily set the amount of money that hand laundries and stores had to donate to the legal cost: each hand laundry was to pay two dollars; each family association, ten dollars; and stores, three, five, ten, or twenty dollars, according to their size. The CCBA threatened that if anyone refused to pay, it would dispatch hatchetmen to "pull out his cash box" or entrust the official debt collector to collect the money.[59] Obviously, the CCBA saw the discriminatory regulation as an opportunity to smash the CHLA and to restore its own absolute power over the community.

The CHLA exposed the secret collusion between the CCBA and the license bureau to the entire Chinese community in flyers explaining the failure of the legal suit against the fingerprinting regulation. The community was shocked, and the CCBA was infuriated. On July 12 the CCBA called a "whole community meeting" intending to "correct the CHLA's falsehood." In the meeting, the CHLA's representatives had an open confrontation with the CCBA's president, Wu Qianchu, and its English Language Secretary, Chen Shutang. Wu and Chen accused the CHLA of slandering the CCBA and demanded that the CHLA representatives present evidence for its criticism of the CCBA. The CHLA representatives cited the CCBA's April 16 meeting as evidence to support its claim that "the CCBA takes [discriminatory] cases as opportunities to extort money," and they asked the CCBA: "You always insisted on using 'political maneuvering' to deal with discriminatory cases, what's the result? Can you show us your achievements?" The CHLA representatives talked emotionally about the case of the fingerprinting rule. They pointed out that on July 3 the judge had hinted that the CHLA had a chance to win the case. A few days later, however, the judge's attitude had changed and the CHLA failed to get the rule abolished. "If there were no secret scheme behind the scene, we would have won. . . . Just mentioning this we feel deeply hurt."[60] Along with the CHLA representatives, the representatives of the Huizhou Gongshanghui (Huizhou Association) and the CAIA also stood up to attack the CCBA.[61] Thus the CCBA community meeting designed to "correct the CHLA's falsehood" ended up an embarrassment to the CCBA itself.

This kind of conflict between the CHLA and the CCBA persisted. In later years, however, the forms and the tones changed along with historical circumstances. For example, from 1937 on, the common interest of all Chinese in the anti-Japanese cause made both organizations put aside their differences for the sake of ethnic solidarity. Nevertheless, the basic fact remained that the two organizations represented two different interest groups in the Chinese community. The CCBA supported the interests of the established elite in the guise of a supreme power representing the entire community. The CHLA, which emerged in a crisis to challenge the autocratic rule of the CCBA, represented the interests of the laundrymen, who constituted a majority in the community.

Viewed from such a perspective, the founding of the CHLA has a profound meaning in Chinese American history. A group of ordinary Chinese Americans established their own organization from the bottom up and developed strategies to defend themselves. Their united militant actions not only reflected their determination to fight for survival, but also constituted a break from the time-honored autocratic rule of the CCBA, which in turn changed the power structure of the Chinese community fundamentally. With this in mind, it is not difficult to see why the founding of the CHLA was called "a revolution in New York's overseas Chinese community."[62] Zhu Xia commented in 1936 that the CHLA "is likely to remake America's Chinatowns while it is remaking American Chinese."[63]

The conflicts between the CHLA and the CCBA suggest that the physical and psychological conditions created by institutional racism often provided the CCBA with means of social and economic control. It acted more often as an exploiting and intimidating institution that received indirect or direct help from anti-Chinese agencies than as a leading organization protecting all its constituency. Its actions deepened the fears of ordinary Chinese Americans living under the shadow of exclusion. Seen in this light, to challenge the CCBA was a way to fight against the oppression and exploitation imposed through the institutions of the larger society. Thus the CHLA's struggles against the CCBA were always part of a larger struggle against racial discrimination.

Chapter Three

The Alliance Is for the Laundrymen

A Democracy Emerges in Chinatown

Growing out of a mass movement against the discriminatory laundry ordinance and the despotic power of the CCBA, the CHLA adopted a democratic electoral procedure that met the demands and was shaped by the experiences of the Chinese hand laundrymen themselves. From the beginning, "the Laundry Alliance is for the laundrymen" was the password among its members.[1] The motto implied that the alliance was set up to serve and defend the common interests of the Chinese laundrymen and that, moreover, it was established by the ordinary laundrymen themselves, in sharp contrast to the structure of the CCBA.

To ensure that the officials of the CHLA were the genuine representatives of the laundrymen, all were elected by and from the members. The procedure was as follows: Greater New York (including Manhattan, Bronx, and Brooklyn) was divided into about three hundred districts. Each district had six to ten laundries located in the same neighborhood. The members in a given district would elect one person as their group leader. (In Chinese, the CHLA members called the group leader *quzhang*: literally, "head of the district.") Each group leader served as the representative of his group (or district) and attended the convention held once a year, usually in November. In the convention the group leaders would nominate 104 candidates for the Executive and Supervisory committees. Then a membership meeting would elect 52 out of these 104 candidates to the committees. After being elected, the members of the two committees divided responsibilities among themselves, assumed different posts, and issued an inaugural statement, which outlined the problems faced by the laundry business and the major work to be done in the following year.[2]

The CHLA bylaws stated that no one could hold office for more than one year. Since there was an election each year, virtually every member would have a chance to be elected to office. Furthermore, the group leaders constituted a network linking thousands of CHLA members scattered throughout New York City and reflecting their opinions to the headquarters. As a rule, any important issue would be decided at the membership meeting. Thus, CHLA members strongly identified with the organization, which they felt to be their own. In contrast, ordinary Chinese were denied the right to participate in the decision making of the CCBA, even though it claimed every Chinese in the greater New York area as an automatic member. CCBA members were responsible for or were forced to pay dues and fees but had no right or chance to express their concerns.

Legal issues were perhaps the most important matters concerning the CHLA members, and the alliance adopted many democratic measures to ensure that the organization would provide extensive and efficient legal services. This emphasis was the result of the laundrymen's actual needs. But of perhaps equal importance was their anger at the CCBA's extortion in the guise of providing legal services.

Two important figures played key roles in the legal services the CHLA provided for its members. One was the legal advisor. Soon after its founding, the CHLA hired a progressive lawyer, Julius Louis Bezozo, the son of Polish-Jewish immigrants, as its legal advisor to offer various kinds of legal assistance to its members.[3] The other was the English Language Secretary, the only CHLA official who received a regular salary (forty dollars per month in the 1930s). The post was usually appointed by the Standing Committee of the Executive Committee, and its occupant remained for long periods of time. Tan Lian'ai, for example, served for more than ten years from the late 1930s to the late 1940s. As a young man, Tan Lian'ai had come to the United States, where he had learned English. One of his successors, Tan Yumin, had learned English in China, where he had worked as an English secretary to a Chinese lawyer before coming to the United States.[4] The function of the English Secretary was twofold: first, because of his language skills and the experiences he had acquired in his dealings with city authorities, he often served as the spokesman and representative of the CHLA in dealing with the English-speaking world. (There was a Chinese Language Secretary who dealt with the Chinese community.) Second, he translated the regulations, or-dinances, and documents related to the hand laundry business as well as the legal advisor's explanations of these documents for CHLA members and other Chinese laundrymen; he was the legal advisor's assistant and interpreter when Julius Bezozo handled complicated legal cases. He also accompanied CHLA members to court whenever necessary.[5]

The CHLA's legal assistance to its members, ranging from applying for licenses to handling customers' complaints, was a major part of its Exec-utive Committee's daily work. According to Chen Shancai, one of the CHLA's active members, the alliance's English Language Secretary and legal advisor helped handle some six thousand such cases between 1933 and 1938.[6] As long as a member had paid the annual membership fee of three dollars, when he asked the alliance for legal help he had to pay only twenty-five cents to cover transportation for the lawyer and the English Secretary. Moreover, the CHLA also extended legal assistance to non-members if they asked for help. Though some members expressed their resentment about those laundrymen who took advantage of the CHLA's legal assistance but never joined the alliance, the CHLA never refused help to anyone who asked for it.[7]

Since the CHLA defended its members' interests responsibly and effi-ciently through its collective actions and legal assistance, its members felt free to refuse to pay the CCBA annual membership fee. Moreover, be-cause the CHLA had a capable licensed lawyer, its members were no longer subject to the total control over arbitration and frequent extortion practiced by the CCBA.[8] This meant that the CCBA lost much of its con-stituency and was thus determined to undermine the CHLA by every means. When its efforts to break the CHLA through the manipulation of racist institutions failed (as discussed in Chapter Two), it tried to destroy the CHLA from within.

In early 1934 a rumor was circulated in New York's Chinatown that the CCBA planned to compromise some leaders of the CHLA and *The Chinese Journal* so that it could first destroy the laundrymen's alliance and then focus its attack on the Chinese left.[9] It was possible for the CCBA to find the individuals it needed within the CHLA, because the lat-ter was indeed an alliance of people of all different backgrounds and po-litical persuasions. Within a few weeks after the rumor was spread, several members of the CHLA Executive and Supervisory committees made public statements in the KMT newspaper, *The Chinese Nationalist Daily*, accusing the CHLA president, Lei Zhuofeng, and other alliance officials of misusing the CHLA's fund in the legal case against *The Chi-*

nese Nationalist Daily in late 1933, spending too much money on the legal case against the fingerprinting regulation in October 1933, and having meetings with Communists in the CHLA headquarters. Privately, some of the signatories claimed that if they could not "control" the CHLA they would "destroy" it.[10]

When asked by a Chinese journalist to comment on these accusations, Lei Zhuofeng said that the decision to fight *The Chinese Nationalist Daily* in court had been taken at a membership meeting and the results had been reported to it, as was the case against the fingerprinting regulation. Moreover, the amount of money spent on the two cases was greatly exaggerated. As for having meetings with Communists in the CHLA headquarters, Lei said, "Since the Communists came to help our struggle at the most desperate moment when the CCBA oppressed the CHLA with all its effort, we ought to accept their help. This is my own as well as many members' view."[11] Lei was not prepared to deal with the troublemakers in the same way as they had attacked him, that is, to make public statements against them. Rather, he was confident in the judgment of the CHLA members and stated that his greatest concern was to work with them to complete the process of establishing the democratic system of dividing districts and electing officials.[12]

At the beginning, Lei might have wanted to conciliate his accusers, but his opponents did not agree with him and with other alliance members on what kind of organization the CHLA should be. The small opposition faction, led by two former country schoolteachers, Zhu Huagun and Li Xinmei, was determined to shape the CHLA according to their own desires. But their very effort to impose their will on the CHLA members led to their failure. Since they published their accusations against Lei and others in the KMT newspaper, which was regarded by most alliance members as a tool of the CCBA to sabotage the CHLA, their action was seen as a conspiracy to destroy the CHLA or to change its nature by colluding with hostile outside forces. Indignation was the membership's response to such actions. On March 11, 1934, a membership meeting unanimously passed a resolution that these individuals, who wanted to realize their personal ambitions at the expense of the membership and who conspired to turn the CHLA into an organization "for their private benefit," be expelled from the CHLA. As it turned out, the group was quite small: only ten out of fifty-two Supervisory and Executive Committee members, and two rank-and-file members out of some twenty-five hundred were expelled.[13]

Zhu Huagun, Li Xinmei, and their followers, refusing to admit their defeat, reacted immediately by publishing statements in *The Chinese Nationalist Daily*. But these statements were contradictory. On the one hand, Zhu and Li claimed that they were the only legitimate CHLA officials and denounced the CHLA membership meeting's decision to expel them; on the other hand, they tried to get CHLA members to resign from the alliance and to found a rival organization.[14] As a result, few CHLA members followed the opposition faction. Moreover, this agitation against the CHLA seemed to enhance the alliance's reputation—within weeks after the opponents were expelled, more than thirty laundrymen joined the CHLA.[15]

In declaring the decision to expel Zhu Huagun and Li Xinmei and their followers, the CHLA denounced them as traitors and accused them of colluding with the CCBA to destroy the CHLA. Soon these expelled members provided evidence to support the accusations. In May 1934 the twelve expelled by the CHLA and a group of KMT members who were engaged in the hand laundry business, with the help of the CCBA, *The Chinese Nationalist Daily*, and the KMT, founded the Chinese Hand Laundry Association.[16] But this puppet association of the CCBA attracted few members. The association in July published a list of "elected officials" in *The Chinese Nationalist Daily* and claimed that it had about one hundred members. In fact, according to one of its members, it had only forty-nine, of whom eleven were KMT party members recruited through the KMT network in New York's Chinatown.[17]

At first the Chinese Hand Laundry Association seemed to pose a threat to the CHLA. An episode in July, however, led many to believe that the new association was as incompetent as the CCBA in terms of providing basic services to its members. In late July the CHLA helped a person by the name of Zhu Qiuli apply for his business operation license. Zhu turned out to be a member of the Chinese Hand Laundry Association, and worse, he had borrowed the membership card of CHLA member Zhu Guanpu to obtain the CHLA's legal assistance. Questioned by CHLA officials, Zhu Guanpu admitted that it had been a mistake to lend his card to a nonmember and asked to be disciplined. The CHLA pardoned Zhu Guanpu but made the event public. Disclosed by *The Chinese Journal*, it became a sensational news story in Chinatown. One Chinese American reportedly said, "How shameful for those who call their organization the Association but failed to get a license for its members!" Another commented, "If Zhu Huagun is unable to provide services to his Association's members, he should have held himself back. The fact that one of their members used false identity to get the CHLA's legal help actually made public their incompetence."[18]

Through its democratic institutions, the CHLA not only provided efficient legal services to its members but also successfully settled internal conflicts caused by several ambitious persons and, as a consequence, maintained its integrity. Contrary to what the CCBA had expected, the CHLA continued to exist and enjoyed an expanded membership. By May 1934, one year after its founding, the CHLA's active membership reached its peak of thirty-two hundred.[19]

It was perhaps the CHLA's success that provoked a call for reform within the CCBA. In March 1934 the newly elected president of the CCBA, Lei Fang, issued a statement in which he admitted that "the Association [CCBA] has become the center of public attack. Complaints and condemnations can be heard far and near." Then he stood up as a reformer: "It's no use to mention all those things happened in the past. [We] will seek a new way to assume our responsibilities in the future."[20] But Lei Fang did not do much more than issue a statement calling for reform of the CCBA. Having failed to find a new way to run the CCBA, he indicated his intention to resign. Since he had not "earned back" the money he had spent to buy the votes for the post, however, he was unwilling to step down.

Then a rumor surfaced in Chinatown that the English Secretary of the CCBA, Chen Shutang, was prepared to pay Lei three thousand dollars for the post.[21] The deal was not realized, and the CCBA did not reform itself to become a democratic organization. Some of the CCBA leaders, however, began to acknowledge their weakness and unpopularity and to take the strength of the CHLA seriously. This new attitude was one of the factors that led to the successful establishment of the Anti-Japanese United Front in New York's Chinatown (discussed in detail in Chapter Four).

When the CHLA celebrated its first anniversary, it was clear that its strength lay in its membership. Its democratic structure distinguished the CHLA from the traditional organizations in which the elite monopolized all power. Democracy was a new idea in Chinatown, and its appeal could be seen in the fact that CHLA members were willing to struggle against the CCBA's public attacks and attempted sabotage. The meaning of the CHLA's democracy can be further understood by taking a look at the damaging effect that the notorious tong wars had on the Chinese community. From 1933 to the end of 1934, the tong wars wreaked havoc in the Chinese communities on the East Coast. Many persons were killed, and a large number of innocent Chinese Americans were arrested and deported by the INS. Newspaper reports described Chinatowns as hells where the Chinese were killing each other ruthlessly.[22]

The tong wars erupted because the various tongs, which usually controlled the gambling houses and brothels in Chinatowns, settled their most intransigent problems through violence. Against such a background, the CHLA's practice of democracy could be seen as a conscious effort, on the one hand, to break away from the traditional ways of settling disputes and, on the other, to counter the negative depictions of the Chinese community.

The basic meaning of the democratic spirit for most of the CHLA's members was that the alliance defended their common interests. This democratic spirit not only distinguished the CHLA from the traditional organizations in Chinatown, but also differentiated it from the radical left forces and defined the CHLA as a grassroots organization.

The Chinese Left and the CHLA: Theory

The CHLA received strong political and moral support from the Chinese left in the alliance's struggle against racial discrimination and the Chinese traditional organizations. But the CHLA's activities were not directed by the left nor did all its members accept Marxist-Leninist ideology. The majority of CHLA members, as hand laundry proprietors, never shared the Chinese left's vision of a proletarian revolution in the United States in which the Chinese Americans' fight against racism and class oppression constituted an integral part. Nevertheless, whenever the CHLA faced problems with either racist authorities or the CCBA, the left offered help. Although accepting this assistance, CHLA members never accepted the left's idea of class struggle. This delicate and sometimes ambiguous relationship between the Chinese left and the CHLA is an important chapter in the history of the laundrymen's alliance, one that provides an opportunity for understanding the dynamics of the changes occurring in New York's Chinatown in the 1930s.

The Chinese left in the New York Chinese community in the 1930s was composed of a small group of young students. They were all born in China and grew up there. They came to the United States for graduate studies after finishing their college education at home. One of the leading members, Xu Yongying (Hsu Yung-ying), was a graduate of the class of

1924 of Qinghua School, which prepared Chinese students for study in the United States. While at Qinghua, Xu became an activist in the May Fourth student movement of 1919 and joined a political society, the Weizhenghui, which advocated "saving Chinese through political reform." Before coming to the United States in 1924, Xu and his friends went to Guangzhou (Canton) to ask Sun Yat-sen for his advice. Sun, the leader of the 1911 revolution, encouraged the young students to take part in the struggle to reform China.[23]

Most of these students joined the KMT in China or in the United States. After the KMT-CCP split in 1927, they identified with the Chinese Communist Party, although it is unclear how many actually joined it. When they founded the Chinese Anti-Imperialist Alliance of America in 1928, they aimed to launch a movement among the "overseas Chinese workers and peasants" to support the CCP against the KMT. After several years, however, they found that they had little success in mobilizing and organizing Chinese Americans. In a self-criticizing article, Xu Yongying explored the reasons for their failure.

Xu's article, "To Overcome the Difficulties in the Development of the Mass Struggle of Overseas Chinese," offered a comprehensive and severe criticism of the left's weaknesses. The left's failure to overcome the "separation between the awakened elements and the overseas Chinese masses" was caused, Xu pointed out, by the left's "close-doorism," which expressed itself in several forms. First, after being "awakened," that is, after understanding that the causes of their sufferings were oppression and exploitation by the capitalist class, leftists began to think about how to overthrow the capitalist system but "became insensitive to the sufferings that [the masses] were enduring." "Therefore, [our] revolutionary consciousness became a sort of religious comfort and reduced our struggling against daily capitalist oppression." The left could not sense what the masses sensed and thus became indifferent to the latter's demands for solutions to their everyday hardships. "We were originally among the masses, but now have walked out on them." Second, the "awakened elements" tended to forget how many steps they had gone through to become "awakened" and had a contemptuous attitude toward those who remained "unawakened." The left condemned the "unawakened" as "stupid" and as "antirevolutionaries" and even labeled some of the poorest elements in the Chinese community "capitalists" or "imperialists" because they would not accept the left's political views. "Then, of course," Xu commented, "the masses condemned the awakened elements as 'crazy' and 'mad.' "[24]

Xu also discussed the social background of the "awakened elements" as an important factor in "close-doorism." These individuals were actually part of the elite within the KMT at the time the CAIA was founded, Xu's article reveals. For example, Xu himself was the editor of the *Guomin Ribao*, a KMT newspaper in San Francisco; Liu Kemian was a member of the Standing Committee of the KMT's Philadelphia branch; Zhao Yue was a member of the Executive Committee of the same branch; Chen Huijian was chairwoman of a trade union in San Francisco; and He Zhifeng was a member of the Standing Committee of the KMT's Chicago branch. When they were in the KMT, "these elements of course did not know what the masses were and were rarely aware of the masses' everyday painful struggle. After they resigned from the KMT, they tried to merge with the masses. However, it was not easy for them to shake off the influences they had been subject to within the KMT for so many years." Even those members of the working class, Xu stated, after joining the CAIA, felt they were different from common people.[25]

Xu listed these weaknesses, he made it clear, to call his comrades' attention to them. He urged leftists to engage in "severe self-criticism" and to correct their mistake of separating themselves from the masses. Xu wanted his comrades to "regard close-doorism as beasts and snakes [that threatened the left's cause]; and after breaking through it, never turn back. And we must overcome various difficulties, and merge with the masses [*zhoudao qunzhong zhong qu*; literally, "go into the masses"]."[26] Xu himself seemed to have been successful in this area, as one of his acquaintances, a former CHLA activist, recalled:

Mr. Xu Yongying was a very nice guy. I respected him a lot. He was from Shanghai, a *liuxuesheng* [Chinese student abroad]. How did we communicate with each other? Well, he learned Cantonese. He managed to talk in broken Cantonese. He was very honest and hardworking. He always had trouble making a living. He once worked as a waiter in Chinatown but soon lost that job. Then he went to 125th Street to polish shoes to make a few dollars. He never had any money. Sometimes he asked me, "Hey, Old Horse (my nickname), give me a quarter. I have no money to go home." I would give him a quarter. Life was tough for him. But he always worked hard. He was a sincere man. He later developed an emotional attachment to the Cantonese community. After liberation (1949), he went back to China and became the head of the Bureau for Foreign Affairs in the Shanghai People's Government. Then he had cancer. He said, "I will die soon. Before I die, I would like to go to Taishan to live for a while. I have so many friends from

Taishan, how can I die without living in their hometown for some time?" So he went to Taishan and lived there for two or three months. Soon after he returned to Shanghai, he died. He died in the '50s.[27]

As Xu and other leftists well knew, however, good personal relations with some "advanced" individuals among the masses did not constitute a mass movement under their direction. As mentioned earlier, in the late 1920s members of the Chinese left had a strong tendency to focus on domestic issues in China. In the early 1930s they began to shift their attention to issues in the Chinese American community. Committed Marxists, they attempted to mobilize the "masses" of Chinese Americans to join a "revolutionary movement" against the "capitalist class" in American society in general, and against the "feudal-capitalist class" in the Chinese American community and in China itself in particular. It is interesting to note that in this theory, the term "feudal-capitalist class" was used to characterize the ruling class in both China and the Chinese immigrant community in America. In their effort to mobilize working-class Chinese Americans, the Chinese left accepted guidance from the CPUSA, whose theoretical analysis they hoped to apply to the reality of Chinatowns. Here they encountered the problem that these theories simply did not seem to work.

Xu Yongying's article had encouraged the left to merge with the masses, but it was not clear which part of the masses the left should approach. A few months later one of his comrades, Yu Xingri, discussed this issue in an article entitled "Applying the Open Letter to the Revolutionary Work among Overseas Chinese." Yu Xingri freely accepted and attempted to apply to Chinatown the prevailing CPUSA approach to mass organization, known as "concentration." The answer to the lack of a mass base, a 1932 CPUSA Executive Committee resolution held, according to Yu's article, was to concentrate work among the industrial working class. Examining the work of the Chinese left, Yu Xingri found that it had failed to concentrate in such major industries as agriculture, canning, textiles, and maritime commerce. Yu attributed this failure to a "lack of political understanding of [the importance] of the concentration." From such a perspective, Yu did not see the founding of the CHLA under the influence of *The Chinese Vanguard* as a great achievement. Instead, he regarded the left's distribution of *The Chinese Vanguard* to small hand laundries as "choosing the easy way" and "working in the least difficult places," and he believed that the left missed "the most important and at the same time the most difficult work," which was to distribute *The Chinese Vanguard* in large factories, ships, and big restaurants and to influence and organize the masses in those places.[28]

Yu admitted that few overseas Chinese were "pure" workers who lived on salaries and that the majority of them were "small craftsmen and small businessmen," whom he considered "petit bourgeoisie." He warned, "Although we should not overlook their revolutionary tendency, . . . as a whole, the petit bourgeoisie often oscillate and lack determination in a struggle." Because the left was weak in organizing the working class, Yu continued, there was a danger that it could not influence the petit bourgeoisie but rather would be influenced by them. To support his point, Yu criticized the fact that the CHLA had joined the New York City National Recovery Act parade. He concluded, "We must concentrate [our work] on the major working class masses, establish and strengthen their independent organizations, so that the overseas Chinese revolutionary movement will not lose its proletarian basis."[29]

Yu's approach to classifying the Chinese community reflected the left's dogmatic application of the CPUSA's theories to overseas Chinese. Many leftist Chinese became Communists in the 1930s, but it is not known whether they joined the CPUSA or founded a branch of the CCP in the United States. In any case, it is clear that from the early 1930s onward they were cut off from the CCP, which was isolated and encircled by the KMT in mountainous areas in southern China, and that they received directives and guidance from the CPUSA, as indicated by the articles in *The Chinese Vanguard*.

Following the theoretical guidance of the CPUSA led to a permanent quandary: how to approach and organize the Chinese "proletariat" in America. Since there were few Chinese industrial workers in the United States, as some Chinese leftists recognized, the left was never able to build a proletarian organization that met its exacting sense of what a genuine proletarian organization should be. Frustrated, these leftists discussed the same issue again and again in the pages of *The Chinese Vanguard*. From February 1933 to May 1934 at least a dozen articles discussed how to work among the proletariat. As a whole, these articles followed the same line of argument and offered quite similar analyses of the issues. Basically, their problem was that they wanted to approach the Chinese American proletariat but could not find it.

Some Chinese leftists tried to explore why they had failed to organize the overseas Chinese proletariat. One simply claimed that "there is no proletarian basis in New York City,"[30] acknowledging the fact that few

Chinese were industrial workers. Others, Xu Yongying among them, approached the issue from a different angle. Xu emphasized that the Chinese left must start establishing a base among the "settled" overseas Chinese proletariat, that is, those Chinese who had settled in the United States permanently. Otherwise, it would be hard to make the Chinese struggle part of the American proletarian revolution. From such a point of view, the "sojourner mentality" of most Chinese Americans was a major obstacle for the left. Xu pointed out:

> Due to the restriction of the U.S. immigration laws, few overseas Chinese can obtain [U.S.] citizenship, [and they] do not have a normal family life. [Thus] most of them have no intention to settle permanently; the majority have the idea "to earn few cents and return to China." The overseas Chinese feudal-capitalist class exploit, promote, and strengthen this idea through various clan and family organizations.... As a result, the starting point to raise the [political] consciousness among overseas Chinese is the China issues, rather than the class struggle in the overseas Chinese community.[31]

This is perhaps the first examination and criticism of the "sojourner mentality" ever offered by a Chinese. It is also interesting to note that the Chinese leftists, most of whom were unable and never attempted to acquire U.S. citizenship, made such observations and regarded the "settled Chinese" as the main target of their revolutionary work. In the ensuing years, as we shall see, the Chinese leftists continued to work to help Chinese Americans give up this "sojourner mentality." The leftists clearly linked their work in Chinatown to a broad proletarian revolutionary movement in the United States. With a vision of a proletarian revolution, they tried to integrate Chinese American struggles into the wider-scale American working-class movement.

To a great extent, this vision defined the nature of the relationship between the Chinese left and the CHLA. In April 1934, when the CHLA suffered its first internal split, in which the opposition faction cited "having meetings with the Communists" as an excuse to attack Lei Zhuofeng and others, the Chinese leftists explained their view of their relationship with the CHLA in an editorial in *The Chinese Vanguard*:

> This newspaper, indeed, stands for the principles and doctrines of the Communist Party. The Communist Party is the political party of the proletariat. But it does not struggle only for the interests of the proletariat.... This newspaper supports the struggle of small hand laundry proprietors in New York City not because we see them as proletarian or because we want to

temporarily "exploit" them in our fight against the Kuomintang and its organ *The Chinese Nationalist Daily*. The reason we support them is because the small hand laundry proprietors are poor laborers, and they are the ally of the proletariat. For these small hand laundry proprietors, real liberation comes to them only after they accept the direction and help from the proletariat and its political party, the Communist Party.[32]

There is no evidence that the CHLA ever accepted the Chinese left's long-term vision of the proletarian revolution. Nevertheless, the CHLA always accepted help from the left in the alliance's short-term struggles against racial discrimination and political oppression. The CHLA never saw its struggle as part of a larger conflict between the working class and the capitalist class in American society, as did the Chinese left.

Despite this great gap, the CHLA and the left communicated through the medium of a shared political language that was entirely Chinese in origin. In its columns, writers for *The Chinese Vanguard* used such terms as "proletarian revolution" and "massive class struggle" to discuss the situation in Chinatown. In the leftists' exchanges with the CHLA, however, the terms were very different: they did not say "capitalist class," but rather "the evil gentry and local despots of the CCBA" (*Zhonghua Gongsuo tuhaoliesheng*); not "proletariat" but "the poor laboring class" (*qiongku laogong jieji*) and "relying on the strength of the mass" (*yikao qunzhong liliang*). These three terms, with distinct Chinese coloring, were widely used in China after the May Fourth Movement of 1919, especially in Guangdong Province, where the CCP and the KMT coalesced to launch a nationalist revolution with the purpose of expelling foreign imperialists and overthrowing the "feudal ruling classes" in the early 1920s.

As immigrants from a radicalized place, Guangdong Province in the 1920s, the Chinese hand laundrymen were familiar with the revolutionary vocabulary used at that time. Even within the context of the Chinese American community, the phrase "evil gentry and local despots" seemed to them adequate to characterize the CCBA officials, whose behavior was similar to that of landlords and local government officials in China. The term "poor laboring class," as ambiguous as it was in China to include all lower-class laborers, helped the laundrymen find a name for their place in American society. The Chinese laundrymen clearly did not see themselves as part of the American proletariat or working class, probably because of the painful memories of that class's anti-Chinese agitation in the past and of their experience of being forced into the hand laundry business by the exclusion acts and white workers' hostility. Nor did they perceive themselves as "petit bourgeoisie," as the Chinese leftists saw them. Within the American context, if an immigrant regarded himself as a "petit bourgeois," he might think of himself as a would-be bourgeois. To the Chinese hand laundryman under the severe restrictions of the Chinese exclusion acts and racial discrimination, the prospect was so bleak that he might never even dream of becoming a bourgeois in American society.

The difference between the CHLA members' self-defined class status and its analysis by the Chinese left suggests that a group's subjective perception of its own status is important to an understanding of its members' mental and behavioral reactions to their circumstances and external influences. "Poor laboring class" was broad enough to include hand laundrymen with various backgrounds and ideas. It was on this basis that a firm occupational organization could be founded. Also, it was because the term "poor laboring class," brought by the immigrants from China to the United States, was so vague and inclusive that the CHLA, with no intention of joining the American proletarian revolution, could still communicate with leftists and accept their help, even if CHLA members did not see themselves as allies of the white American proletariat, as did the leftists. Finally, "poor laboring class," within the Chinese context, called forth a spirit of opposition to exploitation and oppression—the very spirit that undergirded the founding of the CHLA. Condemned by the Chinese left as "temporary zeal," it was nevertheless a spirit that was appreciated and supported.[33]

The Chinese leftists, in contrast, followed orthodox Marxist class theory in their analysis of the class structure in Chinatown and of the status of the Chinese hand laundrymen. The leftists seemed to have no conception of a "service economy" or an "immigrant economy" that would have helped them better understand class relations in American society, and they failed to grasp that entrenched clan and family relationships distorted and complicated the class relations in the Chinese American community. Furthermore, they did not pay much attention to the laundrymen's own ideas of their class status. Nevertheless, as long as they tried to make a breakthrough in their efforts to mobilize Chinese Americans, they had to pay attention to the CHLA, the largest grassroots organization in the New York Chinese community. Therefore, even though the leftists felt an ever-present frustration over their unsuccessful attempts to reach the "overseas Chinese proletariat," which they regarded as their primary revolutionary task, they actually spent a great deal of their energy supporting the CHLA and other "poor laboring class" organizations in the latter's struggle for survival—work that the leftists themselves considered secondary.

The CHLA and the Left: Practice

As noted earlier, when the 254 Chinese laundrymen called for the formation of the CHLA in April 1933, it was a spontaneous movement launched by the laundrymen themselves. But since members of the CHLA faced continuous discrimination in the hand laundry business and, as a result, had to engage in seemingly endless struggles against discriminatory legislation and actions, the organization's contacts with the Chinese leftists, who always initially offered their help, increased. Most CHLA members welcomed such support, but some soon began to feel uneasy about the relationship between the CHLA and the left.

The CHLA's fight against the passport requirement in 1934 is a good example of the complicated relationship between the two. On October 3, 1934, the New York City Commissioner of License Paul Moss issued a new rule requiring all Chinese hand laundry operators to submit their passports or other legal documents to prove their legal entry into the United States when they applied for their operation license or its renewal.[34] Since it was a public secret within the Chinese community that many Chinese laundrymen did not have such legal papers, the rule was interpreted by the community as another attempt to destroy its lifeline—the hand laundry business. The CHLA protested to the license department immediately.[35] Then it called a membership meeting on October 7 to discuss how to fight the regulation. A special committee of six members was chosen to deal with the city government and handle related affairs. Protest letters were printed and distributed to the members, who could simply sign and mail them to the license department. At the same time, the CHLA sent out letters to all organizations in Chinatown asking for their support.[36]

The Chinese leftists were involved in the case from the beginning. Their comments, suggestions, and criticism about how to oppose the regulation suggest that they acted to direct and influence the CHLA in its struggle against discrimination. Some of the CHLA leaders were not ready to launch a massive protest movement against the passport requirement; moreover, they wanted to obtain support only within the Chinese community. They also tended to prefer legal steps to a mobilization of public opinion, prohibiting CHLA members from sending protest letters unless they owned their laundries. Later they even stopped sending the protest letters altogether in order "not to irritate the License Department."[37] The Chinese leftists criticized these CHLA leaders implicitly in *The Chinese Vanguard* and urged the laundrymen's alliance to "rely on the strength of the masses; to coalesce with all mass organizations of Chinese and Americans, especially the revolutionary organizations, such as the CAIA and the International Labor Defense," so as to abolish the regulation.[38] At the same time, the leftists warned the CHLA that it should be cautious about possible sabotage by the CCBA and the KMT, citing the lessons of 1933.[39]

The Chinese leftists not only provided advice to the CHLA on how to develop the protest movement, but also took action to help expand it. The three leftist organizations—the CAIA, *The Chinese Vanguard*, and the Chinatown Branch of the International Labor Defense—all sent protest letters to the license department and, together with the American Friends of the Chinese People, sent representatives to attend the hearings on the passport requirement. After some CHLA leaders decided to prevent their members from sending protest letters, the Chinatown Branch of the International Labor Defense distributed the protest letters among Chinese and American organizations.[40] Furthermore, on October 28, at a "Hands off China" rally attended by representatives of such political organizations as the American Friends of the Chinese People, the International Labor Defense, and the CPUSA, members of the CAIA and *The Chinese Vanguard* raised the passport protest issue. All the organizations agreed to ask their members (numbering 189,000 altogether) to send letters protesting the passport requirement to the license department.[41] Six days later the commissioner of the license department formally announced to the CHLA that the requirement would be withdrawn.[42]

While celebrating victory, many CHLA leaders and members accepted *The Chinese Vanguard*'s conclusion that the case was won, to a great extent, because "many Chinese and American mass organizations" helped and their support enhanced the strength of the protest movement.[43] At a membership meeting on November 4, the support of the sixty organizations of the "Hands off China" rally was cited as an important factor in the success. Xu Yongying, as a representative of the CAIA and *The Chinese Vanguard*, was invited to give a talk. In his speech, Xu emphasized that the laundrymen should understand that "mass organizations have common interests," and that was why so many nonlaundry mass organizations offered to help in the CHLA's struggle against the discriminatory passport regulation. Therefore, Xu said, the CHLA should extend its contacts with other mass organizations. He encouraged CHLA members to participate in activities organized by the CAIA, the Unemployment Council, and the International Labor Defense. His speech was warmly received. Finally, those present decided to send letters to thank all the organizations that had helped defeat the passport requirement.[44]

A week later, on November 11, to further express its gratitude to these organizations in a Chinese way, the CHLA invited their representatives to a banquet in the Chinese restaurant Da Guan Yuan. The guests included representatives from the International Labor Defense, the Friends of China Committee, the CAIA, the Chinatown Unemployment Council, *The Daily Worker*, *The Chinese Vanguard*, *The Chinese Journal*, and other organizations. Once again the guests all pointed out the importance of the unity of the mass organizations in the struggle against discrimination and oppression, and they repeatedly emphasized that this victory over the license department was but "the beginning of the mobilization of mass strength by the overseas Chinese in New York." Julius Bezozo, the CHLA's legal advisor, agreed that the strength of the mass movements was the "primary force," while the legal steps were but "secondary means" in the struggle against oppression.[45]

It is clear that the left's influence was one of the most dynamic forces in the political life of Chinatown in the 1930s and that the leftists were the strongest supporters of the CHLA in its struggles. The fact that the CHLA invited the representatives of the leftist organizations for dinner indicated that many of the alliance's leaders and members appreciated the relationship established between the CHLA and these groups. A formal vote was required, however, before an invitation to Xu Yongying could be issued. Clearly, some CHLA members were hesitant about the relationship with the left. We should remember that when the CHLA experienced its first split in April 1934, one accusation the opponents made against Lei Zhuofeng was that he had held meetings with the Communists in the CHLA headquarters. By early 1936 a small group of anti-Communists within the CHLA had launched another attack against "Communist influence" and caused the second political split of the CHLA. An examination of this split may help us better understand the political atmosphere in Chinatown at that time and the tensions within the CHLA.

After the CHLA won the case against the passport requirement in November 1934, it suffered a loss in April 1935, when the court ruled that

The Chinese Journal was guilty of slandering the CCBA, and its editor, Zhu Xia, was banned from criticizing the CCBA for three years.[46] As noted earlier, *The Chinese Journal* had long been a thorn in the flesh of the CCBA because of its active role in the founding of the CHLA and its constant and severe criticism of the CCBA. In early 1934 the CCBA sued *The Chinese Journal* and Zhu Xia for slander. To defend *The Chinese Journal* and Zhu Xia, the CHLA once again allied itself with the CAIA, *The Chinese Vanguard*, and the Chinatown Branch of the International Labor Defense.

Although the CHLA joined the leftist organizations to defend *The Chinese Journal*, its strategy and slogan were quite different from theirs. The leftists, as usual, wanted to launch a massive protest movement with the slogan, "Oppose political oppression." The CHLA, in contrast, adopted the strategy of appealing to the democratic principles of freedom of assembly and freedom of speech. Apparently, the CHLA's opinion eventually prevailed, for a United Committee to Defend Freedom of Assembly and Speech in the Chinese Community was established, comprising the CHLA and the three Chinese leftist organizations. After more than a year of deliberation and debate, however, the court eventually ruled in favor of the CCBA.

During the trial the judge, showing the protest letters supporting Zhu from the leftist organizations, asked Zhu whether he had any relationship to the Communist party. Zhu announced that he was not a Communist, and the judge finally ruled that "the result of investigation shows that Zhu is not a Communist."[47] This episode seemed to cast a shadow over the CHLA and Zhu himself. Zhu, a liberal intellectual, never accepted the ideology of the Communist party. He had accepted help from the left only to the extent that it would strengthen his attack against the CCBA and get him out of the legal trouble with the association. Once he perceived that the help from the left could have a negative effect on the judge's decision in his case, he asked the leftist organizations not to send the protest letters to the court. The Chinese leftists, for their part, saw the court decision in the Zhu case as the result of collusion between the CCBA and the "American reactionary court," which used the strategy of "red-baiting" to smash the "masses" and "democratic forces" in the Chinese community.[48]

The outcome of the Zhu case and its psychological effect on the CHLA members and the Chinese community showed that anti-Communist sentiments in American society could be a source of great political pressure, which could restrain such potentially radical groups or forces as the

CHLA from developing a close relationship with the left. In the CHLA case, it seems that most of the leaders and members advocated a friendly relationship with the left, although sometimes they did not agree with the left's "massive class struggle" rhetoric and strategy; but some CHLA leaders and members became fearful of being red-baited by the conservative forces in both the Chinese community and American society and attempted to renounce the influence of the left in the CHLA. This situation led to the political split of the CHLA in 1936, the alliance's most serious internal conflict.

In February 1936, when the CHLA was going to have a new election according to its bylaws, Liang Jian, a CHLA member, suddenly put an "open letter to the CHLA members" in the KMT newspaper. Liang claimed that he "hated the Communist Party for its agitation of class struggle, and for its abandonment of the motherland." He demanded that the CHLA expel those "elements who are used by the Communist Party and who intended to *chihua* the CHLA [to make the CHLA "red"]."[49] A few days later some anonymous flyers were posted in Chinatown streets listing twenty-seven CHLA officials and members as "believers of Communism" and asking the CHLA to expel them. The flyers claimed that the CHLA "in recent years was indeed used and controlled by the Communists," and warned that it would be "easily destroyed by the Communists in the near future." As for the evidence, the flyers stated that "we have many facts to prove it, but we'd rather not cite them now."[50]

Liang Jian was probably sent by the traditional forces to infiltrate into the CHLA and destroy it from within. His original name was Liang Qike. When the CHLA was founded in 1933, he was the president of a clan association, Jinglan Gongsuo, and following the practice of the CCBA and the tongs, he posted "long reds" in the streets of Chinatown warning members of his gongsuo not to join the CHLA. Later he changed his name and joined the alliance. After becoming a member, Liang Jian seemed to support all the decisions of the organization. Now his sudden attack on the CHLA led the members to recall his previous effort to destroy it.[51]

Liang's unexpected assault was quickly followed by the actions of a group of CHLA officials and members who wanted to change the direction of the alliance and to place it under their own control. This group included eighteen self-proclaimed "anti-Communists," who also placed "statements" in the KMT newspapers denouncing the "Communist influence" and the current election procedure.[52] On March 8, when the

CHLA held a membership meeting to elect the group leaders, the anti-Communist group questioned the "legitimacy of the election" and claimed that the CHLA "was besieged by the Communists." They wanted to throw out the results of the election and used anti-Communist rhetoric to call for a new one, in which they expected to win. A majority of the members who attended the meeting pointed out, however, that the CHLA's constitution ruled that people of various political persuasions should not be discriminated against; therefore, the demand of the anti-Communist group to expel the Communists was against the spirit of the alliance's constitution. Recognizing that they could not reach their goal through peaceful means, the anti-Communists resorted to force: they initiated a fistfight. Many loyal members were irritated and joined the fight. As a result, four of the anti-Communists were seriously hurt. But they had accomplished part of their purpose: the election of the group leaders failed to proceed.[53]

Until this time the leaders of the CHLA had apparently adopted a conciliatory attitude to the anti-Communists. CHLA officials did not dispute the fact that the alliance had obtained the help of the Communists, but they vigorously denied that the CHLA was either used or controlled by the Communist party. They appealed to the spirit of unity, hoping that the anti-Communists would change their minds. Their goal was to maintain the CHLA as an occupational organization accommodating different political opinions and parties. They stated that it was normal to have diverse opinions within a democratic organization, and they hoped to settle these differences through democratic means.[54]

The anti-Communists, however, were determined to take control of the CHLA. On March 12 they called a membership meeting; refused to allow Lei Zhuofeng, Zhao Shizhi, and others on the list of the so-called believers of Communism to attend, and manipulated the meeting to produce a resolution that denied the results of the preliminary mail-ballot election and set up a "reorganizing committee" to hold a new election.[55]

By this time the CHLA Executive Committee had been forced to abandon its conciliatory attitude toward the anti-Communists and to take action. On March 14 it held a meeting in the office of the CHLA legal advisor, Julius Bezozo (the CHLA office was occupied by the anti-Communists), and unanimously passed a resolution to expel Liang Jian and twenty other anti-Communists from the alliance.[56] On March 25 the Executive Committee issued an "Open Letter to CHLA Members, Fellow Hand Laundrymen, and All Overseas Chinese," making the internal conflicts public and exposing the conspiracy of the anti-Communists. The letter reiterated that the CHLA was an occupational organization with members from all "clan, family, educational, religious, tong, and political groups or associations," and appealed to the leaders of "all overseas Chinese organizations" for their support in the struggle of the CHLA against the "evil forces" that were attempting to disintegrate it.[57]

Then, on March 29, the Executive Committee called a membership meeting that subsequently endorsed the committee's resolution of March 14 to expel the twenty-one anti-Communists and elected the group leaders. Julius Bezozo's support of the Executive Committee seemed to enhance the CHLA's confidence that it could overcome the problems caused by the anti-Communists. Bezozo told the members that the Executive Committee was the only legitimate representative of the CHLA and that all the meetings called by the anti-Communists were illegal, and he assured them that as a legitimate organization the CHLA would be protected by law. Bezozo's speech was reported to have been "applauded vigorously for a long time."[58]

The anti-Communists next challenged the CHLA Executive Committee in court. After the court failed to grant their request for an order to suspend the CHLA election,[59] they sued the new officers of the CHLA, charging that the April election was illegal.[60] The legal battle dragged on for almost a year. Eventually, the New York State Supreme Court decided on April 23, 1937, that the accusations of the anti-Communists against the CHLA were groundless. According to *The New York Times*, "Supreme Court Referee Thomas C. T. Crain upheld the current officers of the association [the CHLA] as having been elected legally. The hearing consumed nine months during which hundreds of ballots in what the Referee's opinion described as 'undecipherable symbols,' were recounted and translated into English."[61]

The court verdict was handed down on the fourth anniversary of the CHLA. To celebrate the victory and the anniversary, the alliance held a banquet at the Joy Far Low Restaurant at 24 Pell Street on Sunday, April 25, 1937. More than three hundred members and guests came. Probably as a diplomatic gesture, License Department Commissioner Paul Moss and Deputy Commissioner Dorothy Kenyon were invited to the banquet. Moss gave a short speech in which he "advised the laundrymen to get higher prices for their work, and his advice was applauded vigorously."[62]

Although the CHLA eventually won the case against the anti-Communists, the political and legal battles were a blow to the alliance. As one of the CHLA members recalled in 1941, "the struggle against the bad elements [in 1936–37] was indeed the most difficult period in the history of our Alliance. In those days, the loyal members not only had to donate money to the legal costs, but also had to stand together and work hard to save the Alliance.... The evil people made all the threats so that the membership was reduced to about 600."[63] Clearly, the red-baiting strategy of the anti-Communists, who obtained the support and help of the CCBA as soon as they started the split in March 1934,[64] worked to produce fear among many CHLA members.

These events suggest that, if it accepted help from the left, the CHLA could be vulnerable to external and internal opposition and attacks that exploited the potentially anti-Communist political atmosphere in American society. Given such a political atmosphere, some members might not have wanted to be associated with the left but they did want its support in their struggle against racial discrimination and economic exploitation. Therefore, the CHLA leaders, during and after the political split of 1936–37, developed a dual strategy of keeping a distance from the radical leftists in order to maintain the alliance as an occupational organization and, at the same time, obtaining the support of the leftists in an indirect way. The Quon Shar was instrumental in making this strategy work.

The Quon Shar and the Leadership of the CHLA

The Quon Shar (in pinyin, Qun She; literally, the "Mass Club") was founded by the core members of the CHLA in June 1935. Its name first appeared in *The Chinese Vanguard* on July 6, 1935. It has been described by some scholars as a cultural, a recreational, or a social club.[65] Actually, the Quon Shar was first founded by the radical members of the CHLA as a separate organization so that they could independently express their opinions on issues concerning China and the Chinese American community. At that time a group of conservatives within the CHLA wanted to keep it a "pure" occupational organization free of politics. The radicals vigorously supported the anti-Japanese movement in the Chinese community, but the conservatives wanted to keep a distance from that movement because the leftists were the most outspoken within it. As a result, the radicals, desiring to express their nationalist enthusiasm but hoping to maintain the unity of the alliance, founded the Quon Shar.[66]

The conservatives were the anti-Communists who caused the political split of the CHLA in 1936. During that crisis the purpose of the Quon Shar was "to support the Chinese Hand Laundry Alliance," "a fact which everyone knows."[67] At one of its meetings it was emphasized that "the progress of the Quon Shar in the past was for the good of the Chinese Hand Laundry Alliance, and that expanding the Quon Shar was the same as expanding the Chinese Hand Laundry Alliance."[68] An examination of the minutes of the Quon Shar meetings reveals that the basic and most frequently discussed subject was how to support and serve the CHLA.[69]

As mentioned earlier, some of the CHLA members, including all the Quon Shar members, recognized the importance of the leftists' support. But they also had to live with the fact that in the political atmosphere of that time many CHLA members were hesitant to get involved in political issues unless they directly and immediately threatened the alliance's survival. Members had seen some extreme cases in which the CCBA and the conservative forces had cooperated with the American authorities to deport their enemies. Since many Chinese laundrymen did not have proper papers, their fear of being exposed by the conservatives was understandable.

The Quon Shar members, perhaps more than anyone else, were sensitive to the fears of their fellow laundrymen and could appreciate their hesitation in participating in political activities, for they themselves were not naive about the danger they faced. Indeed, if they were to fight for justice and better conditions for the laundrymen, they knew they had to face powerful conservative forces determined to use all available means to destroy them. To fight in such an unfavorable environment required not only unity and willingness but also a spirit of self-sacrifice. In the crisis of the second CHLA split in 1936–37, the Quon Shar members were prepared for the worst.

In April 1937 the Quon Shar members had a discussion on how to protect members "endangered because of struggles, such as being summoned for interrogation by the Immigration and Naturalization Service, etc." At that time it was already clear that the CHLA would win the case against the anti-Communists in court. The Quon Shar members agreed, however, "that even though victory may be in our grasp, affairs of the court are too indefinite." Although they believed that "in the event that we should lose, we will still be able to win over the followers," they prepared themselves for the worst possible outcome. The meeting decided that "any member who has not committed any crime and who is arrested by the INS for interrogation should be given as much help as possible"; and if all efforts failed and a member was to be deported, one member said, "if the society members are unwilling to return to China [because of the existing KMT regime], they can go to Soviet Russia, because Soviet Russia has announced that it will take in the working people of any nation who have been deported against their will."[70]

Not every CHLA member was ready to make that kind of sacrifice. Only the most dedicated CHLA members joined the Quon Shar, and there is no way to know the extent of its membership. A reading of the minutes of the club's meetings suggests that there were probably thirty to forty members in the 1930s. By the 1940s, a former member of the Quon Shar estimated, it had some one hundred members. This member recalled, "The Quon Shar was the hard core of the CHLA, the most progressive organization in Chinatown back in the '30s and '40s. To put it simply, the Quon Shar members were the 'hatchetmen' of the CHLA, who protected the CHLA against the CCBA's hatchetmen."[71]

After losing many members in the split, the CHLA understood the potentially fatal blow that the anti-Communists could strike through red-baiting, and it deliberately reduced its contacts with the left. In its statements and letters to its members and the Chinese community in 1936 and 1937, the CHLA talked more about the "solidarity of the fellow hand laundrymen" than the differences between the anti-Communists and the members.[72] During that period it was the Quon Shar that publicly maintained relations with the leftists, and it was through the Quon Shar that the Chinese leftists extended their help to the CHLA.

The Quon Shar members were young, relatively more educated than most CHLA members, and current or former members of the CHLA's Executive or Supervisory Committee. They all strongly identified with the CHLA. Politically active, they were not afraid of CCBA oppression. They also understood, however, that they were the few radicals among the laundrymen. Their efforts to consolidate the CHLA in the years after its split of 1936–37 indicate that they realized that safeguarding the CHLA from attacks and sabotage was a prerequisite to their struggle against the CCBA and the building of a new power order in the New York Chinese community. Thus, from 1936 on, Quon Shar members and CHLA leaders (often the same individuals) made tremendous efforts to strengthen and develop the CHLA.

The CHLA never compromised on one thing: the democratic principle of electing its officials. For many years CHLA members were proud of the fact that from the beginning the alliance had always held democratic elections. The CHLA was able to shape and maintain this democratic system, to a great extent, with the help of the Quon Shar members. Since the CHLA members were scattered all over New York City and most of them did not have a telephone at home or at work,[73] organizing the election of the group leaders involved a great deal of work. It took several years for the CHLA to institutionalize the democratic election system. The records of the Quon Shar meetings show that every year before the CHLA's election of the group leaders, the Quon Shar held a meeting to discuss how to help the alliance and how to handle such problems as the lack of group leaders (who were responsible for the election of new group leaders) in some districts and some members' noncommittal attitude toward the election. Then, on the date of the election, the Quon Shar members went to different districts to help the CHLA members elect the group leaders. The minutes of one of the Quon Shar meetings read:

> *Discussion:* Concerning how to help the Laundry Alliance in its election.
> *Decision:* In the Laundry Alliance election of the past years, the members of this Society have exerted their own efforts in voluntarily directing the election in various districts. If the Laundry Alliance needs people for the election, the members of this Society will give all the help that their time can allow. As for the method for carrying out the election, the Laundry Alliance should handle it.[74]

To protect and develop the CHLA, Quon Shar members as well as CHLA leaders demonstrated a spirit of self-sacrifice. They were themselves all laundrymen working twelve to fifteen hours a day to make a living, but they were willing to give up their self-interest for the good of the collective organization. This spirit of self-sacrifice, together with the spirit of fighting, was emphasized in every year's inauguration of new officials. One CHLA member praised the alliance's leaders in 1943 this way:

> Several years ago, when I was in China, I had learned about the CHLA from my friends' correspondences and the CHLA's bulletins. . . . After I came to New York and I have seen how the officials and members struggle together, I respect them even more. . . .
> The officials of our Alliance serve the membership without pay. However, I have seen that the officials of every year, when there is a lot of work, always work hard; sometime they stayed up until very late to finish the work, going to bed around 3 or 4 o'clock in the morning.[75]

Believing that they were doing meaningful work, the Quon Shar members and the CHLA leaders devoted tremendous time and energy to make the CHLA a "progressive" (*jinbu*) organization. To them and the CHLA members, the notion of progressiveness meant not only that the alliance would "rely on the masses' strength" (*yikao qunzhong liliang*) to fight for survival and justice, but also that the alliance should serve the needs of the members and improve the quality of the hand laundrymen's lives. With the help of the Quon Shar members, the CHLA presented itself as a new and progressive organization.

For this reason, the CHLA opposed what it called traditional Chinese customs and ideas, denouncing them as old-fashioned and corrupt. The alliance's constitution prohibited gambling, a common leisure-time activity in Chinatown, in its headquarters. It also ruled that "all old customs for observing festivals and New Year, e.g., the sending of gifts, shall be abolished."[76] The CHLA developed and sponsored many wholesome recreational and educational programs for its members. Each summer it sponsored a boat cruise on the Hudson River, and many members praised it as "one of the best ways to relax our overworked bodies."[77] Free language classes were set up to teach fellow laundrymen some basic English. A reading room in the headquarters provided Chinese-language newspapers and magazines imported from China and Hong Kong. Dr. Tao Xingzhi, a famous Chinese educator, was invited to teach the laundrymen *xin wenzhi* (new written words, or romanized Chinese). The headquarters collected musical instruments for the members to play, and a Sunday chorus was organized to teach members Chinese patriotic songs.

The CHLA and the Quon Shar often jointly sponsored holiday trips, lectures, and other social and educational programs as an alternative to the old-fashioned activities offered by the traditional organizations, such as playing mahjongg and other forms of gambling, and their headquarters (located in the same building) became an influential center for cultural and recreational affairs in New York City's Chinatown. Because of these social, educational, and recreational programs, many Chinese laundrymen partly changed their old lifestyles. On Sundays, the only day that the men took off from work, the headquarters of the CHLA and the Quon Shar were crowded with laundrymen and young Chinese Americans.[78]

The Quon Shar members not only devoted time and energy but also donated money to these programs. Whenever the CHLA had financial difficulty in sponsoring a program, Quon Shar members made donations. One former member of the Quon Shar recalled, "I have been donating money throughout my life. Back in the '30s, sometimes when I only made six dollars a week, I would donate three. I saved no money. I donated it to the anti-Japanese war, and to the programs our Quon Shar sponsored."[79]

Probably because of their dedication, spirit of self-sacrifice, and political experience, from 1940 on, the Quon Shar members were frequently elected as the CHLA leaders. The CHLA bylaws ruled that no one could hold office for more than one year, but these people were reelected in alternate years. Consequently, the CHLA began to have a stable leadership.

The CHLA, as a grassroots organization, never had a clear idea of the size of its membership. In all its records, the total number of members was vaguely described as "about thirty-two hundred," or "more than two thousand," or "about three or four thousand." This uncertainty was due to the fact that some laundrymen claimed to have joined the CHLA in order to get its legal or other assistance but never paid their annual dues. According to a CHLA Executive Committee report, in the best years "about eighty-five percent of the members paid the annual dues."[80] It is difficult to know if the membership figures given referred to dues-paying members only or to all those who made a claim on the CHLA's services. But it is certain that even in its most successful years the CHLA membership never exceeded even half the Chinese laundrymen in New York City.[81]

This fact suggests that although the average Chinese laundryman was willing to fight discrimination and exploitation when his survival was threatened, only a small group of these men, such as the Quon Shar members, had a strong determination to defend the CHLA even at the expense of their personal interests. Without the support of these backbone elements, it would have been very difficult for the CHLA to overcome its many problems. The significant role of the Quon Shar explains why the CHLA was able to prevail over its opponents and was quite successful, while similar organizations in other cities met a different fate.

According to a contemporary observer's account, within a few months after the founding of the CHLA in New York, "the Chinese Laundry Alliance of New Jersey was founded with headquarters in Newark; another was set up in Chicago; laundrymen in Philadelphia, Washington, D.C., New Haven, and Boston launched campaigns in an attempt to organize themselves."[82] No records show that the laundry alliances in those cities were as successful as the CHLA was in New York, and most of them apparently faded almost as soon as they were founded.[83] No doubt the strong, dedicated, and stable leadership of the New York CHLA enabled it to survive.

Chapter Four

"To Save China,
To Save Ourselves"

The CHLA as a Leader in Chinatown's United Front

By early 1936 the CHLA had emerged as a new leader in New York's Chinatown. It accomplished this remarkable feat not only by proving itself effective in protecting its members' interests, but also by taking a popular stand in the anti-Japanese movement within the Chinese American community.

Shortly after the CHLA began to function as an independent grassroots organization, it actively participated in the anti-Japanese movement in the Chinese community and put forward as its guiding principle the slogan *jiuguo zijiu* (to save China, to save ourselves).[1] This phrase both identified the basic problems that confronted Chinese Americans and epitomized the CHLA's major activities throughout the late 1930s and the 1940s. By upholding such a banner, the CHLA was able to unite other Chinese-American patriotic organizations around itself and emerged as a new leader in the New York Chinese community. In that role, it made great contributions both in the pursuit of nationalist activities and in the struggle against the political discrimination and economic exploitation suffered by Chinese Americans. The phrase also suggests that the CHLA consciously linked its patriotic support for China to its struggle against exploitation and discrimination in the United States.

When the CHLA was founded in 1933, China was facing a national crisis—the Japanese invasion. In September 1931 the Japanese Kwantung Army, which had been stationed in Manchuria since the early twentieth century, staged a surprise attack and quickly drove Chinese troops and government officials out of the provinces of northeastern China. This action was followed by the creation of the puppet state of Manchukuo. In 1932 Japanese troops attacked Shanghai and, in the following year, occupied Rehe Province in northern China and threatened to cross the Great Wall. Most Chinese nationals, both inside and outside China, recognizing that Japan's ambition was to conquer all of China, devoted themselves to the movement to save China from the Japanese invasion, even though the ruling Kuomintang party-state did nothing to repel the Japanese advances.

Before the emergence of the CHLA, some Chinese patriotic organizations had been established in New York's Chinese community and had engaged in the *jiuguo* (to save China) movement. After September 1931 Chinese Americans organized "Anti-Japanese Associations, National Salvation Associations and National Salvation Fund Savings Societies,"[2] which sponsored anti-Japanese rallies and parades and launched a fundraising campaign to support China. In the battle to defend Shanghai in 1932, the Chinese Nineteenth Route Army, led by General Cai Tingkai (Tsai Ting-kai), bravely resisted the numerically and technologically superior Japanese army, and Chinese Americans spontaneously donated a tremendous amount of money to Cai's army. According to a contemporary account:

> [Community] organizations, [both] family and territorial, raised funds among their members; even individuals cabled money to the responsible military leaders. The Chinese Women's Patriotic Association collected almost eight thousand dollars by a Sunday afternoon parade. Five- and ten-dollar bills cascaded into the war chest. A laundryman named George Kee turned out his pockets for the cause. He had over one hundred dollars which he had intended to give a creditor. But the creditor could wait, he said, and then walked back to his laundry in Columbus Circle because he lacked a nickel for carfare. Kee is by no means a rare example. There was Wu Hing, who cabled a thousand dollars, almost every cent of many years' saving, and gave all but thirty dollars of his month's wages. One restaurant alone gave $2,500, and a family organization with a membership of little more than one hundred contributed $20,000.[3]

The Chinese patriots had to carry out their national salvation movement in an unfavorable atmosphere. In China, although the Japanese occupation of Manchuria and northern China deepened the national crisis, the Nationalist government (and its ruling party, the KMT) led by Chiang Kai-shek pursued a policy of nonresistance toward Japan.

Chiang insisted on *annei rangwai* (first pacification [of Communists and local warlords], then resistance). Between 1930 and 1934 Chiang conducted five massive "bandit annihilation campaigns" against the Communist forces in southern China.[4] Advocates of immediate military action against Japan urged broad national unity and popular mobilization, and Chiang's pursuit of civil war in the face of Japanese aggression was increasingly unpopular among Chinese at home and abroad.

In the United States Chinese patriots faced intimidation by KMT branches and the Chinese diplomatic apparatus for daring to express opinions that differed from official KMT policy. After it established a national government in Nanjing in 1928, the KMT strengthened its control over the overseas Chinese communities. The KMT government acknowledged dual citizenship and counted every Chinese abroad as a citizen of China regardless of his or her chosen citizenship.[5] In 1928 the Overseas Chinese Affairs Commission (OCAC; *Qiaowu Weiyuanhui*) was set up within the government. Functioning as an independent ministry, the OCAC was designed to guide and control Chinese life overseas. With the power of "monitoring of movement of the *Hua-ch'iao* [*huaqiao*; overseas Chinese] both to and from China and between various portions of the overseas Chinese world" and *jiandu* (supervising) "every public institution in the Hua-ch'iao community," according to historian Douglas Lee, "the OCAC possessed a great deal of influence and sheer power, which local organizations were hard pressed to resist." "In the era before and during World War II, the OCAC became an active and vital agent in the Chinese American community."[6]

To control the overseas Chinese community, the OCAC, the KMT branches (each had an Overseas Chinese Committee), and the Chinese consulates aimed at commanding political loyalty and soliciting financial donations. Many Chinese Americans, however, demonstrated their patriotism not only through contributing to the war-relief funds but also through their disapproval of the KMT policy of nonresistance. The most vigorous critic of that policy was, not surprisingly, the Chinese left. From 1931 on, every issue of *The Chinese Vanguard* carried articles calling on Chinese Americans to participate in the anti-Japanese movement. Because Chiang Kai-shek pursued nonresistance, Chinese leftists regarded him as a traitor and saw his overthrow as a prerequisite to a successful war of national salvation, well expressed by their slogan *kangri daojiang* (resist Japan, overthrow Chiang).[7] Since Chiang's policy of nonresistance was unpopular among many Chinese, these attacks sometimes paralyzed the KMT fundraising campaigns in America's Chinatowns after the spring of 1932, when the Nineteenth Route Army was forced to withdraw from Shanghai.[8]

Although it was the KMT's own policy that alienated Chinese Americans, KMT agencies in the U.S. blamed the Chinese left for their loss of Chinese American loyalty. They accused the Chinese left of being anti-Chinese because of its criticism of Chiang and the KMT, and they banned the leftist newspaper, *The Chinese Vanguard*, from Chinatown newsstands. Moreover, they even threatened that anyone reading the paper would be denounced to the INS as a Communist.[9] The KMT seemed determined to crush the left's forces by any available means. In 1933, with the cooperation of U.S. immigration officials, it succeeded in deporting Xie Chuang, a left-wing critic of the KMT regime and of Chiang Kaishek and an organizer of Chinese workers in San Francisco.[10] According to *The Chinese Vanguard*, the KMT even sent its secret agents, members of the Blue Shirts Society (the KMT counterpart of Nazi Germany's Brown Shirts), to Chinese American communities to keep surveillance over the dissidents. The paper listed the names of the agents in Washington, D.C., and New York and hinted that the split within the CHLA in 1936 was a result of the Blue Shirts' conspiracy.[11]

Despite its unpopularity, the KMT dominated the Chinese community through its control over the established forces: the CCBA and the clan and family organizations. For their own vested interests, these groups supported the KMT regime in China and followed the KMT politically in the United States. Nevertheless, anti-Japanese sentiment still ran high within these traditional organizations. Although they dared not attack Chiang's policy of nonresistance publicly, they did not support it either. Their enthusiasm in donating money to the Chinese troops that bravely fought the Japanese indicated their support for military resistance. But when the KMT suppressed its opponents by branding anyone who publicly called for immediate military resistance a "traitor," "anti-Chinese," and a "Communist agitator," these organizations chose to remain silent. As we shall see, however, this alliance between the KMT and the traditional organizations was not unbreakable, even though the silence of these organizations before 1936 seemed to confirm the KMT's dominance and isolate the advocates of immediate military action.

Outside the Chinese community, people were largely indifferent to the anti-Japanese cause. Deeply bogged down in the Great Depression, the American public and government were preoccupied with their own economic and political problems, and the crisis in China did not seem to them a real and important concern. From the outbreak of the Manchuria Incident (1931) to the Marco Polo Bridge Incident (1937), the primary goal of the U.S. government was to prevent war between the United States and Japan.[12] Although President Roosevelt broke his long silence on the East Asian situation in his quarantine speech in 1937,[13] the United States had neither a plan of action nor a policy of trade sanctions against Japan. The United States was not willing to risk itself to defend China. In fact, in December 1937, when Japanese planes provocatively destroyed the U.S. Navy gunboat *Panay* (then escorting Standard Oil barges on the Yangtze River), the U.S. government quickly agreed to accept apologies and compensation from Tokyo.

If the *Panay* incident showed the Roosevelt administration's reluctance to "quarantine" Japan and to support China, the influential Hearst Press's headline "We Sympathize. But It Is Not Our Concern" during the Manchuria crisis revealed the strength of isolationism among Americans.[14] In short, the CHLA as well as other Chinese American patriotic organizations faced a difficult situation in pursuing anti-Japanese activities from 1933 to 1938.

It was against this background that the CHLA emerged as a new leader in the New York Chinese community. The CHLA was the first grassroots organization independent of the established forces through which ordinary Chinese Americans could collectively express their demand for immediate military resistance against the Japanese invasion. As mentioned in Chapter Two, most CHLA members were single males, reluctant members of a bachelor society. It was only natural that they were deeply concerned about their relatives in China to whom they regularly remitted their hard-earned money. The Japanese military invasion posed a real threat to the Chinese nation as well as to the Chinese Americans' families and relatives. Anxious about their kin in China, most Chinese Americans expected China to resist Japan's military invasion. They hoped that their financial donations would contribute to an efficient military campaign to drive the Japanese out of China.

Within the traditional organizations in the Chinese community, few dared to run the risk of being labeled "anti-Chinese" for challenging Chiang Kai-shek's policy of nonresistance, even though many were actually sympathetic to the Chinese left's anti-Japanese stand. Therefore, the establishment of the CHLA provided an opportunity for many ordinary Chinese Americans to speak out against the Japanese and to express their strong desire for China to engage immediately in military resistance. Indeed, although the primary cause for the CHLA's founding was the 1933 laundry ordinance and the alliance's initial struggle was against the discrimination these laundrymen suffered in American society, as soon as it was established the CHLA endorsed the *jiuguo* cause and quickly initiated the campaign "to save China, to save ourselves."

The CHLA's campaign clearly related Chinese Americans' patriotic feelings to their struggle for survival in American society. It reflected the problems confronting Chinese Americans and their desire to seek solutions. To Chinese Americans in the 1930s, "to save China" and "to save ourselves" were inseparable. Since the 1850s Chinese immigrants had come to the United States, which they called "the Gold Mountain." Although they made great contributions to the agricultural development of the West and to the construction of the railroads in the 1860s and 1870s, the Chinese immigrants were insulted, discriminated against, excluded from most industries, and deprived of the right of naturalization.

Chinese Americans attributed their humiliation and low status in American society to China's weakness and backwardness. For this reason, aiding China became a tradition in Chinese American communities. Many studies in Chinese American history suggest that the Chinese in the United States supported China's self-strengthening or revolutionary movements in hopes that their contributions would help build a powerful China, and that a powerful China would, in turn, help elevate their own status in America. Before 1911 they donated large amounts of money to Sun Yat-sen's revolutionary cause and even went back to China to join the fight against the Manchu dynasty. They also enthusiastically supported any educational, economic, and political reform that might turn China into a modern, democratic, and powerful country.[15]

Many overseas Chinese had even stronger nationalist sentiments than their compatriots in China because they personally and directly experienced the humiliation Chinese nationals encountered in a foreign land. In the 1930s the Japanese invasion was demeaning to any Chinese national living anywhere in the world. To Chinese Americans, the reports in the American press of China's weakness and disorder, of Chiang Kai-shek's policy of nonresistance, and of the American public's negative assessments of China's ability to resist deepened their sense of humiliation. Most of the news coming from China was bad enough to discourage them from arguing with those Americans who contemptuously mocked Chinese troops for "using chopsticks to fight their enemies."[16] According to a contemporary account, before the Marco Polo Bridge Incident of 1937, the Chinese in New York City had to hide their heads while walking in the street or riding on buses and subway trains to avoid direct humiliation from unfriendly Americans.[17]

Many Chinese Americans believed that this negative view of China strengthened Americans' contemptuous attitude to and discrimination against them. It was in response to this humiliation and the persistent discrimination in American society, in addition to a deep concern over their homeland's fate, that Chinese Americans actively participated in the anti-Japanese movement. The CHLA's patriotic activities in the 1930s and 1940s, therefore, can be seen, on the one hand, as Chinese nationals' patriotic support of their homeland's national salvation movement and, on the other hand, as a struggle to improve their image and status in American society.

From their own experiences in fighting discrimination, CHLA members recognized the importance of unity and collective action and called on all Chinese Americans to unite in the anti-Japanese campaign. Because of the KMT's dominance, the CHLA worked hard for many years to organize an effective anti-Japanese movement in New York's Chinatown. The first opportunity came in late 1934, when the anti-Japanese hero General Cai Tingkai visited the United States and urged all Chinese to give up partisan conflicts and join the anti-Japanese movement.

General Cai, whose Nineteenth Route Army of forty thousand men resisted eighty thousand Japanese troops for more than a month in Shanghai in 1932, visited New York's Chinese community in August and September 1934. A native of Guangdong, tall and charismatic, Cai was "the Chinese official most welcomed by overseas Chinese in history."[18] All Chinese Americans, most of whom came from Guangdong, were proud of Cai and his army, which was made up of "the sons and brothers of Guangdong people." Not a single soldier of his army deserted during the Shanghai battle, Cai told Chinese Americans. In his speeches Cai extended to Chinese Americans his deep appreciation of their moral and financial support of his army. But he also told them that his army had received less than one-third of the donations from overseas Chinese—the rest was embezzled by officials in the KMT government, who even refused to pay the soldiers of the Nineteenth Route Army during and after the war, claiming that the donations from abroad were payment enough. Moreover, Cai made it clear that he first took a stand against Chiang Kaishek's order of nonresistance, then went to fight the Japanese. Everywhere he went, his sad story of the suppression and dismantling of the Nineteenth Route Army by Chiang Kai-shek after the Shanghai battle brought many Chinese Americans to tears.[19]

General Cai's visit aroused Chinese Americans' anti-Japanese enthusiasm to a new level, and his call for united efforts by all Chinese to resist Japan and to force Chiang to declare war on Japan received an immediate warm response. The newly founded New York Chinese Anti-Japanese Society (Niuyue Huaqiao Kangri Jiuguo Hui), which consisted of the CHLA and such leftist organizations as the Chinese Anti-Imperialist Alliance, the Unemployment Council, *The Chinese Vanguard*, and the Chinese Worker's Center, exchanged opinions with General Cai on how to build a united front in the Chinese American community and asked him to urge the influential Zhigongtang (Chee Kung Tong; the Chinese Free Masons) to join them. Cai replied that he would be happy to use his influence to persuade the Zhigongtang to become part of a united front.[20]

With Cai's help and the CHLA's efforts, the Anti-Japanese Society's attempt to form a united front with the Zhigongtang proved to be successful. The Zhigongtang, with a long history of supporting anti-Manchu struggles and the anti-imperialist cause in China, comprised radical nationalists who opposed any imperialist aggression in China, as well as conservative members of the established power structure in the Chinese American community. It was suspicious of leftist groups such as the Chinese Anti-Imperialist Alliance, whose rhetoric against traditional organizations was repugnant to conservatives. As part of the established forces in the Chinese community, it was determined to maintain the status quo. Since some of its members were also members of the CHLA, however, the Zhigongtang maintained generally cordial relations with the laundrymen's alliance.

As radical nationalists, members of the Zhigongtang had gradually become disgusted with Chiang Kai-shek's nonresistance and the autocratic behavior of the KMT branches in the United States. Situ Meitang (Soohoo Meihong), the leader of the Zhigongtang, who later became a dominant figure in New York's Chinatown, was especially angered by the KMT's attempts to assassinate General Cai. Once General Cai set foot on American soil, Situ Meitang guaranteed his safety with the protection of the Zhigongtang. He openly challenged the KMT agents: "Anyone who wants to kill General Cai has to walk over my body."[21] He himself accompanied the national hero in his visits to the Chinese communities in major American cities. On September 2 the CHLA invited General Cai to give a speech at a welcoming banquet. Cai was warned by "several anonymous letters" from the "evil gentry" that his life would be "endangered" if he attended the CHLA banquet, because the CHLA was "a Communist organ." Accompanied by Situ Meitang, Cai ignored the threat and addressed the laundrymen at the banquet, reaffirming his proposal to unite all Chinese, including all political parties and every variety of organization, into an anti-Japanese movement.[22] These KMT actions and threats, which clearly put its own partisan interests above the national interest and ignored the popular anti-Japanese sentiment among Chinese Americans, alienated a large proportion of ordinary people as well as some leaders in the Chinese community and thus created a situation in which the CHLA and its allies were able to build a united front from the bottom up.

The CHLA was the basic and efficient driving force in the formation of the united front in New York's Chinatown. As a grassroots organization, the alliance had members who came from and maintained relations with almost every family/clan and district association in Chinatown. Also, because most of its members were single males who often met and chatted at the gongsi fang (the mutual-aid group, discussed in Chapters One and Two), the CHLA had influence in these basic and important social units in the bachelor society.

Furthermore, some CHLA leaders, with proven capability in their service to the alliance, were also elected as important officials in their family or district organizations. For example, Tan Lian'ai, the English Language Secretary of the CHLA, was elected by the Zhaolun Lianyi Gongsuo (Chew Lun Lin Yee Association, a united clan association of people with the surnames Tan, Tan, Xu, and Xie) as its English Language Secretary;[23] Zhu Simei and Yu Hongyao, two of the most active CHLA members since 1933, became representatives of the Zhu Kaoting Fang (Gee How Hing Association) and the Yu Fengcaitang (Yee Fong Toy Tong), respectively; and Chen Sancai, one of the radicals within the CHLA, was elected as a member of the Executive Committee of the Chong Zheng Hui (Tsung Tsin Association), one of the Hakka people's associations.[24] All these individuals, incidentally, were members of the Quon Shar and had once served on the CHLA Executive Committee.

With these connections, the CHLA leaders and members were entrusted by the New York Chinese Anti-Japanese Society to invite other grassroots organizations to join the united national salvation movement. In September 1935 Chen Sancai, Lei Zhuofeng, Zhao Shizhi, and other CHLA leaders and members, with the help of the Jinglan Gongsuo (Kim Lan Association), a tong that was affiliated with the Zhigongtang, contacted such family and district associations as Dingjiao Fang, Weishan Fang, Yanqing Fang, Lisi Fang, Binzheng Fang, Aoshan Fang, Tongqing Fang, Jiulong Renyi She, Duqing Gongsuo, Dongguan Gongfang, Longgang Gongsuo, and others, urging them to take part in the anti-Japanese salvation movement.[25] In October many of these grassroots organizations participated in anti-Japanese rallies and parades organized by the CHLA and the Anti-Japanese Society. Catching this new nationalist enthusiasm, in November the CHLA and other patriotic organizations united these fangs to found the New York Chinese Anti-Japanese Salvation Association (Niuyue Huaqiao Kangri Jiuguo Lianhehui), a much larger organization that replaced the Anti-Japanese Society.[26]

This rapid organizational development alerted the leaders of the traditional groups to the challenge they faced: if they remained indifferent to the patriotic movement, they could lose the support of the people who increasingly identified with the salvation movement led by the CHLA. The CCBA definitely did not want to see CHLA influence expand through the promotion of the anti-Japanese cause. Thus, in December the CCBA called three whole-community meetings to discuss how to coordinate the anti-Japanese efforts. The CHLA welcomed the CCBA's move and participated in all three meetings, as did the leftist organizations.[27]

Although some die-hard conservatives within the CCBA (such as Chen Shutang) opposed the united front, its president, Lei Fang, frightened by the possibility that the CHLA would gain even greater influence and power, decided to join the anti-Japanese movement, in which the CCBA, with its influence in the community, could hope to have a dominant voice and thereby maintain its power as Chinatown's supreme leader. After long discussions, debates, and verbal fights (Situ Meitang, the leader of the Zhigongtang and the On Leong Tong, once shouted at the opponents of the united front, denouncing them as traitors at a CCBA community meeting),[28] a genuine united front organization, the All-Chinatown Anti-Japanese Salvation Association (AASA; Niuyue Quanqiao Kangri Jiuguo Hui), was founded on January 19, 1936, with General Cai Tingkai as one of its honorary presidents.[29] The AASA included the major organizations in the Chinese American community. The only organizations that refused to join were the KMT's New York branch and its organ, *The Chinese Nationalist Daily*, and a few traditional groups under the influence of the KMT, such as the Hip Sing Tong.[30]

According to its constitution, the aim of the AASA was "to unite all Chinese people regardless of their political opinions, carry out military self-defense, oppose one-party dictatorship, promote [the formation of] a National Defense Government, resist Japan actively, and eradicate all traitors."[31] This statement shows that the opinion of the CHLA and its leftist allies prevailed. Indeed, anti-Japanese and anti-nonresistance feelings ran so high that at its founding meeting the AASA sent a telegram to the Nanjing government:

> To the Nanjing Kuomintang Government:
>   This Association has been founded today. We ask you to return power to the people. Do not sell out our country. We hope you recover your national consciousness soon.
>
>   —The AASA[32]

A New Stage of Overseas Chinese Nationalism

The AASA was a loose coalition of various interest groups. The common anti-Japanese sentiment reduced but never eliminated the conflicts among the organizations representing different interests. Through promoting the campaign "to save China, to save ourselves" and helping to form the united front in Chinatown, the CHLA demonstrated its capacity to bring together grassroots organizations. Faced with this new development, the CCBA chose to accept the united front so as not to lose its power base in the community. On appearance, the rival groups now worked together in the anti-Japanese movement. But underneath this seeming patriotic harmony, conflicts between the CCBA and the CHLA and its leftist allies continued. Moreover, the KMT's New York branch, though now isolated in the community, exploited the cracks in the AASA to undermine the united front and to harass the CHLA and the Chinese left. It was from such a complicated experience within the anti-Japanese movement that the CHLA and many other Chinese Americans carried overseas Chinese nationalism to a new stage of development.

Sun Yat-sen's revolutionary movement against the Manchu dynasty had given Chinese Americans their first chance to express strong nationalist feelings. In that period (1890s–1910s) the elites dominated the scene and the major role of ordinary people was to donate money. Presumably, when Sun's revolution succeeded and a strong Republic of China was founded, Chinese in the United States would return to their homeland, leaving behind all the humiliation they had suffered in the Gold Mountain. Sun's efforts to build a modern, independent, and powerful China failed, but Chinese Americans continued their campaign to save China, and Guangdong peasants continued to come to the United States to join the bachelor society.

The slow progress in China disappointed Chinese Americans. In the 1930s, even while facing the crisis of Japanese invasion that threatened the nation's very survival, Chiang Kai-shek and his KMT regime failed to resist effectively the aggressors and, moreover, tolerated no criticism and suppressed domestic patriots who called for military action. When New York's Chinese Americans expressed their anti-Japanese demands, they likewise experienced the KMT's autocratic actions in the United States.

Shortly after its founding, the AASA came under attack from the KMT's New York branch, which issued a statement to the community denouncing the united front coalition as "a subversive organization" "manipulated by the Communists" and "other opponents" of the KMT regime and accusing it of "sowing discord [among Chinese] and agitating civil war in the disguise of 'unity' and 'salvation movement.'"[33] Many people in the AASA were furious at these accusations. The general reaction was a mixture of hurt, grief, and indignation, as expressed in a short statement of the AASA that countered the KMT's accusations:

> The KMT statement shows that there exist some misunderstandings. . . . This Association is an open organization including all overseas Chinese organizations [in New York City], and we believe that no single party or faction can monopolize the anti-Japanese movement. . . . Any organization and any Chinese at any time can come to our meetings, and we welcome all suggestions on how to promote the salvation movement. From now on we will ignore all senseless slanders. Our sole purpose is to fight the Japanese and save China.[34]

Nevertheless, whatever the policies of Chiang's Nationalist government, it remained the sole, legitimate, internationally recognized government of China. Under the shadow of the exclusion laws and facing the possibility of losing the support and protection of the Chinese consulates, some community leaders and a few traditional organizations gave in to the KMT's pressure and became reluctant to promote the anti-Japanese cause independent of the KMT's control. In late February, Lei Fang, president of the CCBA and the AASA, perhaps frightened by KMT threats, "took a sick leave."[35] In the Chong Zheng Hui, one of the associations of the Hakka people, an internal conflict was instigated by KMT agents, and the group withdrew its membership from the AASA.[36]

The successful formation of the AASA, according to *The Chinese Vanguard*, "to a great extent, is owed to the organizational efforts of the

CHLA, and its [previous] active participation in the work of the Anti-Japanese Society and the Anti-Japanese United Association."[37] Thus it was no surprise that the KMT focused its attacks on the CHLA and vigorously supported the "anti-Communists" within the alliance. During that period, as discussed in Chapter Three, the CCBA, sharing the KMT's anti-Communist ideology and representing the interests of the elite in Chinatown, helped the anti-Communists within the CHLA. In fact, the CCBA was eager to see the disintegration of the CHLA because then the association could resume its control over the hand laundries.[38]

Overwhelmed by internal troubles in early 1936, the CHLA was unable to devote much of its energy to the work of the AASA. Without the active participation of the CHLA, the AASA ceased to exist except in name. For months it held no meetings and did no salvation work, and by May, three months after its founding, it was "controlled by a few reactionary elements" who were concerned more about personal prestige and power than the anti-Japanese cause.[39]

The internal split weakened the CHLA and in turn reduced the weight of its voice in the AASA. On May 2 Zhao Shizhi, the CHLA representative serving on the Standing Committee of the AASA, proposed that the united front organization sponsor a mass meeting in late May to commemorate the eleventh anniversary of the "May 30 Incident" (an anti-Japanese demonstration in Shanghai in 1925) and take the opportunity to promote the anti-Japanese movement in the New York Chinese community, which had been sluggish for a while. But his proposal was ignored, and the AASA held no mass meeting.[40]

This episode showed the CHLA that those groups dominated by the elite were not willing to share power with grassroots organizations. The CCBA had joined the AASA united front and sat side by side with the CHLA because the laundrymen's alliance had a large membership and considerable influence in the community. Now that the CHLA membership was greatly reduced by internal conflict, the CCBA changed its attitude toward the organization of hand laundries.

To recover from its loss of influence, the CHLA launched an anti-Japanese campaign of its own. On July 26 it founded the New York Chinese Hand Laundry Anti-Japanese Salvation Association (CHLASA; Niuyue Yiguan Tongye Kangri Jiuguo Hui), which proclaimed itself to be an "occupational anti-Japanese organization," aiming "to unite all Chinese hand laundry workers regardless of political opinions and affiliations, and to work with all Chinese compatriots in China and overseas, for the purpose of resisting Japanese invasion."[41]

According to the CHLA's statement, its intention in founding the CHLASA was "to expand the *qunzhong* [mass] base so as to consolidate the anti-Japanese coalition of overseas Chinese."[42] This purpose does not sound much different from what the alliance had said earlier in its efforts to form the AASA. Having experienced internal division and persistent KMT attacks, however, the CHLA had become more sophisticated in Chinatown politics and in its understanding of the relationship between overseas Chinese and China.

First, the founding of the CHLASA suggests that the CHLA realized that within a united front organization the relative strength of the participating groups was the basis for sharing power. Only with enough strength was it possible for a grassroots organization, such as the CHLA, to talk to the elite-dominated organizations and to exert influence on them while simultaneously maintaining its own independence. Second, from the frustrations and dissatisfactions with Chiang Kai-shek and the KMT regime, the CHLA, as well as other Chinese American organizations, began to think of what kind of China it wanted and what kind of contribution it should make.

Experiences in Chinatown politics propelled the CHLA members to reconsider their role in building a new China. They were no longer satisfied with being the mere financial donors, though they contributed almost everything they had to help the anti-Japanese war; they began to develop political opinions, which reflected both their experiences and their expectations, and they wanted their voices to be heard.

With the founding of the CHLASA, the CHLA hoped to increase its force. Indeed, a few months later the CHLA, with the CHLASA, demonstrated its strength by pushing the AASA to resume the national salvation work. On September 18 the AASA issued a strong anti–Chiang Kai-shek statement to commemorate the fifth anniversary of the Manchurian Incident. It accused Chiang of being "concerned only with personal power" and "ignoring the sufferings of the people." Moreover, it directly attacked "Chiang's policy of *annei rangwai* [first pacification, then resistance]" and pointed out that this policy was "actually one of internal slaughter and external surrender [*duinei cansha, duiwai qufu*]."[43]

This was the first time that the AASA had dared to attack Chiang Kai-shek personally. The statement signaled an increasing opposition to Chiang and the KMT. How far this popular anti-Chiang, anti-KMT sentiment would have gone and how it would have affected Chinatown politics will never be known, for that winter the Xi'an Incident changed everything. In December 1936 General Zhang Xueliang, who had obeyed

Chiang's order of nonresistance and retreated from Manchuria to north-west China after 1931, kidnapped Chiang in the city of Xi'an and forced him to promise to stop the civil war and to engage in military resistance against Japan. The incident not only dramatically changed the relationship between the KMT and the CCP, which soon thereafter formed a united front with other anti-Japanese forces in China, but also tremendously reduced the tension between the KMT branches and overseas Chinese in the United States.

Half a year after the Xi'an Incident, Japanese troops provoked the Marco Polo Bridge Incident (July 1937) and launched a large-scale military campaign, and Chinese troops began to engage in serious military resistance against the Japanese. Chiang Kai-shek became the supreme leader in the national defense war, and overseas Chinese immediately stopped criticizing him and pledged their political and financial support. Now all Chinese organizations joined the united front with the sole purpose of driving the Japanese out of China.

In the New York Chinese community, after the Marco Polo Bridge Incident, a new united front organization, the New York Overseas Chinese Anti-Japanese Salvation General Committee for Military Funds (OCASGC; Niuyue Quanti Huaqiao Kangri Jiuguo Couxiang Zhonghui), was established in November 1937.[44] Every Chinese organization was a member of this group, and its Executive Committee comprised representatives from the CCBA, On Leong Tong, Hip Sing Tong, Zhigongtang, CHLA, CAIA, the U.S. branch of the CCP, and the KMT's New York branch, among others.[45]

The new united front, which cut across all clan, district, and political lines, pledged its loyalty to the Nationalist government with the hope that it would effectively assume responsibility for defending the country. While the KMT was anxious to collect financial donations from overseas Chinese, it also wanted to control them. In the case of the New York Chinese community, the KMT was uneasy about the new political order established through the united front. It did not want to see the growth of the political influence of the grassroots organizations in the anti-Japanese movement. When the KMT tried to increase its dominance over the community through controlling the united front, however, it encountered resistance from the CHLA and other organizations.

In August 1937 the Chinese ambassador to Washington, Wang Zhengting, sent a letter to all Chinese in the United States, demanding that they "deposit all collected funds in the Bank of China in New York City," and "if the money was for purchasing military equipment, it should be put in the account of the Chinese Embassy."[46] Many Chinese Americans expressed their suspicions about this order. They were anxious to send their money "earned with sweat and blood" to the Chinese soldiers fighting the Japanese at the front, but their knowledge of the KMT government's embezzlement of the overseas Chinese donations during the Shanghai battle weakened their confidence in the KMT agencies. The CHLA ignored the ambassador's order and sent the money it raised in July and August to Madame Sun Yat-sen, a "democratic figure" who vigorously opposed the KMT one-party dictatorship and thus won the respect of overseas Chinese, who entrusted her to give the money to the soldiers engaged in the fighting.[47]

Available evidence shows that the CHLA tried to keep its independence within the united front in the following years, too. In 1938, with the money it collected among its members and their customers, the CHLA purchased four ambulances, of which it sent two to the Eighth Route Army led by the Chinese Communist Party and two to the KMT army. The alliance described it as "two for the North, and two for the South," on the principle that any army fighting the Japanese, whatever its political complexion, deserved an equal share of the laundrymen's donations. This meant that the CHLA wanted to make autonomous decisions about the money it raised: its members had the right to decide to whom the money should be sent.[48]

The KMT's intention to tighten its control over the Chinese communities in America was also reflected in one of its abortive plans to reorganize and rename the existing Chinese American anti-Japanese organizations. After the Marco Polo Bridge Incident the Chinese ambassador to the United States presented a proposal to rename these organizations "Chinese patriotic associations" and place them under the leadership of a national organization: "The Patriotic Association of the Chinese in the United States" (Lu Mei Zhonghua Aiguo Hui). Ambassador Wang himself would become the president of the national association, and the staff members of the "patriotic associations" in different Chinese immigrant communities "should be appointed by the president."[49]

Most Chinese Americans resented the idea. At a community meeting held in the CCBA's headquarters, representatives of different organizations raised questions about Ambassador Wang's proposal. First, they asked why the term "anti-Japanese" should be dropped from the name of the proposed new organization. Wang's representative to the meeting, Yu Junji (James Tsunchi Yu), the Chinese consul general in New York

City, explained that Wang was a diplomat, and if the term "anti-Japanese" were used in the name of the new association, "the Japanese will protest to the U.S. government." Also, Yu Junji said, the term "anti-Japanese" would alienate the U.S. government, which had passed a neutrality act.[50]

Some Chinese American representatives were irritated by such "diplomatic considerations." If Ambassador Wang feared this and that, they asked, why did he appoint himself the president of the proposed association? "We may give him a title of 'honorary president' if we see fit," some commented mockingly. They also asked, since the staff members of the anti-Japanese associations were elected by Chinese Americans, who gave the power to the ambassador to appoint new staff members? Who invited him to write a new constitution for these associations? Moreover, some representatives stood up "with intense sorrow" to attack "those weak-kneed Chinese government officials who made concessions to Japanese in the past."[51] In short, the representatives who attended the meeting made it clear to Consul General Yu that Ambassador Wang's idea was unacceptable.

Failing to respect the Chinese Americans and treating them merely as financial donors without any rights in decision making, the KMT-appointed ambassador alienated Chinese Americans before he even had a chance to set up a patriotic association that would neither alienate the Americans under the neutrality act nor provoke Japanese diplomatic protest. One of the CHLA leaders, Zhong Huitang, wrote an article to expose the authoritarian nature of the ambassador's proposal. In the United States, Zhong argued, many American citizens publicly expressed their opposition to the three fascist regimes—Japan, Italy, and Germany—and openly called for the abolition of the neutrality act. Zhong asked: "Is it because we are Chinese that we have to obey that neutrality act 100 percent? Is there any clause in that act that prevents us Chinese from using the term 'anti-Japanese' in the name of our organizations?" Moreover, Zhong pointed out, "under the constitution of the United States, overseas Chinese have the freedom of assembly and the right to decide the name of their own organizations. It has nothing to do with the neutrality act."[52]

After refuting Ambassador Wang's "diplomatic considerations," Zhong further explicitly exposed the essence of the name-change proposal: the KMT wanted to use the "patriotic associations" to cultivate influence for "their followers" and to exclude "their opponents." Zhong concluded his article by stating, "I'd rather believe that this is not Ambassador Wang's real intention. And I hope that Ambassador Wang would listen to and accept the opinions of overseas Chinese, promote the democratic spirit, so as to really fulfill the purpose of resisting Japan and saving China."[53]

This episode was but one of the conflicts between the Chinese Americans in New York and the KMT that continued throughout the anti-Japanese war (1937–45). Given the political and psychological conditions created by the anti-Japanese national salvation movement, the KMT failed to build its influence among the laboring class of Chinese Americans (at least among those in New York City), to a great extent, because of its authoritarian approach to these people. To them, it was apparent that the KMT distrusted them; ignored their needs, opinions, and demands; and, in many cases, abused them politically and exploited them economically.

In their struggle to maintain their independence and resist the KMT's authoritarian control, many Chinese Americans demonstrated a new kind of overseas Chinese nationalism through their own organizations, such as the CHLA. The essence of this new nationalism included an awareness of the basic political rights of citizens and the willingness to claim those rights, the development of political consciousness and the courage to voice political criticism, and most significantly, the use of political concepts learned in American society to criticize China's politics. Many studies have praised the financial contributions of Chinese Americans to their homeland during World War II but have ignored this important aspect of their lives in that period. Moreover, because these Chinese Americans consciously linked their struggle for survival in America to China's national salvation movement, they even began to develop a new consciousness of themselves as Chinese Americans. A scrutiny of the political opinions of the CHLA members and their allies as expressed in their own newspaper, the *China Daily News*, will help us to understand what that means.

The Founding of the China Daily News

The *China Daily News* (CDN) is the English title of the Chinese-language newspaper *Meizhou Huaqiao Ribao*, founded in 1940 mainly with funds solicited from members of the CHLA. The English translation of the paper's name, as that of many Chinese names, is not very accurate. Literally, *Meizhou Huaqiao Ribao* means "[North and South] Americas'

Overseas Chinese Daily." It had the longest history among the half dozen Chinese-language newspapers published in New York's Chinatown, circulating in the Chinese community without interruption from 1940 to 1989.

CDN was founded by CHLA members to meet the needs of Chinese laundrymen and other Chinese Americans. *The Chinese Journal*, the CHLA's ally, was ordered by the court in 1935 to stop criticizing the CCBA for three years. After that it lost much of its political influence in the community. By 1937 the paper had been sold to a company; its name was changed and, along with it, its sympathetic attitude toward the hand laundrymen.[54]

Then, in late July 1938, *The Chinese Vanguard* went out of business because many of its editors and staff members returned to China to join the fight against the Japanese.[55] Its successor, the *Chinese Salvation Times*, also a left-wing newspaper, originally published in Paris and brought to New York by Yao Sushi (then a Chinese student and later a top CCP leader) in 1938,[56] lasted for only half a year and was shut down because of a shortage of funds and manpower.

With the disappearance of these papers, the CHLA found it difficult to make its voice heard in the community. The KMT newspaper, *The Chinese Nationalist Daily*, subsidized by the Nanjing government, represented the official policies of the KMT and reflected only the opinions of the elite. Many Chinese Americans felt that they could not get accurate information about the situation in China from the paper. For example, *The Chinese Nationalist Daily* often reported stories of the KMT troops' successes, but people learned from English-language newspapers that the KMT troops were actually retreating.

Thus, in order to "reflect ordinary Chinese Americans' opinions and to get objective information about China's domestic situation, especially about the conditions of the overseas Chinese community [in Guangdong]," the CHLA proposed to establish an "overseas Chinese daily newspaper" in late 1939. Funds were collected mainly from CHLA members. The original plan was to raise ten thousand dollars; by July 1940 some three hundred eighty shareholders had put together about eight thousand dollars. Most held one or two shares (ten dollars each); only "five or six owned shares worth more than two hundred dollars."[57]

On July 7, 1940, *CDN* was born. Its introduction made a remarkable observation about Chinese Americans: "This paper is founded by overseas Chinese in the United States. Among the overseas Chinese in this country, many have acquired U.S. citizenship. To them, to love and defend [their] motherland is a bound duty [*tianzhi*], and to be loyal to the United States is an obligation [*yiwu*]."[58] Three weeks later an editorial made the same point: "So we regard overseas Chinese concern about their motherland as a natural expression of normal human feelings [*renqing zhi zhiran*], and their efforts to permanently develop their settlement [in the U.S.] as a rational development [*shili zhi dangran*]."[59]

This observation was noteworthy because it was perhaps the first elaboration by a Chinese American newspaper on the nature of the attitude of American citizens of Chinese ancestry toward China and the United States.[60] It seems to mark the start of what may be called "the awakening of Chinese American consciousness" as a group of first-generation Chinese began to think positively of themselves as Americans with a Chinese heritage. In its first issue the newspaper proclaimed that its sole purpose was "to serve the interests and welfare of the overseas Chinese in America."[61] To inspire, encourage, and help Chinese Americans to understand, obtain, and exercise their political rights became one of its basic services to the community.

Throughout the 1940s *CDN* persistently encouraged its readers to vote in local, state, and national elections. "Election is the most precious system in a democratic country," one *CDN* editorial stated. "The most remarkable progress in human political life is that the ballot has replaced the gun to obtain power, and has become the basis of policy making."[62] The paper urged "the overseas Chinese with franchise" "not to give up your right to vote," which was seen as a "sacred right and duty of citizens in a democratic country."[63] Moreover, it provided information about the backgrounds and platforms of competing candidates and ran editorials and commentaries analyzing issues and the results of elections to help readers understand the American electoral system. In October 1942, before the New York State elections, *CDN* sent letters to different candidates asking them about their positions on the issues of American aid to China, services for Chinese American communities, the Chinese Exclusion Act, and elimination of prejudice against Chinese.[64] The replies from the candidates of the Democratic party, the Republican party, and the Communist party were translated into Chinese and published in the paper.[65]

As a long-term editorial policy, the encouragement of Chinese Americans to exercise their political rights was a decision made by the *CDN* board of directors, which was dominated by CHLA members. In carrying out the policy, two figures played a significant role: Thomas Tang (Tang Mingzhao) and Eugene Moy (Mei Cantian). Both were U.S. citizens.

Tang acquired his U.S. citizenship through his birth on American soil, while Moy obtained his because his father was a native-born U.S. citizen. Tang was born in 1910 in San Francisco and grew up in that city. He received his college education in Qinghua University in Beijing, China. After he returned to the United States, he taught English to Chinese immigrant children in Brooklyn, New York. In 1937 he joined the CHLA and became an influential figure in the New York Chinese community, where he appeared as the representative of the CHLA at many community meetings.[66]

Moy was born in 1903 in a small village in Taishan and came to the United States in 1921. He first worked in a hand laundry shop in Boston, then as a waiter in Chinese restaurants in various cities: Worcester, Philadelphia, Buffalo, and Washington, D.C. While struggling to make a living, Moy "undertook to educate himself in two languages at the same time." After many years' efforts, Moy, with only a grammar school education in China, "became literate in Chinese and English simultaneously and cut his eye-teeth on philosophy and literature in both languages. . . . His formal education was limited to the assistance of an ex–Sunday school teacher he met while working in a restaurant."[67]

A self-made writer, Moy was greatly influenced by the ideas and style of Lu Xun, the most celebrated writer and thinker in modern China. Indeed, Moy was called the "Lu Xun of the overseas Chinese community" by his contemporary admirers.[68] His "Old Moy Column," a five-hundred-word commentary on every aspect of Chinese life in the United States, became one of the most popular features of the paper.

Although the editorials that encouraged Chinese with U.S. franchise to vote in elections were written by the well-educated Thomas Tang and the self-made intellectual Eugene Moy, their perspective was shared by many laundrymen. *CDN* offered the CHLA the privilege of having a CHLA Special Column ("Yilian Zhengkan") to be published in the paper. This column, which appeared once a month, provided information and advice about the hand laundry business, presented the plans and the work reports of the CHLA Executive Committee, carried eulogies for deceased members, and even contained some poems in classical Chinese style composed by laundreymen. In addition, in almost every issue CHLA members expressed their political opinions in short articles.[69]

Although the new idea espoused by *CDN* and CHLA members represented remarkable progress in the development of Chinese American consciousness, it translated into very limited results. In 1940 the total Chinese population in the United States was about seventy-five thousand.

According to *CDN*'s estimate, among them fewer than twenty thousand were citizens eligible to cast ballots.[70] Such a small ethnic group had little leverage in American politics. Thus, the candidates' replies to *CDN*'s inquiries into their platforms seemed to be only token gestures rather than pleas to a powerful constituency.

Furthermore, this desire to participate in electoral politics came from and to a certain extent was defined by the campaign "to save China, to save ourselves." *CDN* editorials and the CHLA Special Column articles indicated a major concern over the candidates' positions on America's China policy and on issues concerning Chinese Americans, such as the repeal of the Chinese exclusion acts. Only those who promised to support China's war against Japan and to defend the legal rights of Chinese Americans were worth supporting, these editorials and articles suggested. In 1944, for example, Li Chengzhu, one of the active CHLA members, urged his fellow laundrymen to vote for Franklin D. Roosevelt, because FDR "carried out a positive aid-China policy and played a part in abolishing the Chinese Exclusion Act."[71]

Because of the scarcity of documents, it is difficult to know how many enfranchised Chinese voted and, if they did, for whom in the national, state, and municipal elections in the 1940s, and how they reflected on the consequences of their voting. *CDN* editorials and the CHLA Special Column articles suggest that, first, the CHLA and its allies had reached a new sophistication in approaching political issues in American society and in seeking solutions to their problems. These Chinese Americans began to think of themselves as an integral part of American society as they set out to consider their franchise as a positive means to improve their conditions. This was a significant development in Chinese American history. Contrary to the conventional stereotypical depictions that assume Chinese Americans to be apolitical and "inassimilatable," the CHLA case suggests that by the 1940s a group of Chinese Americans had tried hard to exercise their political rights. Within this context, how much they in fact achieved does not matter (they seemed to have achieved little). What matters is that this group of Chinese Americans made positive and active efforts, a point neglected in most of the literature in Chinese American history.

Second, the CHLA's attempts to participate in American politics were developed and shaped in their campaign "to save China, to save ourselves," in which the fate of Chinese Americans was closely linked to the destiny of China. Therefore, the extent of the success of these attempts was, to a great degree, determined by the state of U.S.-China relations and American domestic circumstances that responded to changes in these relations. In the 1940s the fact that the United States and China became allies created a favorable climate in which Chinese Americans were able freely to express their political opinions; but in the 1950s increasing hostility between the two countries in the Cold War made such free expression very difficult. Therefore, if these once politically active Chinese Americans became relatively silent again in the 1950s, it was not because of their "inertia" or "Chinese cultural heritage" of political apathy, but rather because their political efforts were vulnerable to changes in U.S.-China relations. Nevertheless, they tried to help improve that relationship, as the CHLA did in its "people's diplomacy" in the 1930s and 1940s, discussed in the next chapter.

Chapter Five

"The People's Diplomacy"

"Please Help China"

In the CHLA campaign "to save China, to save ourselves," "to save China" was essential to the struggle "to save ourselves." If Chinese nationals did not dare to protest and fight against their country's invaders, they could never expect other Americans to respect them as dignified human beings; if they made no effort to save China and if their homeland were conquered by Japan, there would be no hope for them to stand up in American society. At the same time, "to save ourselves" became a major part of the campaign "to save China." Here was something Chinese Americans could do in the United States: improve the image of the Chinese in the American mind and win American sympathy and support for China's war of resistance against Japan through their own actions.

The patriotic activities of the CHLA in the 1930s and 1940s can be seen as a continuation of the community tradition of aiding China. As many Chinese American organizations had done in the past, the CHLA stressed financial contributions. During the depression years Chinese laundrymen often earned only five or six dollars a week.[1] After paying taxes, rent, and various fees, they had little money left on which to survive. Even under such circumstances, the hand laundrymen, as well as other Chinese Americans, managed to make donations to support the war of resistance against Japan. Since the CHLA had a large membership, the amount of money that the alliance raised, bit by bit, from its members was impressive. For example, from July to October 1937, it collected more than five thousand dollars from its members and sent that sum to the Chinese government.[2]

The CHLA's patriotic campaign had a striking new feature that represented a departure from the Chinese American *jiuguo* (to save China) tradition: the alliance consciously pursued a campaign that it called *guomin waijiao* (people's diplomacy).[3] As part of the campaign "to save China, to save ourselves," the basic purpose of the CHLA's "people's diplomacy" was to win the sympathy of Americans and to enlist their moral and financial support for China's war of resistance against Japan. Through pursuing people's diplomacy, the CHLA greatly extended its contacts with American people and institutions (civic organizations, civil rights organizations, and so on). These contacts helped CHLA members understand American people and society better and to a certain extent facilitated the laundrymen's integration into American society.

Before the 1937 Marco Polo Bridge Incident, Chinese Americans had felt humiliated by the Japanese invasion and by Chiang Kai-shek's nonresistance policy. That sense of humiliation discouraged any appeal they might have made to the American public for support, for if Chinese did not stand up to defend their own country, who could help much? After the Marco Polo Bridge Incident, as China showed a determination to resist Japan's military invasion to the last drop of the nation's blood, the CHLA and other Chinese American organizations felt less embarrassment about seeking American support. Their voice was, they believed, strengthened by China's desperate but heroic actions.

Although the CHLA sent many letters and telegrams to politicians urging them to adopt policies to support China against Japan, it mainly appealed to the American public. The fact that the Chinese hand laundrymen affiliated with the CHLA were scattered throughout the city and encountered American customers every day put the alliance in a better position than most other Chinese organizations to launch people's diplomacy. The first action of the CHLA in its campaign was to distribute "Aid China against Japan" flyers through thousands of Chinese hand laundries.

In August 1937 the CHLA printed one hundred thousand English-language flyers and sent them to hand laundries for distribution. Entitled "A Letter to the American People," these flyers "described the brutal Japanese actions [in China] in detail" and "explained that Japan's aggression not only threatened China's existence but the world peace." They called on the American people to urge their government "to condemn and sanction the aggressor politically and economically, to stop shipping military materials to Japan," and "to extend moral and material support to China." These flyers were to be distributed to customers with their clean laundry, and non-CHLA members were also encouraged to help distribute them.[4]

In the following month the CHLA printed and distributed another set of flyers asking Americans "to boycott Japanese goods."[5] These actions received positive responses from the hand laundries' customers, most of whom were from the lower middle or lower class.[6] Some customers even made suggestions to the laundrymen on how to improve their people's diplomacy and to achieve more effective results. In October 1937, for example, "many customers" suggested that the CHLA "should expand the fundraising movement." The winter was coming, these customers advised, so the CHLA should launch a campaign to raise "medicine- and relief-fund" for "wounded soldiers and refugees."[7]

Acting on these suggestions, the CHLA made and placed five thousand relief-fund boxes in Chinese hand laundries all over the city. This campaign was so successful that in February 1938 the alliance announced that with the donations collected from the relief-fund boxes it had purchased four ambulances.[8] Later the ambulances were shipped to China.

Edgar Snow, the famous American journalist who was reporting on wartime China, saw one of the ambulances in Yan'an (Yenan), headquarters of the Chinese Communist army, in 1939.

> The limousine which coughed tubercularly at the bottom of the path leading down from my cave looked like a Black Maria. When I got close enough I saw that it was an ambulance, and on its paneled door was neatly lettered:
>
> Presented to the Heroic Defenders of China
>
> By the Chinese Hand Laundrymen's Association of New York City
>
> [Chinese Hand Laundry Alliance]
>
> ... A number of these laundrymen's gifts had accumulated in Yenan, where sometimes they were used to carry civilian air-raid victims to nearby hospitals. But generally they remained idle; there was no petrol to move them.
>
> Motor ambulances were actually of little use on a guerrilla front; the mobile character of the war, the roadless countryside, and lack of fuel and servicing facilities indicated a medical service of a special type. If overseas Chinese and foreign friends had sent to Yenan the money they spent on costly ambulances and foreign drugs it would have had permanent value once invested in local production—in the expansion of drug factories and guerrilla industry.[9]

From a practical point of view, the CHLA ambulances might not have been very useful in a guerrilla war, but the decision to buy ambulances for China was not made out of a lack of understanding of the conditions in China's countryside. It was shaped, rather, by the considerations of people's diplomacy. The CHLA's perspective on the matter was different from Snow's.

Before being shipped to China, the four ambulances participated in several significant events. On January 30, 1938, the CHLA held a rally to celebrate the sixth anniversary of the battle to defend Shanghai. A special guest speaker from the Medical Bureau and North American Committee to Aid Spanish Democracy was invited to give a talk on the "experience of American people in aiding the Democratic Republic of Spain." According to the speaker, within a year (1937), the committee had set up eight hospitals in Spain, sent 150 doctors and nurses and some sixty ambulances there, in addition to financial donations. The speaker declared that "American people will aid China with the same spirit."[10] In the march immediately after the rally, two of the four CHLA ambulances were placed in front, slowly passing the stores, restaurants, and apartment buildings in Chinatown. "Many Chinese and Americans were deeply moved by the scene, some to tears."[11]

In February, cooperating with the American League for Peace and Democracy and the American Friends of the Chinese People, two civic organizations that demanded that the U.S. government adopt a policy of sanctioning aggressors, the CHLA launched a large-scale sidewalk fundraising campaign. From February 7 to 28, CHLA members were dispatched to different sections of the city, "holding 'special relief-fund' boxes to solicit donations in the sidewalks." On the twenty-seventh, a Sunday, the CHLA and the two civic organizations cosponsored a massive parade in the Lower East Side, again with the ambulances leading the march. Thousands of Americans and Chinese Americans attended, and some "white Americans" explained why they came to join the march: "I put some bucks into the relief-fund box [in the Chinese hand laundry where I take my laundry]; I want to see the ambulances they bought."[12]

The ambulances had at once symbolic meaning and practical purpose in the CHLA's people's diplomacy. First, the idea of purchasing ambulances was partly inspired by the American movement to aid the Spanish loyalist republicans, and the CHLA had learned from the experiences of other American civic organizations. This gave the campaign a remarkable Chinese American character quite different from the people's diplomacy conducted and directed by the KMT's official People's Foreign Relations Association (to be discussed below). Second, the ambulances became a symbol of ordinary Americans' support for China to inspire more donations. As a commentator in *The Chinese Vanguard* pointed out: "The majority of Americans sympathize with and are willing to help China, but many of them do not know how. Once they see the ambulances, they will immediately think of the Japanese brutal, inhuman killings of Chinese women and children, and think of the need of the Chinese refugees and heroic soldiers for material support. Then they will think about how to follow the example of the CHLA [and make donations]."[13]

Third, the parades led by the ambulances were opportunities to present a new image of the Chinese to the American public. *The Chinese Vanguard* commented: "[When Americans] see the ambulances, the orderly conducting of the parades and rallies, and high spirit of us Chinese, they will recognize the unyielding spirit and the organizational capacity of the Chinese nation, which will defeat the invaders."[14]

The last point is the key to understanding the nature of the people's diplomacy of the CHLA. Consciously, the alliance tried to play a specific role in U.S.-China relations in the 1930s and 1940s: the members presented themselves to the American people as a new image of the Chinese. Knowing that negative impressions of the Chinese as a passive, divided, and disorganized people were deeply rooted in American minds, the humble Chinese laundrymen united themselves and stood up as dynamic and dignified human beings. Through the people's diplomacy and "to save ourselves" campaigns, both the fluent English-speaking CHLA representatives and the ordinary laundrymen struggled to cultivate a new image of the Chinese in the American mind.

While members of the CHLA stood on the sidewalks soliciting donations from passing Americans or encouraging their customers to contribute to the relief-fund boxes, its representatives reached out to participate in many rallies and meetings organized by American civic and political organizations, promoting international sympathy and support for China. In those years the CHLA developed relationships with numerous American civic organizations, such as the League for Peace and Democracy, American Bureau for Medical Aid to China, and American Friends of the Chinese People. Cooperating with these organizations, the CHLA sponsored or jointly sponsored many rallies and parades to appeal to the American public for moral, financial, and other kinds of support for China. The spirit of the CHLA was praised and its members and representatives were accepted by these organizations as dignified and self-respecting people. The CHLA's representative, Thomas Tang, attended the national congress of the League for Peace and Democracy in 1937 and was elected a member of the league's National Committee.[15] Tan Lian'ai, another representative of the CHLA, was elected to the National

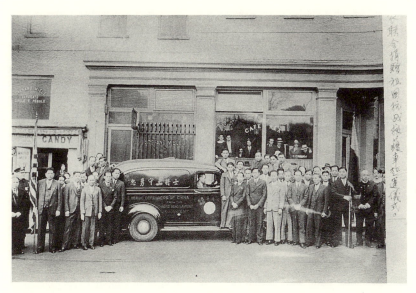

CHLA members with one of the four ambulances bought with funds raised in the campaign "to save China," 1938. All photos herein courtesy of the Chinese Hand Laundry Alliance of New York.

One of the four ambulances that the CHLA shipped to China, 1938. Figures in this picture unknown.

A "people's diplomacy" parade, 1937.

CHLA members march in New York City in an attempt to win American sympathy for China's war of resistance against Japan, 1938. Julius Bezozo (*at rear left, with moustache*) was the CHLA's lawyer in the 1930s and 1940s.

◁ 形情會宴念紀年週四祝慶會本 ▷

The CHLA's fourth anniversary banquet, 1937.

Amateur musicians of the CHLA, 1947.

The CHLA chorus, 1947.

Eugene Moy, editor-in-chief of the *China Daily News*.

Executive Committee of the American Youth Congress[16] and was frequently invited by civic and student organizations to give speeches on various issues related to China and the Chinese community in the United States.[17]

Evidence suggests that the CHLA's people's diplomacy produced a positive influence. At a mass meeting held on February 27, 1938, Byron N. Scott, a Democratic congressman from California, impressed by the high enthusiasm of the Chinese, promised to continue to urge congressional aid for China.[18] *The New York Times* reported the shipment of the CHLA ambulances to China in April, though it inaccurately stated that there were five ambulances and "the money for the ambulances was donated by 1,500 Chinese laundrymen in the metropolitan area."[19] The president of the Borough of Manhattan, Stanley M. Isaacs, clearly influenced by the efforts of the CHLA and other Chinese American patriotic organizations, endorsed an American policy to impose an embargo on Japan. In July 1940, one and a half years before the United States declared war on Japan, Isaacs expressed his support for China in a letter to the editor-in-chief of *CDN*:

> I am deeply interested in the gallant struggle of the Chinese people for national freedom and like millions of other Americans I am hopeful that your great people will fight their way to complete national freedom. Like many other Americans I blush with shame that we have not yet imposed an embargo upon Japan and have provided it for so long with so much of the death-dealing weapons which they were using against China. In my own humble way I have tried to do what I can by prohibiting the export of the scrap metal of the Sixth Avenue "L" demolition to aggressor nations. This was aimed particularly at Japanese aggression against China.[20]

It would be wrong, of course, to suggest that the people's diplomacy of the CHLA as well as other Chinese American organizations greatly influenced Roosevelt's China policy or significantly changed American stereotypes about the Chinese. But the CHLA's people's diplomacy was from beginning to end a grassroots movement. It was a campaign initiated by humble Chinese laundrymen to win ordinary Americans' sympathy and support for China, and at this level it seems to have had considerable success. Historian Michael Schaller observed that by late 1938 the United States had begun to adopt a policy of supporting a "pro-American China" against the Japanese aggressors. Among the "complementary factors" that facilitated this policy transformation, Schaller thought that "the most emotional [reason] must have been public shock at reports of the brutality of the Japanese army in China."[21] Seen in this context, the CHLA's activities in the people's diplomacy campaign played a positive role in winning American support for China.

Of course, focusing on the CHLA limits the scope of the examination of the actual role of Chinese Americans in wartime U.S.-China relations, a subject neglected in most of the literature on U.S.-China relations.[22] This study, however, by concentrating on the CHLA, suggests that before drawing generalizations about the experiences of Chinese Americans as a whole, we must have solid, in-depth case studies. In the case of New York's Chinese community, although most Chinese Americans aimed to obtain American moral and material support for China and their ultimate goal was to win an official American pro-China policy, the tactics of the various groups were different.

As noted earlier, the essence of the CHLA's people's diplomacy was to rally ordinary Chinese laundrymen to present a new image of the Chinese to the American public. A similar emphasis on dignity was missing in the official secret diplomacy of the KMT government. Using recently declassified U.S. State Department documents, Michael Schaller revealed that the KMT government employed some devious means to obtain American material support. In late 1940, Schaller found, "threats of surrender had become standard KMT negotiating practice" in order to gain American aid.[23] For example, Chiang Kai-shek sent a message to the State Department in November 1941 through his brother-in-law, T. V. Soong, then the representative of the KMT government in Washington. In the message Chiang stated that if the United States did not give more aid to China,

> then the Chinese people would consider that China has been completely sacrificed by the United States. The morale of the entire people will collapse and every Asiatic nation will lose faith . . . in democracy. . . . The Chinese army will collapse and the Japanese will be enabled to carry through their plans. . . . Such a loss would not be to China alone. . . . The certain collapse of our resistance will be an unparalleled catastrophe to the world, and I do not indeed know how history in future will record this episode.[24]

This kind of "diplomacy" was perhaps part of the reason that Chiang was able to get tens of millions of dollars from the U.S. government, but it also earned him the contempt of many American officials, diplomats, and generals.[25] Indeed, China needed American support desperately, but Chiang's appeals to the United States lacked all dignity. There was no way for ordinary Chinese Americans to learn about Chiang's secret diplomacy with the U.S. government, but when certain Chinese organizations in the United States used similar tactics to press the U.S. government, the CHLA and other groups expressed their own opinion on the matter.

In January 1942 U.S. Secretary of the Navy Frank Knox, reflecting the Roosevelt administration's Europe-first policy, stated that Hitler must be defeated first and that "full-scale action by the United States Fleet against Japan in the Pacific could not be expected in the near future."[26] A few days later sixteen Chinese organizations in New York City sent a telegram to President Roosevelt, protesting against the plan outlined in Knox's statement. The tone of the telegram was very much like that of Chiang's messages to the State Department:

> Most important of all, do not try our Chinese patience too far, and do not assume Chinese have no feelings to be hurt. . . . Have you ever considered what its effect on the Chinese people will be if the grand strategy of the Allies, as outlined by Secretary Knox, is followed? Mr. President, we feel it is our duty as citizens of China and friends of America to tell you the blunt truth. What we feel, we know the hundreds of millions in China are feeling today. A spirit of deep dissatisfaction is growing all around, in China, as well as in Australia, Dutch Indies and in London itself. If Singapore is lost and the Burma Road is threatened and the American fleet still persists in doing nothing in the Pacific, then we have the right to be disappointed with our Allies and will be forced to decide our own destiny. You cannot blame us for being impatient, for our people have suffered more than any of the Allies and by our suffering and our help to the democracies we have earned the right to speak.[27]

Among the sixteen organizations that signed the telegram were the CCBA and two major traditional district associations, Ning Yang and Lian Cheng; two powerful tongs, On Leong and Hip Sing; and most important, the Kuomintang and its affiliated organizations, the San Min Chu I Youth Corps, Kum Ai Association, and Chinese Foreign Affairs Association.[28] The name Chinese Foreign Affairs Association was an inaccurate translation of the name of a KMT agency, the New York Branch of the People's Foreign Relations Association of China.[29] This organization was founded in January 1938 in Wuhan, China, with important KMT officials, such as Chen Lifu, as its leaders, to promote "substantial support for China" among "friendly countries" and "communication between China and America."[30] Its New York branch was set up in July 1940,[31] three years after the CHLA launched its people's diplomacy.

The tone of the telegram seemed to be set by the KMT and its affiliated agencies, most probably by the People's Foreign Relations Association of China, following the usual practice of KMT diplomacy in America. These KMT agencies and traditional organizations represented only a part of the Chinese people, however. The CHLA, *CDN*, and some other Chinese American organizations resented the defeatist tone of the telegram. *CDN* immediately published the Chinese translation of the telegram and simultaneously carried several editorials criticizing the way the sixteen organizations were conducting their people's diplomacy.[32]

The day after the telegram was published in *CDN*, the CHLA held a membership meeting to discuss it. The members were so upset by the "disgraceful way" the sixteen organizations had presented themselves that they decided to express their own opinion to President Roosevelt. On January 18 the CHLA sent a telegram to FDR, telling him that "the Chinese in the United States can understand that you will make the strategic plans based on overall considerations of the conditions in this prolonged war.... This Alliance, representing thousands of the Chinese hand laundries, sincerely supports your overall strategy." The signature on the telegram, "The CHLA Membership Meeting," emphasized that it represented ordinary people's opinion.[33] On the same day, the CHLA sent a telegram to Chiang Kai-shek, expressing its disapproval of any defeatism and urging him to uphold Chinese morale. The Quon Shar sent similar telegrams to Roosevelt and Chiang.[34]

Two days later the CHLA received a reply telegram from Knox, who stated that Roosevelt had passed the CHLA telegram to him and asked him to respond. "I am pleased that your Alliance correctly understands my statement at the Conference of Mayors," Knox said. Then he promised that the United States "of course" would do everything "to defeat Japan."[35]

The point here is not that the CHLA understood the U.S. Europe-first policy better than did the KMT and the traditional organizations, nor that the CHLA supported the policy while the KMT wanted to change it. The CHLA did its best to solicit all possible support for China, and no less than anyone else it was eager to see the U.S. government adopt a more active policy of aiding China. The telegram episode simply suggests that the CHLA, a grassroots organization without knowledge of how KMT officials were trying to obtain aid from the United States, was disgusted by what it called the "disgraceful" tactics the sixteen organizations had used. It wanted to present another image of the Chinese to the U.S. president as well as to the American people and press—the implicit message being that the heroic and unyielding Chinese people deserve the support of the peace-loving American people. Ironically, it was these innocent Chinese laundrymen (compared with the American-trained KMT diplomats, such as T. V. Soong, who tactfully manipulated the American bureaucracy) who took at face value the rhetoric both of Chiang Kai-shek, who claimed that the Chinese people would fight against Japan to the last drop of blood, and of American politicians, who insisted that a special relationship existed between China and the United States and that the latter would do everything to save the former.

Unfortunately, while *The New York Times* took the telegram of the sixteen organizations as the "opinion of the Chinese in New York City" and said that they "begged" the president "not to commit to such a policy [of concentrating on Europe],"[36] the opinion of the CHLA was basically ignored by the American mass media. Within the Chinese community, however, the CHLA's courage to dissent from KMT policy was applauded by many. For weeks *CDN* received letters from Chinese laundrymen and restaurant workers supporting the CHLA's position.[37] The CHLA's influence went even beyond New York City. The Chinese Workers' Mutual Aid Association in San Francisco, founded in 1937 and active in promoting cooperation between Chinese and American workers, sent an open letter to all the Chinese in the United States denouncing the sixteen organizations' telegram and supporting the CHLA's point of view.[38]

To differentiate themselves from the defeatists and to present an image of the Chinese that was dignified and deserving of American aid, CHLA members passed a resolution at a membership meeting held on February 1, two weeks after the telegram was sent to FDR, to buy American war bonds.[39] A three-man committee was set up to promote the purchase, and the organization's fund was used to buy the first $300 worth of bonds. Enthusiasm ran so high among the members that within the first week $2,850 worth of war bonds were bought.[40] By June the total value of the bonds purchased by CHLA members amounted to more than $13,000.[41] Although the first drive of CHLA members to buy war bonds was intended to nullify what they perceived as the "bad influence" caused by the telegram of the sixteen organizations, it soon became a consistent war effort. Li Chengzhu, one of the CHLA's core members, wrote an article in 1944 urging his fellow members to continue their (American) patriotic actions: "Now the Government is selling the fifth-term war bonds. We shall all buy. Let every hand laundry in every corner become a buyer of the war bonds, so as to increase the amity between us and our customers and, to set an example for those 'cheap' customers, inspiring them to follow us to buy the war bonds ."[42]

Clearly, this article reflected the opinion of Chinese Americans rather than that of Chinese nationals. After the Japanese attack on Pearl Harbor, CHLA members and many other Chinese Americans, especially those with U.S. citizenship, felt that they "now have double national hatred" toward Japan.[43] The CHLA campaign "to save China, to save ourselves" gained a new meaning in the new context: it was equally important to support the war efforts of both China and the United States, which now had a common interest in defeating Japan. Therefore, the CHLA's drive to buy American war bonds can be seen as another step toward the formation of a Chinese American consciousness among first-generation Chinese immigrants. This drive had a symbolic significance: pursuing people's diplomacy in the American context, CHLA members began to reflect on their position in American society from a new perspective. The more they became involved in promoting the development of a friendly and equal relationship between the United States and China, the more they developed the sense of being Chinese Americans. Thus, through its activities the CHLA played a leading role in shaping a new community identity in New York's Chinatown during the war years.

"We and the Oppressed Nations"

During the period 1937–45 the conflicts between the different interest groups in New York's Chinatown still existed but were greatly lessened by the collective effort to save the homeland from Japanese invasion. As the programs and activities sponsored by the CHLA made positive contributions to the cause of saving China, its allies in the community increased. Although the CCBA appeared to be the community's leader, a position that the CHLA acknowledged within the context of the united front, it was the CHLA and other progressive organizations that most actively responded to the issues concerning the community. Therefore, the CHLA frequently acted as a spokesperson for the whole community. Fulfilling that role, the CHLA, on the one hand, pursued some activities on its own initiative while, on the other hand, it challenged the CCBA's leadership by pushing the "supreme power" to do what it proclaimed to be doing.

By the late 1930s and early 1940s the CHLA leaders had become more experienced, and they made the alliance more active and more visible both inside and outside the Chinese community. By 1941 the CHLA had recovered from the losses of 1937 and its membership had risen to more than two thousand again.[44] In the following years, although many CHLA members were drafted into the U.S. armed forces, new members joined the alliance, and its membership remained stable between two thousand and three thousand.[45]

The people's diplomacy campaign expanded the contacts between Chinese and Americans, an important step in breaking the barriers that had caused and perpetuated the isolation of the Chinese hand laundrymen. Little documentation exists that reflects the Chinese laundrymen's perception of their position in American society and their relations with other groups. Fortunately, *CDN* consistently carried out a policy of "cultivating freedom of speech among overseas Chinese,"[46] so that ordinary Chinese Americans were encouraged to express their opinions in the paper's two special columns, the Letters column and the Op-Ed column. Through these letters and articles, we can see how first-generation Chinese immigrants began to deal with various issues in their relationship with other ethnic groups. Their thinking was strongly influenced by people's diplomacy—that is, their attitude toward a certain ethnic group was greatly affected by that group's attitude toward China's war of resistance against Japan. Most interesting, these Chinese Americans began to reflect on and self-criticize their "incorrect" attitude toward "weak groups" such as Jews and blacks, attributing it to the "bad" influence of the dominant "white racist culture."

Of all the letters and articles published in *CDN* in the 1940s, Xiao Lin's article "We and the Oppressed Nations" was most representative and is worth quoting at length:

> Our Chinese war of resistance [against Japan] and this world war are related. We shall struggle to win the liberation and freedom not only for the Chinese nation, but also for all mankind in the whole world. Therefore, doubtlessly, we must unite with [other] oppressed nations in the world. . . .
> In the United States where we now live, there are at least two groups that are oppressed, one is Jews, the other, blacks. According to the above-mentioned theory of uniting with [other] oppressed nations in the world, we Chinese should be the best friends of Jews and blacks, uniting together closely. However, the reality is the opposite.
> I once taught a group of Chinese kids in a church. When I mentioned Jews, these kids would contemptuously say: "Jewish devil! None of them is any good." I tried different ways to explain to them that there are both good

and bad people among the Jews, just like there are both good and bad people among our Chinese. We must not judge a whole nation based on one or two bad or good persons. What should we Chinese say if [some] foreigners claimed that all Chinese were bad because there were one or two bad Chinese? However, no matter how hard I tried, the kids still kept their contemptuous attitude toward the Jews. I do not blame the kids. They are the products of the environment. They in their schools, their parents in American society, often come into contact with the anti-Semitic whites and, as a result, many of them also become anti-Semitic. But, we must remember: anti-Semitism is one of the means that Hitler attempts to use to conquer the world, and we should never fall into his trap.

Many [Chinese] criticize the Jews for being cunning and stingy. How about we Chinese? If other people say we Chinese are cunning and stingy, what would we think? Some [Chinese] believe that every Jew is a rich man. In fact, this world is full of poor and oppressed Jews. As the [Chinese] saying goes, "Those who have the same illness sympathize with each other." Especially in this fight against the Japanese, we should unite with the oppressed Jews all over the world.

Several best friends of mine are Jews. They sympathize tremendously with China's resistance against Japan, they have donated a lot of money to China, and they want to unite with Chinese.

In the United States, blacks suffer the most. Anywhere and at any moment, they are discriminated against, insulted, even slaughtered. According to the above-mentioned theory of uniting with the oppressed nations, we shall unite with black people. However, in fact, many Chinese discriminate against blacks.

In the largest black newspaper, the *Pittsburgh Courier*, one black writer wrote: "The Chinese proudly socialize with white people, but discriminate against us blacks." Unfortunately, there are many such cases.

We feel angry at the fact that our Chinese seamen were discriminated against in South Africa and in the United States, but we discriminate against black people. Some say that "if we treat black customers well we will offend white customers." We should tell white customers: "We Chinese and blacks are both colored people. We are comrades in the same front." Some say: "Harlem is full of thieves." Is there any place without thieves? It is the deliberate exaggerations of those anti-black newspapers that make the impression that Harlem is a horrible place, just like the exaggerations of Chinatown as a den of vice made by some anti-Chinese agitators in the past. If someone warns people not to go to Chinatown, what should we think?

What's the black people's attitude toward our Chinese? The whole world knows that the best-known black singer [Paul] Robeson voluntarily did some benefit performances for China's war against Japan. Many of the poor blacks donated their sweat-and-blood money to support China. Recently, the *Pittsburgh Courier* invited Chinese writers to report on China's war efforts. All this indicates that black people are willing to unite with the Chinese people and engage in a common struggle against oppression.

My fellow Chinese! Never forget that we were discriminated against and oppressed five years ago [before the Marco Polo Bridge Incident], and that we are now still being discriminated against and oppressed. In our struggle for equality and freedom, we must unite with the oppressed nations![47]

Despite constant calls for unity with black people, there is no evidence that Chinese Americans established substantial relationships with black organizations. The CHLA was exceptional among Chinese American groups in its effort to contact black organizations. The black community was one of the targets of the CHLA's people's diplomacy. The black singer Paul Robeson was often invited to CHLA rallies during the war years. Some black organizations came to know the CHLA as an influential organization in the Chinese community and requested its cooperation in some programs. In May 1942, for example, when the United Service launched a fundraising drive in the Harlem area to supply musical instruments to servicemen, it asked the CHLA for help. The CHLA responded warmly. It requested its members with hand laundries located in the area between 110th Street and 155th Street to give a hand to the fundraising campaign.[48]

The most meaningful progress in Chinese-black relations during the war years came from the discussions led and encouraged by *CDN* on the relationship between the two ethnic groups and what kind of attitude the Chinese should have toward black people. If most members of the early generations of Chinese Americans felt sorry for blacks but never came to the realization that Chinese and blacks had a common fate, those Chinese Americans who wrote to *CDN* in the 1940s began to think in such terms.

In 1943 the news that Chinese restaurants in Washington, D.C., were suffering a rapid decline due probably to a black boycott stirred the Chinese community, and some Chinese Americans began a soul-searching self-criticism of the Chinese attitude toward blacks. In June 1943 a Chinese named Chen Sheng wrote to the editor of *CDN* reporting that "the business of the Chop Suey restaurants in the black communities in D.C. recently declined greatly. Many Chinese here suspected that the blacks are boycotting [us]." Chen Sheng mentioned that a black customer "frankly told me that blacks are really disappointed at the Chinese." According to Chen, the black customer stated that blacks had sympathized with the Chinese and always supported the Chinese resistance against

Japan. But though both were discriminated against by white racists, some Chinese discriminated against blacks, "sometimes worse than the whites." The black also complained that even Chinese leaders, such as Madame Chiang Kai-shek, had made contemptuous remarks about blacks.

Chen said that he explained to his black customers that Chinese had no intention to hurt the feelings of black people; as for those incidents of some Chinese restaurants serving mainly white customers, with black customers being led to sit in the corner or shown icy faces, it was because white customers discriminated against blacks. "If whites do not discriminate against blacks," Chen Sheng told his black friend, "from a 'business is business' point of view, we Chinese of course would welcome both white and black customers." Chen Sheng's explanation was not persuasive to his black customer, who told him that "blacks generally believed that Chinese discriminate against blacks." So Chen wrote to *CDN* hoping the newspaper could lead an educational movement to help solve the problem.[49]

In the following days *CDN* ran two editorials calling the attention of Chinese to the problem in order to develop a "correct attitude" toward blacks. The editorials admitted that there were "some individuals in the Chinese community who were influenced by the general contemptuous attitude to blacks in American society" and "had insulted our fellow-sufferer blacks." Chinese should never do such shameful things again. Though the rumor that the Chinese chop suey restaurants used cat meat to replace beef and pork was outrageous, the editorials warned, the Chinese "must calm down, and should not act emotionally. Never try revenge." The editorials further suggested that the Chinese restaurant owners and waiters should be friendly to black customers and especially to lower-class blacks, and that the Chinese who operated chop suey restaurants in black neighborhoods should organize themselves and elect their leaders to communicate with "the leaders of black religious and other organizations." Since most black organizations were supportive of China against Japan, the editorials expected that the leaders of black organizations would help resolve the tension between the two ethnic groups. Finally, the leaders of all Chinese organizations should be aware of the problem and actively seek solutions to it.[50]

Liu Liangmo, one of the CHLA's allies and the leader of the People's Chorus, a patriotic organization very close to the CHLA, asserted that "a fundamental change of the Chinese attitude toward blacks is the only way to solve the problem." A Chinese patriot from Shanghai,[51] Liu

Liangmo was invited to write a special column on China's war efforts for the black newspaper *Pittsburgh Courier* during the war years.[52] He joined the discussion on the black-Chinese relationship with an article "On the Black Attitude to Chinese." He told his fellow Chinese that black leaders and the black press were "very sympathetic with China," "many blacks donated money to our fight against Japan," and "all black newspapers supported the repeal of the Chinese Exclusion Act [which was then being debated in Congress]."[53]

Liu Liangmo also reported that blacks and their leaders were "very disappointed" with the Chinese leaders "who dared not speak out for the struggle of blacks for justice and equality because they did not want to offend the Southern politicians who oppressed blacks." Many blacks were "often treated poorly and often heard insulting words in Chinese restaurants," Liu went on, "so their disappointment turned to anger." Liu insisted that blacks had a friendly attitude toward Chinese, but "some Chinese" had a "poor" attitude toward blacks. He urged all Chinese Americans to treat blacks as brothers. "We should understand that blacks and we Chinese are like each other—we are the nations being discriminated against and oppressed. We have no reason to discriminate against our black brothers."[54]

These discussions suggest that the campaign "to save China" and people's diplomacy created an opportunity for Chinese Americans to rethink their relations with other ethnic groups, especially with blacks. Basically, these Chinese Americans realized that they shared a common experience with blacks and with Jews as "oppressed nations" in American society. In addition to the discussion on black-Chinese relations in June and July 1943, *CDN* continued to carry editorials, essays, and letters to urge Chinese Americans to renounce their bias against blacks and Jews.[55] It was not until the 1970s, however, that Chinese Americans in New York City began to establish substantial relationships with the black community. In 1984 and 1988 the CHLA was one of the Chinese American organizations that vigorously supported the Reverend Jesse Jackson's presidential campaigns.[56]

In the 1940s both the Chinese and black communities had their own urgent issues to deal with so that cooperation between the two groups did not become an item requiring immediate attention in their agendas. After World War II Liu Liangmo's column in the *Pittsburgh Courier* was discontinued because "the *Courier* received reports about China's 'disdain' for blacks."[57] Meanwhile, *CDN* gave more coverage to the domestic situation in China. Thus a possible meaningful communication between the two groups was interrupted. Nevertheless, the frank self-criticisms of the Chinese discriminatory attitude toward blacks, the positive calls for improving the relationship between blacks and Chinese, and the proposals for communicating with the black community were part of the efforts made by the CHLA and its mouthpiece, *CDN*, as well as other progressive Chinese Americans, to shape a new community identity—an identity defined in the contexts of American conditions and of U.S.-China relations.

Group and Community Identity

In addition to a new perception of their relations with other "oppressed nations," the campaign "to save China, to save ourselves" prompted the CHLA and its allies to rethink many other issues within the Chinese community. In the 1930s and 1940s, supporting China's war of resistance against Japan dominated Chinatown politics and other aspects of communal life. The mobilization of the people also led to many social changes. The most noticeable was the rise of the younger generation, whose members became more and more active in community politics and social activities, emerging as a new and important force among Chinese Americans. Together with the CHLA and its allies, young people became part of the progressive forces that sought a new direction for the community.

As previously noted, the younger and more active members of the CHLA organized Quon Shar in 1935 to promote the cause of Chinese salvation. After the outbreak of the anti-Japanese war in China in 1937, these young members felt the need to establish a broad youth organization to attract young people in other occupations. More important, they wanted to merge with the U.S.-born Chinese American youth. On April 11, 1938, at the initiative of several CHLA members, the Chinese Patriotic Youth Club (Niuyue Huaqiao Qingnian Jiuguo Tuan) was founded with about twenty members. A few years later the membership had increased to more than two hundred, and the club became the largest of the youth organizations in New York's Chinatown.[58]

The Youth Club was an independent organization, but it had a close relationship with the CHLA and was under its influence. The organizational and language abilities of Tan Lian'ai, the CHLA's English Language Secretary, and Eugene Moy, the editor of *CDN*, made them the guiding forces of the club. Some CHLA leaders and active members, such

as Li Guhong, Chen Jingjian, Chen Kangming, and Yu Zhiming, were at
the same time the leaders of the Youth Club. The CHLA, Quon Shar, and
the Youth Club all had their headquarters in the same building on Canal
Street.[59]

To meet the needs of the youth, the club sponsored many social and recreational programs (sometimes with the help of the CHLA and the
Quon Shar), such as classes in Mandarin (the Chinese national language),
music, and photography, and a chorus. The club even organized a drama
group, providing opportunities for amateurs to perform on stage. Chen
Kangming, one of the CHLA's core members, became an amateur play-
wright after many years' practice. The club also published its own magazine, the bilingual (Chinese and English) *Chinese Youth*, which linked
New York's Chinese young people with those in other cities, such as
Washington, D.C., and San Francisco. From May 1941 on, the club ran
a special monthly youth column in *CDN*. Both the column and the magazine provided a forum for Chinese youth to express their opinions on the
issues concerning them.[60]

One of the purposes of the Youth Club was to unite the U.S.-born and
China-born Chinese youth. An article published in 1941 addressed the
lack of communication between the two groups before 1937:

> Because the native-born and China-born were educated and grew up in dif-
> ferent cultural environments, they have different habits and ideas. These dif-
> ferences cause them to misunderstand each other and worse, they even look
> down on each other. While the native-born look down on the China-born
> because they believe that they are better than the China-born since they have
> the superior Western culture, the China-born think of themselves as "real
> Chinese" and regard the native-born as "neither Chinese nor Western," a
> hopeless group. This phenomenon has existed [in the community] for a long
> time, ever since our grandfathers.[61]

To remove the wall that separated the two groups of young people, the
Youth Club consciously worked to pull them together. The club membership included both the China-born and the U.S.-born, and its leaders
were elected from both groups. "We worked together, and cooperated
with each other quite well," one work report of the Youth Club stated.[62]
To expand the communication between the two groups, the Youth Club
sponsored dancing parties, inviting U.S.-born and China-born youth in
New York City to meet and understand each other.[63]

The Youth Club tried, without much success, to sponsor a discussion
of the future of Chinese youth in America involving both the U.S.-born

and the China-born with the hope of eventually reaching a consensus. Although only a few of the former articulated their opinions, these discussions provide us with some valuable insight into the second-generation Chinese Americans' reflections on their future in America and their relations with the older generation.

An article by Frank Leung entitled "Our Future in America," published in *Chinese Youth*, offered a comprehensive view. According to Leung,

> Chinese Youth staying in this country are all confronted with the problem of providing economic security for themselves[,] at least of caring for the basic needs of life. The present economic possibilities for the second-generation may roughly be divided into the following four groups: to take over or to work within those businesses established by the older generation, to develop new trades and services within the Chinese communities, to seek employment with American organizations, or to create new jobs by selling new services and new products in the American markets.[64]

By "those businesses established by the older generation," Leung was referring to "the restaurants and laundries in the East, the groceries in the South, and tourist trades, restaurants, and different service industries in the West." It is interesting to note that although Leung believed that the restaurant and laundry businesses "have little appeal" to "the Chinese youth who intend to make a home in this country," and that "the chances of the youth in the East to make a fair living in the laundries or restaurants are small," he still listed them as the number-one choice for the second generation. Leung pointed out that "Chinese youth seeking employment with American organizations have always faced numerous obstacles and only a small percentage have succeeded in obtaining jobs. The reasons are many but we must not forget that in seeking jobs we are competing with thousands of unemployed American youth also trying to fill those positions. Competent training is necessary. Do we always have it?" But he was more optimistic about the chances for Chinese young people to find employment in government agencies. He observed that "most of these opening[s] are under the jurisdiction of the Civil Service Commission and there is no discrimination as to the candidates," so he thought the Chinese youth should try. Nevertheless, in his conclusion Leung stated that "the present businesses established by the older generation are generally stable sources of income." But he urged improvement: "If improvements are made through applying new business knowledge the incomes will increase[,] hence affording the much desire[d] economic security to exist. However, in some businesses where better conditions are desired, remedies should be made gradually if necessary, rather than abandoning those businesses now if better conditions cannot immediately be gotten, for this will only decrease the sources of income."[65]

Leung's arguments suggest that even second-generation Chinese Americans, limited by a variety of restrictions, considered the laundry business one of their prime economic choices; however, they chose laundry work only as a temporary, transitional, and least-desired option. Because of their knowledge of English, their opportunities were better than those of the first-generation Chinese immigrants in finding other jobs in the labor market. Therefore, few of them entered the hand laundry business as a lifetime job or joined the CHLA, which was overwhelmingly dominated by Cantonese-speaking, first-generation Chinese.[66] Nevertheless, a natural and meaningful result of the discussion of the economic possibilities in the United States was that some of the second generation developed a greater respect for the older generation, and on that basis they seemed to have established a positive identity with the community in which they had grown up. The spirit of the older generation became part of the heritage of the community, which was seen by the second generation as a source of inspiration and strength. As Leung put it: "If we all apply the same enterprising spirits our fathers applied when they reached this country we cannot help but to succeed in bringing ourselves into the realm of the American way of life."[67]

While promoting a more positive community identity, the CHLA forged a stronger group identity among its members. By the early 1940s many members felt that the foundation of the CHLA as an occupational organization should be further strengthened. Summing up the opinions of the members, Chen Houfu, a former activist in the Washington, D.C., Chinese community who joined the CHLA in 1943,[68] made several proposals. First, Chen suggested, the CHLA should buy a building as a permanent headquarters, so as not to pay high rent every year. This goal was realized immediately after the end of World War II when the CHLA bought the building at 191 Canal Street for thirty thousand dollars.[69] Second, the CHLA should set up a membership cooperative store, buying and selling laundry supplies so that the members could avoid being exploited by the merchants who controlled the business. Also, the profit from the store would enable the CHLA to sponsor some welfare programs for its members. Finally, the CHLA should organize various "study groups" to meet the needs of members of different age groups. "We should study hard to catch up with the progress of the society, to learn more to enable us to understand the complicated affairs," Chen said. Through mutual help, Chen hoped, the members would enhance their "ability to deal with problems."[70]

The CHLA failed to set up its co-op store but founded its own wet-wash factory (discussed in the next chapter). In addition to collective efforts to defend its members' common economic and political interests and rights, the alliance set up its own welfare programs. One of them concerned death benefits. If a member had fulfilled his membership duties and paid his dues and fees, when he died the CHLA would collect a quarter from each member to pay for his memorial service and burial and to give his family a small sum of money.[71] Moreover, members would write articles and poems (in classical Chinese style) in memory of the deceased. These pieces demonstrated that many members had developed a strong identity with the CHLA.

In October 1944 Luo Fu, a veteran member of the CHLA, died of a stomach ailment. His old friend Chen Sancai wrote an article to express his grief and to praise Luo Fu's contribution to the CHLA:

> I feel deeply sad upon hearing the bad news that Luo Fu died in hospital. Luo Fu had been in the United States for almost twenty years, working as a laundryman in New York City. I met him after the CHLA was founded. We have worked together ever since. From my ten-year friendship with him, I know him as a loyal member devoted to the common interests [of the membership]. He was able to make correct judgments, especially when our Alliance faced difficulties. He was honest and dared to stand up and speak out, never blindly following others. He made great contributions to the CHLA success in overcoming the opposition to the democratic procedures for elections, and to the strengthening of the CHLA....
>
> Last year, when we protested the wet-wash companies, one fellow laundryman (I do not remember whether he was a member or not) was oppressed [by a wet-wash company that refused to do his work]. After learning the news, Luo Fu immediately closed his own laundry on a weekday and went to help the suffering fellow laundryman. He used his connections to find a wet-wash company for the man, and rent a car to send his work to the wet-wash company....
>
> Later, when the CHLA was to establish our own wet-wash factory, Luo Fu hired hands to operate his hand laundry, but he himself went all over the city to persuade fellow laundrymen to buy shares in the CHLA's wet-wash factory.... Even when he lay in the hospital bed, he was still concerned with

Alliance affairs. When we went to the hospital to see him, he asked us to be well prepared for the celebration of the Alliance's eleventh anniversary....

The death of Luo Fu is a great loss to the CHLA. However, his selfless spirit will be alive with us and with the whole Chinese community![72]

Occasionally, the memorial articles, while praising the spirit of the deceased members, urged the laundrymen to pay more attention to their health. Perhaps because of long working hours under unclean conditions, some hand laundrymen died of hematemesis at an early age—in their thirties or forties. In one article in memory of Tan Yunsheng, who died of hematemesis, Chen Houfu called fellow laundrymen's attention to the sanitation conditions in their laundries.

Tan Yunsheng had been a staff member of the CHLA for several terms. This year he was once again elected as a member of the Executive Committee. Tan was a typical old overseas Chinese [lao huaqiao], honest, diligent, and a man of few words. I used to tease him when he came to the headquarters on Sundays: "Do you work on Sundays? That's against the law." I always tried to persuade fellow laundrymen in a joking way not to work on Sunday, the only day we can take a rest and recover from our exhausting work. I believe that the death of Tan was mostly because he worked too hard and suffered too much. How sad!

I remember that Tan used to sigh when we talked about issues of sanitation. He seemed to be gloomy. Now I would like to discuss some issues here, on the one hand, in memory of Tan, on the other, hoping my fellow laundrymen could learn a lesson. Hand laundry work is tough. The store space we rent is usually small, and the sanitary conditions very poor. However, shall we live with this forever and never plan on any improvement? I dare to tell my fellow laundrymen: money is important, but life is much more important. Even though we may earn less, we should have enough sleep. Sleep at least eight hours every day. Never work on Sundays no matter what happens....

... In the hand laundries, there accumulates lint, which makes the air inside very dirty. Breathing this kind of air for a long time one's lungs must be vulnerable to disease. So, please keep the windows open, and sweep the floor frequently. These are of course little things, but we cannot afford to ignore them. Ignoring these little things could lead to fatal problems.[73]

Working together in common political and economic struggles and participating in social activities initiated by themselves, CHLA members developed friendships and mutual concerns that strengthened with the passage of time. This unity enabled the alliance to achieve remarkable goals and to endure great difficulties and hardships.

Repeal of the Chinese Exclusion Acts

The repeal of the Chinese exclusion acts in 1943 had a profound impact on the Chinese American community. All the Chinese exclusion laws were abolished, Chinese were allowed a quota of 105 immigrants to the United States per year, and they became eligible for naturalized citizenship. In the process of debating the repeal bills, however, Congress and the press, as well as the organizations that vigorously supported the repeal, virtually ignored the voice of the Chinese Americans themselves. The fundamental argument for the repeal was that it would help end the war and further U.S. postwar commercial relations with China. Some religious and humanitarian groups emphasized "racial equality" and "human rights," but in a patronizing tone.[74] "When Chinese-Americans sought to help the campaign, they were asked to refute the argument that Chinese were unassimilable rather than state their specific group interests."[75] The Citizens Committee to Repeal the Chinese Exclusion, an organization founded in New York on May 25, 1943, which played a key role in the campaign, for tactical considerations limited its membership "to American citizens not of Asiatic origin so as to give the impression that the demand was completely indigenous and not fostered by the Chinese or anyone with a personal 'axe to grind.' "[76]

As a result of this deliberate neglect by both the oppositional and supportive groups to the repeal, there are few records of how Chinese Americans responded. This section documents the response of the CHLA, as well as its mouthpiece, *CDN*, to the repeal.

Even before Congressmen John Lesinski, Martin Kennedy, Vito Marcantonio, and Warren Magnuson presented their proposals to amend the immigration laws and to repeal the Chinese exclusion laws in February and March 1943, the CHLA had been actively seeking a way to push Congress to do so. Part of the alliance's effort was to try to work with other immigrant communities and those civic organizations that advocated the rights of immigrants. On January 30, 1943, the CHLA sent Tan Lian'ai to a meeting attended by some three hundred representatives of organizations and trade unions supporting the rights of the foreign-born. The meeting, organized by the American Committee for Protection of the Foreign Born and the New York Guild of Lawyers, discussed how to press Congress to amend the immigration laws. A seven-person committee was set up to draft proposals for presentation to Congress, and Tan was elected as one of its members.[77]

Tan presented the Chinese case to the meeting. He pointed out that the Chinese exclusion laws were evidence of the injustice and mistreatment that Chinese suffered; furthermore, Tan continued, Chinese Americans had to confront many problems deriving from the exclusion laws, such as whether Chinese American GIs were eligible for citizenship and whether their families were entitled to the benefits of the government's GI family programs that other ethnic groups enjoyed. The seven-person committee drafted several proposals for submission to Congress, of which one was to repeal the Chinese exclusion laws—possibly due to Tan's efforts.[78] Later the American Committee for the Protection of the Foreign Born sent a letter to the House of Representatives supporting the repeal of the Chinese exclusion acts, though the committee's main effort was to push for the removal of all racial discrimination in the naturalization laws.[79]

On February 17 Congressmen Martin Kennedy proposed a bill in the House (H.R. 1882, "Chinese Citizenship Act of 1943") that would repeal the Chinese exclusion acts and make Chinese eligible for naturalization. On February 26 Congressman Vito Marcantonio submitted his bill (H.R. 2011), "To Amend the Nationality Act of 1940," which also proposed to offer Chinese the right to become U.S. citizens.[80]

On March 15 *CDN* published the first of a series of editorials dealing with the repeal, entitled "To Struggle for the Repeal of the Exclusion Laws." Without knowing that some organizations, such as the Citizens Committee to Repeal the Chinese Exclusion, did not want their active participation in the campaign, the editorial encouraged Chinese Americans to involve themselves in the fight.

> We believe that many ways could be used to promote the campaign to repeal the exclusion laws. Here are some: (a) all Chinese Americans and their organizations across the United States should immediately write letters or send telegrams to the Secretary of State, senators, and representatives, demanding the repeal of the [Chinese] exclusion laws; (b) mobilize all pro–Chinese American organizations and individuals to engage in the same action; (c) mobilize all Chinese mass media (both Chinese language and English language) to publicize the campaign among both the Chinese and American people; and (d) using all our connections to mobilize the American press and public opinion to support the repeal.[81]

Throughout 1943 *CDN* and the CHLA actively promoted Chinese participation in the campaign to repeal the exclusion laws, and they worked together closely. Three days after the *CDN* editorial appeared, the CHLA sent a cable to Samuel Dickstein, chairman of the House Committee on Immigration and Naturalization, expressing its "excitement upon learning of the Kennedy and Marcantonio proposals" and requesting the committee to "quickly discuss and pass the bills."[82]

The CHLA also sent its legal advisor Julius Bezozo and secretary Tan Lian'ai to attend the House hearings on the repeal. Apparently, they did not have a chance to speak to the House committee. With Song Feng (pen name), the special correspondent of *CDN*, however, they reported to the CHLA and the Chinese community on the House hearings and debates.[83] Song wrote a series of reports and analyses about the campaign, which helped to inform the Chinese community of the arguments of both the supporters and the opponents of the repeal bills.

Believing that Chinese participation in the campaign was necessary and important, *CDN* consistently urged all Chinese to do something to facilitate its progress. In May the paper provided a printed letter on its seventh page for the use of its readers:

> Hon. Samuel Dickstein, Chairman
> Committee on Immigration and Naturalization
> House of Representatives
> Washington, D.C.
> Sir:
> May I urge upon your committee to report favorably and recommend the enactment of H.R. 1882 to repeal the provisions of the Exclusion Laws. These laws repudiated all concepts of democracy and violate the fundamental principles of American government.
>
>   NAME _____
>   ADDRESS _____[84]

When the House hearings began, *CDN* once again urged Chinese American organizations to express their opinion and to support the repeal. The paper's editorial of May 4 emphasized that "the hearings are vital to the fate of the Bills to repeal the exclusion laws." "We especially urge the CCBA and all Chinese organizations and individuals in this city, if possible, to send representatives to attend the hearings and to express our Chinese opinion so that to abolish the Chinese exclusion laws and to enable Chinese to have equal rights as American citizens."[85] Acting on this push, the CCBA called a community meeting and passed a resolution to support the repeal bills. It was decided to take the following steps in the name of the whole community: to send 531 letters to the senators and representatives asking them to support the bill, H.R. 1882; to send cables to the four congressmen who initiated the bills, encouraging them to continue the cause; to send cables to the leaders of the Senate and the House and the two senators from New York asking for their support; to send a letter to the Chinese ambassador to the United States, Wei Daoming, requesting him to send legal advisors to the hearings; and to set up a nine-person committee to study related issues.[86]

From May to October, when Congress held hearings and debated the bills to repeal the exclusion laws, *CDN* devoted a great amount of its space to the coverage of these events. Its special correspondent, Song Feng, sent reports on every development in the process from Washington, D.C., to the paper's New York headquarters each night through long-distance telephone calls.[87] To help readers gain a comprehensive understanding, the paper reported in detail on the viewpoints and arguments of both the opponents and supporters of repeal. The testimony of "friendly American individuals," such as Dr. Arthur Hummel of the U.S. Library of Congress and the writer Pearl Buck, as well as the opinions of some anti-Chinese organizations and individuals, were translated into Chinese and published in the paper. Song Feng reported that he interviewed more than half the members of the House Committee on Immigration and Naturalization, who told him that "the issue [of the repeal] may encourage the Southern black people to demand equality too," and "that may threaten the special status of the Southern whites." "Nevertheless," Song Feng wrote, "all of them claimed to be the best friends of China and Chinese!"[88]

Song Feng warned his fellow Chinese Americans in a special essay that the "biggest obstacle to the repeal of the exclusion laws is the opposition of the House representatives from the South." According to him, these representatives, whether Democrats or Republicans, "all had very deep racial prejudice and a mentality of discriminating against colored people. Most of them do not want to share equal rights with us Chinese." Song Feng asked Chinese Americans to unite with American supporters of repeal to fight against these southern racists. At the same time, he was also critical of Chinese Americans who "did very little" in the campaign, and he attacked the Chinese embassy and consulates in the United States for "remaining silent from the beginning." If the Chinese remain passive and silent, Song Feng asserted, "the goal of repealing the exclusion laws cannot be easily reached."[89]

Song Feng observed that "many pro-Chinese Americans were confused by the silence of the Chinese government officials on the repeal."[90] Many other Chinese Americans also expressed their anger at the reticence of Chinese government officials. Madame Chiang Kai-shek, who was on a state visit in the United States in 1943, made no public comments on the repeal bills. Although she did make some efforts in private to promote the repeal campaign,[91] Chinese Americans had no way of knowing it, and as a result, their humiliation was deepened by the weakness and seeming indifference of the Chinese government.

CDN did not openly criticize the passivity of the Chinese official representatives in the United States, but the paper did attack this official policy of silence in an indirect way by borrowing from some American newspapers. On May 7 the daily printed a Chinese translation of a report from the Boston *Christian Science Monitor*. Carried on the second page, a location usually reserved for editorials and important essays, the report pointed out that "it should be noted that although the discrimination in the American immigration laws has been a sore point with Chinese, they had not initiated this repeal. Inquiry at the Chinese embassy here has always brought the reply that the immigration laws are solely a matter for Americans' own decision."[92]

Two months later, when a proposal to repeal Canada's Chinese exclusion laws was made in that country, *CDN* ran an editorial that clearly indicated a hope that the Chinese government might express its support for the repeal of the exclusion laws in both the United States and Canada:

> The campaign in Canada [to repeal the exclusion laws] will certainly meet difficulties as did the one in the United States. So, our compatriots in Canada must work hard to pursue people's diplomacy, to win the support of the Canadian people, and to push Parliament to repeal the exclusion laws.... But the Chinese government also should engage in active diplomacy and initiate negotiations with the Canadian government [on the issue]. We should not treat the repeal of the Chinese exclusion laws as the internal affairs of the Canadian government. We should not say that we ought not to intervene.... Only through pursuing government diplomacy and people's diplomacy simultaneously we can hope to repeal the exclusion laws and to wipe out our shame.[93]

The Chinese government and its diplomats, however, ignored these demands and remained inactive throughout the entire process of repealing the exclusion laws in the United States, though some of the Chinese officials did work for repeal through nonofficial channels.[94] One explanation for this stubborn and consistent silence on the part of the Chinese government is that the Chinese officials, advised by their American friends, refrained from making public statements on the repeal because they feared such statements might have a boomerang effect. The Citizens Committee to Repeal the Chinese Exclusion believed that "Japanese Ambassador Hanihara's protest against the exclusion provisions of the 1924 law was the final stroke which caused Congress to accept the clause." With that lesson in mind, the Citizens Committee "continued to encourage the Chinese to speak only confidentially, and not to make public statements about repeal until after the House had passed the repeal bill."[95]

From a tactical and realistic point of view, by persuading Chinese not to speak publicly, the Citizens Committee succeeded in avoiding fatal counterattacks on the part of the most conservative opponents to the repeal. This strategy, however, sacrificed the right of Chinese Americans to speak out. It is a cruel irony: over an issue that was vital to the fate of Chinese Americans, they did not have the opportunity to speak to the American public.

The CHLA and *CDN*, acting as representatives of the community, wanted to and did express the thoughts of Chinese Americans. *CDN*'s series of editorials and essays on the repeal bills, because they were published in a Chinese-language daily, were confined to a Chinese American audience. From the beginning, *CDN* attacked the exclusion laws as racist and counter to the spirit of American democracy. The laws were portrayed as the root of many problems—social, economic, and political—in the Chinese community because they institutionalized the discrimination against Chinese and forced them to live in ghettos. They created a permanent fear among Chinese Americans that they could be investigated and deported at any time and therefore made them vulnerable to the manipulation and exploitation of both white and Chinese racketeers. Under the exclusion laws, the wives Chinese immigrants had left behind were not allowed to join them. As a result, prostitution and gambling became features of a socially impoverished bachelor society. "In short," one editorial asserted, "most of the sorrows, darkness, and various problems in the Chinese community are the products of the Chinese exclusion laws."[96]

Implicitly, this kind of analysis expressed a hope that the repeal of the exclusion laws would provide Chinese Americans an opportunity to build a better community. Clearly, it was in tune with the CHLA's and *CDN*'s previous analysis of the Chinatown power structure and with their criticism of the traditional elite, whose power in Chinatown was partly based on institutionalized racism against Chinese.

In May and June many editorials and essays in *CDN* echoed the argument that the repeal would help win Chinese hearts and end the war earlier by undermining Japanese propaganda that the United States was a racist country and the common enemy of Asian people. But from July on, perhaps as a result of its observation that there was virtually no voice representing Chinese Americans, the paper began to concentrate on appealing to the fundamental principles of American democracy and to express more Chinese American than Chinese nationalistic opinions. An editorial, "Celebrating Independence Day," summed up such opinions:

> Generally speaking, the United States claims to be a democratic and free country. However, in fact, the country is far from having reached the goal [of building a democratic and free society]. The Chinese exclusion laws and the discrimination against blacks and other colored people are against the principles of equality enunciated in the Declaration of Independence and the Constitution, the fundamental creed of the United States.
>
> . . . [The existence of the Chinese exclusion laws and racial discrimination] means that the U.S. Independence War has not yet been won. . . . The American people should carry forward the dauntless spirit of the revolutionary martyrs, boldly engage in self-criticism, work to eliminate racial discrimination, thereby to complete the Independence War by realizing real freedom, democracy, and equality.[97]

The day after the House passed the repeal bill, *CDN* ran an editorial to express the delight and hope of Chinese Americans:

> The Chinese in the United States will be affected by the repeal bill the most. After the repeal of the Chinese exclusion laws, we Chinese will be eligible for naturalization and, as taxpayers, will have the right to participate in politics. We then can use the right to vote and to run for office to present our needs and to express our opinions. This will provide us many direct opportunities and advantages to solve the problems and to promote the welfare of the Chinese community. Furthermore, the Chinese in the United States, now that they can directly participate in all kinds of activities in American society as citizens, will make more contributions to the political, economic, social, and cultural development of the United States, and become more influential. This will benefit both the Chinese themselves and American society as a whole.[98]

These opinions offer insight into how Chinese Americans, or at least a certain group of Chinese Americans, reacted to the successful end of the repeal campaign. While the repeal bill was passed mainly in consideration of the war effort and of U.S.-China relations, those Chinese Americans who expressed their opinions through *CDN* had based their argument for repeal on the fundamental principles of American democracy and the ideals of the American Revolution. They also viewed repeal as vital to the future of Chinese Americans. This attitude suggests that this group of Chinese Americans had come to believe in the promise of American democracy, despite the fact that their experiences in the United States had made a mockery of democratic principles.

American democracy was not something ready-made for Chinese Americans to enjoy. They had to fight for it. The campaign "to save China, to save ourselves," which encompassed many aspects of the political and social life of the community in this period, was a unique vehicle through which Chinese Americans tried to gain their rights under the American system. The development of what might be called a Chinese American consciousness during the 1930s and 1940s can also be seen as a contribution made by Chinese Americans to the full realization of American democracy.

Chapter Six

The Struggle Over a Penny

In the winter of 1946–47 the Chinese Hand Laundry Alliance led a struggle against a price increase imposed on the hand laundries by the Chinese power laundries. The Chinese hand laundries in New York City were in a position different from that of their counterparts in other cities. Since the 1920s the Chinese hand laundrymen in New York City had not done the washing in their shops, although these shops were still being called "hand laundries." They received the laundry from the customers, sorted it, and sent it to the wet-wash factory (in Chinese, they were called "power laundries") to be washed. The next day the wet-wash factory delivered the clean laundry back to the hand laundry shops, where the laundrymen would iron and fold the clothes to be picked up by the customers. By the 1940s most of the Chinese hand laundry shops in New York City had equipped themselves with shirt-press machines to replace hand ironing. The Chinese hand laundrymen in many other cities, however, still did the wash in their own shops and continued to iron by hand as late as the 1940s.[1]

The struggle between the hand and power laundries was not only economic but also political. With the strength it had acquired in previous struggles, the CHLA, now in its fourteenth year of existence, once again challenged the power structure of the Chinese community in New York City. When the popular protest movement under its leadership failed to reach a compromise with the power laundry owners, the CHLA mobilized its members and supporters to found their own wet-wash factory to protect and promote the interests of ordinary hand laundrymen. The establishment and successful operation of the CHLA wet-wash factory once again demonstrated the organization's increasing influence in the New York Chinese community.

In the struggle between the Chinese hand laundries led by the CHLA and the Chinese power laundries, several important issues emerged: a class conflict between the hand laundries and the power laundries within the Chinese laundry business, the interplay of this class conflict with racial discrimination in the larger society and its impact on Chinese Americans, and the function and application of the concept of ethnic solidarity in the community.

In the same years several organizing drives of the Laundry Workers Union (AFL) failed to unionize the Chinese hand laundries because of the persistent resistance of the CHLA. This failure raises the question of why the CHLA, a self-styled "progressive" organization, rejected the labor union. This chapter discusses these issues.

"Charlie" in the Paper

On December 9, 1946, *The New York Times* reported:

> Hundreds of thousands of New Yorkers will have to find some other way to get the family wash done when 4,000 Chinese hand laundries stop accepting soiled clothing today, though they will keep their shops open until next Monday. The laundrymen are protesting a price increase of one third imposed on them by the eleven laundries of the Chinese Power Laundries Association, the group that does all the washing for the individual operators. In a series of bitter charges leveled at the power laundries, the hand laundrymen, members of the Chinese Hand Laundry Alliance ..., contended that it would be "unpatriotic" for them to pass on the increase, which went into effect Nov. 30, to their customers.[2]

The Chinese hand laundries' boycott might be inconvenient for many New Yorkers, but it was easily circumvented; if the Chinese hand laundry on the corner were closed for a couple of weeks, one had to walk only several blocks away to do one's laundry in the newly opened self-service laundries (launderette or laundromat). Or, if one could afford it, one could simply make a phone call to a laundry company that picked up and delivered laundry. The introduction of more efficient modern equipment into the laundry industry began to provide the urban population with cheaper and more convenient service.[3] Thousands of "Charlie," the Chinese hand laundrymen in many neighborhoods in New York City, in contrast, now faced a new and difficult situation.

The price increase that the Chinese power laundries announced was one penny more per pound for wet wash, but the increase rate was 33 percent. According to one estimate, each Chinese power laundry monopolized the wet washing of no fewer than two hundred Chinese hand laundries. If the hand laundries complied with the increase, each of them would have to pay at least five more dollars for the wet washing per week. Accordingly, each power laundry would earn one thousand dollars more each week.[4] Moreover, it was reported that the owners of the power laundries planned to impose a new rule on the hand laundries. They would have to contract their work with the power laundry with which they did business in August 1946. This move was perceived by the hand laundries as a conspiracy to deprive them of "freedom of wash." Above all, the hand laundrymen resented the way in which the power laundries announced the price increase: they placed an advertisement in the Chinese newspapers instead of notifying the hand laundries individually, and they gave only two days' advance notice.[5]

The CHLA, now representing more than two thousand members, tried to negotiate with the power laundry owners but was rebuffed.[6] The angry hand laundrymen decided to wage a boycott. An emergency meeting was called and attended by five hundred hand laundrymen, and an "All [Chinese] Hand Laundry Action Committee" was set up on December 1 to organize and coordinate the boycott.[7] Thomas Tang, the manager of *CDN* and a former secretary of the CHLA, spoke at the emergency meeting. He pointed out that the price increase revealed the contemptuous attitude of the power laundry owners toward the hand laundrymen—no advance consultation and no negotiation. He encouraged the hand laundrymen to carry out the boycott and to force the power laundries to cancel the price increase, and he assured them that if they united they could win. To strengthen his argument, Tang noted that a month ago a boycott launched by white hand laundries successfully forced the white power laundries to make a compromise: the price increase rate was reduced from 15 to 8 percent.[8] This was a unique phenomenon: Chinese hand laundrymen were waging a boycott against the Chinese owners of wetwash companies. It provides a rare opportunity to examine the class struggle within the Chinese community.

The Chinese hand laundry business in New York City experienced a boom from 1942 to 1945. After the United States entered into the war in 1941, many women joined the labor force, and in order to save time, they sent many items, such as sheets, towels, and even underwear, which they ordinarily washed themselves at home in the prewar years, to the hand laundries to be washed.[9] The sudden increase in demand, plus the fact that many young men in the hand laundry business were drafted into the armed forces, created a serious labor shortage for the business. The Chinese laundrymen grasped this golden opportunity to expand their business by extending working hours to meet the rapidly increasing demand. As a result, in spite of the labor shortage caused by the draft, the Chinese hand laundry business obtained many new customers and prospered during the war years.[10]

The boom did not last long, however. After the war the small Chinese hand laundry shops faced competition from the large laundry companies owned by white Americans, which tried to monopolize the market and drive the small hand laundries out of business by providing better and cheaper services. With huge capital and much more advanced equipment, the large laundry businesses could provide pick-up and delivery service to their customers. Furthermore, they employed some drastic means to compete with the hand laundries for customers. For example, in 1946 some large laundry companies gave away pillow cases and sheets (which were then in short supply) to attract customers. The small Chinese hand laundries could only complain about but not compete with these extravagant gestures of the large companies.[11] With little capital to invest in new equipment, the hand laundries had to improve the quality of their service and to reduce service charges if they were to survive.

In addition, after the war many newly manufactured washing machines appeared on the market. Before long a lot of families might buy the machines and wash their clothes at home, an editorial in *CDN* warned, and as a result, the demand for the hand laundry service would decrease.[12] Another threat to the hand laundry business was the emergence of the launderette, whose cheap self-service attracted many lower- and lower-middle-class housewives, on whom most of the Chinese hand laundries had depended.[13] It was against this background that the conflict over the price increase of wet wash broke out between the Chinese hand laundries and the power laundries.

"We Are Brothers" versus "You, the Blood Sucker"

An easy relationship had never existed between the Chinese hand laundries and the power laundries, although they were known in the Chinese community as the "two pillars" of the Chinese laundry business, comprising an "ethnic economy" on which the Chinese community heavily depended. But the struggle was conducted in unique ways shaped by the political and social conditions in the Chinese community. The basic characteristic of this struggle was that both ordinary hand laundrymen, who considered themselves the "laboring class," and the power laundry owners, who saw themselves as the "gentry class" exercising power over the community by virtue of their wealth and education, promoted their own interests in the name of "ethnic solidarity."

Since its founding in 1933, the CHLA had made every effort to promote solidarity in the community in order to support China's war against Japan, and it had attained considerable influence as a spokesperson for the hand laundries. During the war years the various interest groups worked together within a united front organization for the common goal of supporting China. Every group tended to agree that the survival of the homeland should transcend the particular interest of any individual group. An atmosphere was created in which every interest group spoke in a patriotic language, defined and defended its own interest in terms of the common interest, and accused rival groups of being selfish and unpatriotic. Moreover, to maintain ethnic unity, it was emphasized that disputes (both political and economic) among the interest groups should be resolved within the community. Thus the rhetoric of ethnic solidarity became a language of persuasion and community mobilization, useful to all groups and frequently masking deep conflicts of interest. Ironically, once the CHLA acquired influence within the community, it began to participate in the power game of Chinatown politics and lost its sharp and militant tone when it attacked the establishment.

Within the context of Chinatown politics, the CHLA approached the conflict between the hand laundrymen and the power laundry owners in terms of ethnic solidarity and sought to solve it in that framework. But once that strategy failed to yield the desired result, the CHLA was not afraid of adopting more aggressive means, such as appealing to forces outside the community.

One basic problem that existed between the two types of laundries was that the power laundries always attempted to shift the burden of cost increases to the hand laundries in the form of increasing the price for wet wash. In theory, the hand laundries could raise their service charges after the power laundries raised the price for wet wash. For the hand laundries, however, providing cheaper service was the only way they could survive because of their disadvantages in competing with the non-Chinese laundries: no English-language skills, lack of capital to buy equipment, and racial discrimination. In 1933, when there was a dispute over the service charge between the Chinese and the non-Chinese hand laundries, the white laundries agreed that the Chinese laundries could

charge one to two cents lower for each item of washing, on the understanding that only in this way could the Chinese hand laundries survive.[14]

The Chinese hand laundries did not resist every price increase. They
themselves had been trying to increase their service charges but were unable to do so. In 1941 there was an extensive discussion among hand
laundrymen about how to increase service charges, and the practice of reducing service charges among the hand laundries as a means of competition was criticized as "suicidal" and seen as a threat to the business.[15] In
addition to the internal competition, the Chinese hand laundries faced resistance from their customers to price increases. In January 1946, for example, when the CHLA attempted to organize a service-charge increase
in several districts for its member laundries after the Bureau of Price Control relaxed its regulation, it met strong resistance from the customers. In
the end, the CHLA's efforts failed.[16]

Because they could not raise their service charges, the hand laundrymen found the price increase of the power laundries unfair and unacceptable. When the Chinese power laundries imposed the price increase, the
Chinese hand laundrymen felt they were being doubly exploited—by
white laundry companies and by the Chinese power laundries. When the
power laundries ignored their protests, the hand laundrymen angrily denounced them as traitors who betrayed Chinese interests. Thus an essen-
tially class issue was clothed in the language of ethnic solidarity and
betrayal.

In this persistent struggle the CHLA played a significant role. Only
through the CHLA could the individual hand laundries make their voices
heard. The CHLA's capable leaders and legal advisors could articulate
the interests of the hand laundries and argue on their behalf and, when
necessary, organize collective actions and seek legal recourse.

Before the 1946 boycott two major confrontations had occurred between the Chinese hand laundries and the Chinese power laundries. The
first was in 1938. The power laundries were forced to modify significantly their price increase after the CHLA successfully organized a massive protest. During the negotiations between the CHLA and the power
laundries, the CHLA's representatives defended the interests of the small
hand laundries in terms of ethnic solidarity and argued that if the power
laundries imposed the price increase on them, the hand laundries' income
would be reduced and their ability to donate money to the anti-Japanese
cause would be affected.[17]

The CHLA's tactic of appealing to ethnic solidarity won community
sympathy and support in 1938, but it did not always work so well. In

1942, for example, the power laundries were determined to increase the price for wet wash by 25 percent, ignoring the CHLA's appeal to ethnic solidarity. They even refused to negotiate with the CHLA. Only after the CHLA members collected money in preparation for the establishment of their own wet-wash factory did the power laundries make concessions, agreeing to postpone the price increase.[18]

One interesting aspect of the 1942 dispute was that the CHLA demonstrated its willingness to employ other means after its failure to reach an agreement with the power laundries. Because the power laundries refused to talk with it, the CHLA reported the case to the City Bureau of Price Control, a wartime agency. When the power laundry owners angrily attacked the CHLA as a Chinese traitor who revealed internal disputes among the Chinese to outsiders, one CHLA member replied:

> The power laundry owners accused us of being Chinese traitors who indict Chinese. . . . The United States is a country of law. . . . We CHLA members are good citizens. We report the illegal action of the power laundries to the Bureau of Price Control because we help the government to enforce the wartime regulations. The power laundry owners themselves are Chinese traitors because they attempted to increase prices illegally.
>
> The CHLA's action of reporting the illegal acts of the power laundries to the Bureau of Price Control is a decent act that shows that the CHLA knows and obeys the law and seeks its protection. The power laundry owners knowingly violate the law and do not allow others to report them. You are uncivilized, but how can you ask others also to be uncivilized?[19]

This case illustrates the way the idea of ethnic solidarity was used instrumentally—as rhetoric to serve the interests of these two rival groups. It was a language used primarily in negotiation and for propaganda. The power laundries bowed to the protest of the hand laundries when the Bureau of Price Control intervened in the latter's favor, not because they were persuaded by the ethnic solidarity rhetoric of the CHLA. It is essential to understand the notions hidden behind such rhetoric, for the vocabulary used in Chinatown politics, developed and shaped by historical conditions, often obscured the harsh reality of class conflicts in the community. Even when the poor hand laundrymen were extremely angry at the power owners, their strongest accusation was that these people had abandoned Chinese morality and obligations and had forgotten the common interests of the Chinese community.

When the Chinese Power Laundry Association announced the price increase on November 28, 1946, the first response of *CDN*, which always represented and defended the interest of the hand laundries, was to appeal to ethnic solidarity. The paper's editorials urged the power laundries not to be "shortsighted" and concerned with only short-term profits. As a whole, the editorials pointed out, the Chinese laundry business was facing a crisis due to the competition of the large white laundry companies, inflation, and a coming economic recession. The Chinese in the business, whether power laundry owners or hand laundrymen, should cooperate with each other to cope with the situation.[20] One editorial used as its title two lines from a famous classical Chinese poem, "Both grew from the same root; why hurry to burn each other up?"[21] "The Chinese power laundry owners and the hand laundrymen are the same descendants of Huang Di,[22] sharing the same fate of coming to a foreign land to make a living under other people's ceiling. Those Americans who discriminate against Chinese will treat both Chinese power laundry owners and hand laundrymen the same. They will not discriminate solely against the hand laundrymen and spare the Chinese power laundry owners as 'high-class Chinese.'"[23]

The objective of such an appeal was to arouse a popular sympathy in the Chinese community for the hand laundries and to force the power laundries to abandon the price increase, as they had done in 1938. The CHLA first presented the case to the community as an urgent issue that should concern everyone, because the ups and downs of the laundry business would affect the business of restaurants and stores in Chinatown. Given the fact that all these businesses were linked to one another in the community, the CHLA pointed out that the power laundries would not be able to exist by themselves. Therefore, the action of the power laundries to raise prices was both unethical and ungrateful.[24] Making such an argument, the CHLA portrayed the power laundry owners as selfish and greedy and made the hand laundries' struggle over the penny a concern of the entire community.

Initially, the CHLA hoped these pressures would make the power laundry owners come to the negotiating table, where a compromise could be worked out. The power laundry owners' refusal to do so angered the hand laundrymen and prompted them to express their resentments against the power laundries. Many hand laundrymen wrote letters to *CDN* attacking the power laundries. These letters revealed the real feelings of the hand laundrymen.

A letter by Chen Yanchuan was representative. It was given the title "Why We Must Fight Against the Power Laundries" by the *CDN* editor. In the letter Chen argued that the power laundry owners enriched themselves by exploiting the hand laundries. He said, "Power laundry bosses have earned a great deal in recent years. Some have bought buildings, some have expanded their business, and these are the facts well known to everyone in the community. I would like to ask them to search their conscience in the night: where does the money come from?"[25]

Chen Yanchuan, like other letter writers, was particularly upset by the way the power laundries treated the hand laundries. "They did not do a good washing job," Chen complained. "The white shirts turned yellow after ironing because the power laundries were sloppy doing the washing. Our customers were dissatisfied and our business hurt." Moreover, Chen continued, "when they weigh the wet-wash cloths, they threw them to the scale. While the scale needle was still waving, they arbitrarily set the weight and charged. Also, they did not write clear bills and if you dared to argue with them, they would threaten not to take your work."[26]

What upset the hand laundries the most was the power laundries' plot to control them. It was revealed that the Chinese power laundries had just formed an association of their own (the Chinese Power Laundry Association) and had made a secret plan to monopolize the wet-wash work. Before they suddenly announced the price increase on November 28, the power laundries had signed a contract by which the participants agreed to follow uniform steps to raise the price for wet wash. The plan showed that the power laundries anticipated a protest by the hand laundries. Each of them deposited one thousand dollars in a fund to pay lawyers in case the hand laundries brought the issue to court. Once their plan to increase the price succeeded, the power laundries would divide the market among themselves. The hand laundries had to contract their work with a designated power laundry. If a hand laundryman refused to contract his work with the power laundry assigned to him, all other power laundries would refuse to do the job for him. In this way, the power laundries felt they could control the hand laundries.[27]

The hand laundrymen's determination to boycott the power laundries caused anxiety in the community. Some wealthy merchants, worried that their businesses would be affected by the confrontation between the hand laundries and the power laundries, urged the CCBA to intervene. The CHLA welcomed this suggestion. Although the CHLA often openly criticized the CCBA and had no illusions about the "supreme power," the two organizations had worked together within the anti-Japanese united front during the war. The rhetoric of ethnic solidarity left room for both sides to accept the CCBA's mediation.

On December 12, 1946, four days after the hand laundries launched the boycott, the CCBA invited representatives of the CHLA and the Chinese Power Laundry Association to its headquarters to discuss the crisis. After three hours of shouting and heated debates, both sides accepted the CCBA's proposal to set up a "mediation committee," consisting of nine merchants who had prestige in the community, to investigate the issue and work out a solution.[28] On December 17 the committee presented a proposal that the price for wet wash be increased half a cent to three and a half cents per pound and the price for flat work remain the same. After five hours of discussion in the CCBA's headquarters, the proposal was accepted and an agreement was signed by the representatives of both sides.[29]

The CHLA hailed the agreement as a success for the hand laundries. The power laundries had been forced to compromise with hand laundrymen, even though it was through the mediation of the CCBA. The mediation itself revealed that the humble laboring class could also employ the idea of ethnic solidarity to defend its interests. Left-wing Chinese intellectuals in the mid-1930s had exposed the class exploitation that ethnic solidarity camouflaged, but they had failed to realize that the exploited class could use the same idea for its own purposes. Now they joined the hand laundrymen in exercising this strategy through writing editorials for *CDN*.

Moreover, the CCBA mediation showed that the hand laundrymen, once organized under the leadership of the CHLA, could exploit the conflicts among the different groups within the establishment to their own advantage. To avoid the potential damage that a hand laundry boycott against the power laundries could inflict on their business, the merchants of other businesses had persuaded the power laundries to talk to the CHLA and to make concessions.

There has been a myth that Chinatown was ruled by unique Chinese traditional values and customs that were inscrutable to outsiders, that the CCBA was a de facto government in Chinatown and enjoyed arbitrary power. But the struggle between the CHLA and the power laundries in 1946 indicates that different groups in the Chinese community acted and related to one another according to their own interests and that behind the rhetoric of ethnic solidarity each group strove to defend and expand its own interests. The CHLA was able to function increasingly effectively in Chinatown politics as it became more familiar with the political environment and more skillful in manipulating it.

Within Chinatown politics, the old rule was that the merchants divided and distributed power among themselves according to their relative strength. The CHLA represented a new force that disturbed the old political game. Its strategy, the use or the threat of use of popular protest movements such as boycotts and strikes, had been exercised for a decade and could not be ignored. In the eyes of some elite merchants, such as the owners of the power laundries, the rise and growth of the CHLA's influence was a threat to their power and prestige. That the CCBA had to be asked to mediate meant a decline in the ability of the established power holders to settle disputes among themselves. Now they had to sit side by side with the humble laundrymen.

Nevertheless, the power laundry owners were confident of their economic and political power and were determined to advance their cause. Two weeks after the signing of the mediation agreement, the Chinese Power Laundry Association broke its promise and unilaterally announced on January 3, 1947, that it would charge one cent more for each sheet from January 18 onward.[30]

The Wah Kiu Wet-Wash Factory

The power laundries' action, naturally, angered the hand laundrymen. Since the mediation agreement was signed under the supervision of the CCBA, on January 7 the CHLA sent a protest letter to it and asked it to take steps to enforce the agreement and to punish the power laundries for violating it. The CCBA did not do anything. Five days later the CHLA sent representatives to meet with the president of the CCBA, Chen Zhonghai (Jung Hai Chan), to urge him to act. Chen Zhonghai said in a typical bureaucratic manner that the CCBA "will pay attention" to the case. When the CHLA representatives pressed him on how he intended to deal with the violation by the Chinese Power Laundry Association, Chen replied, "We have done a lot of work. To take the interests of the whole into account, we did it secretly."[31]

Under pressure from the CHLA, the CCBA held a community meeting on January 15 to discuss the issue. Members of the Chinese Power Laundry Association refused to attend. The CHLA's representatives demanded that the CCBA denounce and punish them. Several merchants who were involved in the mediation angrily condemned the power laundries and demanded that the CCBA force them to obey the agreement. Otherwise, they asked, where is the power of the CCBA? Where is the "face" of the CCBA?[32] The CCBA, however, did nothing to stop the power laundries from increasing the price they charged.

Having failed to reach a satisfactory agreement with the power laundries, whether through a boycott or through the CCBA's mediation, the CHLA decided to mobilize the hand laundrymen to establish a wet-wash factory of their own. In fact, before the CHLA signed the mediation agreement with the Chinese Power Laundry Association on December 17, 1946, some hand laundrymen had expressed their desire to build their own wet-wash factory in order to deal with the oppression of the power laundries. A "Tall Guy Gao" wrote a letter to *CDN* on December 10 stating, "The power laundry owners are insatiably avaricious and they always try to oppress the hand laundries. In addition to uniting ourselves in a boycott to deal with the current crisis, we have to build our own wet-wash factory. Only with our own wet-wash factory can we get away from the oppression of the power laundries."[33]

This call was echoed by several hand laundrymen.[34] A letter by a "Coolie Worker" bluntly stated, "We are facing an imminent disaster." "In order to release ourselves from the oppression and to protect our freedom of wash, we must found our own wet-wash factory. This is the only solution."[35] By January 1947, when the power laundries violated the mediation agreement and announced the price increase for sheets, the establishment of a wet-wash factory had become a popular demand among the hand laundrymen.

The CHLA became the instrument for making the popular demand a reality. On Sunday, January 19, 1947, CHLA members held a meeting and unanimously passed a resolution to raise money to found a wet-wash factory. Twenty-one members were elected to set up an ad hoc committee charged with the responsibilities of raising money, purchasing a factory, and managing the business. It was decided to name the would-be wet-wash factory Wah Kiu (Hua Qiao), or Overseas Chinese. The ad hoc committee set the amount of capitalization at three hundred thousand dollars, to be raised among hand laundries in the form of shares, each share being two hundred dollars. The immediate goal was to raise one-third of the amount within two weeks.[36]

The most striking characteristic of the creation of the Wah Kiu Wet-Wash Factory was that it was a collective effort by the hand laundrymen to oppose the oppression of the power laundries. At the beginning the popular resentment against the power laundries was so great that the hand laundrymen did not even discuss whether or not the wet-wash factory would make money. The laundrymen wanted to build their own factory primarily because they wanted to keep their freedom and dignity as self-reliant laborers. A wet-wash factory of their own would free them from the constant humiliation and oppression of the power laundry owners in the form of price increases and rejection of their jobbers. In the history of Chinese American business, this was perhaps the first time that the opening of a business was motivated not by profit-making but by a desire to defend the right to be treated decently and to maintain freedom.

One strong motivation behind the drive to found the Wah Kiu Wet-Wash Factory was to win respect for the hand laundrymen. Many of them believed that the power laundries saw the hand laundries as being so disorganized and lacking in unity that they could be treated with contempt;[37] moreover, the hand laundrymen were unhappy with their dependence on the power laundries. Lin Judai expressed this feeling in a letter to *CDN*: "I and my friends are fed up with the power laundries' oppression in recent years. We often said that we should open a wet-wash factory to win credit for us poor laundrymen, and we were willing to run it even at a loss. Unfortunately, we did not have the money to do it. Now our dream is coming true, thanks to the effort of the CHLA. . . . I am very excited."[38]

This feeling was shared by many hand laundrymen, especially CHLA members. Since December 1946 many members had come to the alliance's headquarters demanding that the CHLA assume leadership in organizing hand laundries to found a wet-wash factory.[39] Reflecting this mood, the CHLA ad hoc committee's advertisement to raise capital by floating shares for the Wah Kiu Wet-Wash Factory, placed in the local Chinese papers, emphasized that the Wah Kiu was initiated by hand laundrymen, with the purpose of serving hand laundries, and that "whatever its prospects, we have to do our best to realize the plan." In plain language, the advertisement did not promise huge profits or dividends, but encouraged hand laundrymen to join the fight by purchasing shares.[40]

The hand laundrymen's sentiment against the oppression of the power laundries ran so high that within four weeks the CHLA had raised more than one hundred thousand dollars (about five hundred shares bought by three hundred shareholders). While many of those who bought the Wah Kiu shares were CHLA members, some were not. But these nonmembers joined the CHLA when they bought the shares.[41] With the money, the CHLA ad hoc committee made the first payment for a wet-wash factory located at 136 East Street, the Bronx, in February 1947.[42] On March 9 the committee announced that it had stopped further capital-raising,[43] and on March 16 it held the first meeting of all shareholders of the Wah Kiu Wet-Wash Factory. After a few hours of discussion the meeting passed several resolutions. A charter was discussed and passed, and a board of directors was elected to replace the ad hoc committee.[44] The progress of the new wet-wash factory was reported in the local Chinese papers.

As the Wah Kiu Wet-Wash Factory was being built, some of its shareholders began to contemplate its possible effects on the laundry business and the relationship between the Chinese power laundries and the hand laundries. One obvious outcome would be that the hand laundries would no longer be subject to the bullying and threats of the power laundries. The founding of the Wah Kiu would break the Chinese power laundries' monopoly of the wet wash and thereby deprive them of the means to control the hand laundries. Some hand laundrymen who suffered from the sloppy work of the power laundries hoped that the Wah Kiu would do good wet-wash work, thereby forcing the power laundries to improve their work and their attitude toward the hand laundrymen. The result would be a general improvement in the service of the Chinese laundry business, which could then become more competitive in the market. Some, however, suspected that the power laundries would reduce their prices to compete with Wah Kiu.[45] This prediction, unfortunately, proved to be accurate.

Once the hand laundries under the leadership of the CHLA demonstrated their determination to build their own wet-wash factory, the Chinese power laundries fell into disarray. After the CHLA ad hoc committee began its capital-raising campaign, one laundryman reported, "The power laundries are not as reckless as before. Also, they do not charge 7¢ for each sheet [as they recently announced]; instead they only charge 6¢ [the old price]."[46] One power laundry even approached a CHLA staff member, suggesting that the CHLA stop its effort to found the wet-wash factory and in return the power laundries would abandon their plan to increase prices. The suggestion was ridiculed as "the biggest joke under heaven."[47]

Nevertheless, the power laundries had reason to believe that the CHLA might compromise if they softened their stand. In the past the CHLA had twice tried to organize the hand laundries to establish their own wet-wash factory without success. The first time was in March 1938. When it failed to reach a compromise with the Chinese power laundries in a month-long negotiation over the price increase for wet wash, the CHLA set up a committee to collect capital from hand laundrymen and prepared to build a wet-wash factory. After the CHLA committee collected more than twenty thousand dollars, the power laundries gave in and withdrew the price increase.[48] In the summer of 1942 the power laundries again attempted to raise the price for wet wash. The CHLA resumed its efforts to raise funds to found a wet-wash factory, this time collecting forty thousand dollars. But it returned the money to the hand laundrymen after the power laundries promised not to increase prices.[49]

Based on these previous experiences, the power laundries underestimated the strength of the hand laundrymen. They hoped that their temporary abandonment of the price increase would undermine the CHLA's effort to build the wet-wash factory. This time they were wrong. By 1947 the CHLA had established itself in the community. Its leaders had acquired political experience in the wartime united front activities and were determined to maintain and expand the CHLA's influence. To them, it was clear that the establishment of a wet-wash factory of their own would have a profound effect on the struggle between the power laundries and the hand laundrymen. Only with such a factory could the CHLA protect the hand laundries' interests against the power laundries. In other words, the wet-wash factory would be the most powerful weapon in their economic as well as political struggle against the elite establishment in Chinatown.

After several months' preparation the Wah Kiu Wet-Wash Factory was opened on May 3, 1947. In the following days the hand laundries reported that the Chinese power laundries' attitude toward them immediately changed. "Charlie Chan" (pseudonym) wrote to *CDN*:

> The Wah Kiu Wet-Wash Factory has been opened. . . . Last week the power laundry men came to collect money. They called me "Mr." upon entering my shop and declared their intent to maintain "friendship" with me forever. And they automatically reduced the price [for wet wash]. I have never seen such a friendly manner in many years. Watching them, I could not help but make a forced smile. Why are these guys now so easy to get along with, but so ferocious just a few weeks ago?
>
> I do not have to explain this. I trust that all my fellow hand laundrymen understand [why the power laundries changed their attitude]. I only hope that my brothers will not be fooled by the present sweet words of the power laundries. . . . We have to support our own Wah Kiu Wet-Wash Factory. No matter how nice the power laundries are now, we should not forget their ferocious behavior in the past.[50]

Many other hand laundrymen reported the same experience: the owners of power laundries not only changed their attitude, but also improved the quality of their service and reduced prices. The price for wet wash was reduced from three and a half to three cents per pound, and for each sheet from seven to six cents.[51]

A more significant development than the changes in attitude and prices was the dissolution of the Chinese Power Laundry Association. As mentioned earlier, the association was founded for the purpose of dividing the market among the Chinese power laundries and controlling the hand laundries. Once the CHLA successfully founded the Wah Kiu Wet-Wash Factory, the power laundries saw that there was not much that could be done and decided to dissolve the association.[52]

Nevertheless, the Wah Kiu Wet-Wash Factory still faced many difficulties, as expected by some CHLA members from the beginning. The most serious challenge was not from the outside but from within. In the first few months of its existence Wah Kiu encountered tremendous problems because of its personnel's lack of experience and managerial skills. The urgent situation of an open confrontation with the power laundries drove the CHLA to make hasty decisions, some of which proved to be inadvisable. The first problem was that the alliance bought an old and dilapidated factory that required extensive renovation. The limited funds raised by the CHLA were spent on new machines and equipment. Thus the factory had very little floating capital with which to expand its business and compete with the established Chinese power laundries.[53]

The second problem was the lack of experienced and skilled managers. As the Wah Kiu Board of Directors reflected later, when the factory was first opened "those with experience [in running a wet-wash factory] were not willing to provide any help, and those who offered to help were suspected—we were not sure whether or not they were reliable. As a result, we had no choice but to try it by ourselves."[54] Moreover, the inexperienced managers and workers had to cope with an extraordinary problem created by the situation—they had more business than they could handle. Many Chinese hand laundries turned to Wah Kiu to do their wet wash in the first two weeks, so huge heaps of soiled clothes piled up everywhere. Although the managers, workers, and machines of Wah Kiu worked to their full capacity, they still could not meet the demand of their customers. A lot of wet-wash jobs could not be finished on time, many items got lost because of mistakes in the process of wet-washing or in delivery, and a great deal of money was wasted on poorly planned renovations.[55]

It was the firm support of the loyal shareholders that enabled Wah Kiu to survive. Some Chinese power laundry owners had predicted that Wah Kiu would be closed down within a few months because of its lack of experienced managers. They had said that it was not difficult for the hand laundrymen to raise the money, but it would be very difficult for them to run the factory.[56] To prove that this prediction was wrong, the Wah Kiu customers (who were also its shareholders) endured many hardships and made tremendous sacrifices. Most of them persisted in doing business with Wah Kiu despite the temptation of lower prices offered by the Chinese power laundries. If Wah Kiu made wrong deliveries, the laundrymen would check with each other and exchange the laundry bags on their own or return them to the Wah Kiu delivery truck. "Without this spirit of unity and the selfless support [of our shareholders]," a Wah Kiu Board of Directors report concluded, "the Wah Kiu Wet-Wash Factory would not have lasted to this day."[57]

The problems that emerged in the first few months, however, forced the Wah Kiu Board of Directors to seek improvements. In August the board appointed Tan Yumin, a veteran CHLA member and a capable man, to be chief manager of the factory. Tan spent a month investigating and then instituted a series of management reforms. By November his reforms had made great improvements in Wah Kiu's business management. A standard procedure for running the business efficiently was set up, business and income stabilized, and Wah Kiu's wet washing was praised for being better than that of the Chinese power laundries. Some of the power laundries even indicated their interest in changing their delivery route after the pattern set by Tan.[58] By the end of 1947 it was clear that Wah Kiu was going to survive.

Ironically, while Wah Kiu was making progress in its business management, the cut-throat competition from the Chinese power laundries cast a shadow on its further development. The power laundries tried to drive Wah Kiu out of business through luring customers away from it by charging lower rates. Unfortunately for Wah Kiu, over the long run this strategy proved to work very well. Even some Wah Kiu shareholders shifted their work to other Chinese power laundries, using many excuses (some said that their hand laundries were closer to a given power laundry, some said Wah Kiu's pick-up and delivery route did not fit their schedule, and so on). But it was obvious that these hand laundrymen were attracted by the lower rate—the power laundries' price for wet wash per pound was slashed to half a cent cheaper than Wah Kiu's.[59]

This pricing strategy presented a dilemma for Wah Kiu: if it decided to reduce its price to compete with other power laundries, the power laundries would reduce their price even further and, in such a competition, Wah Kiu could not hope to beat the other power laundries; but if it maintained the same price, it would not be able to attract more customers and to expand its business. Nevertheless, the establishment of Wah Kiu freed the hand laundries from fear and the oppression of the power laundries and helped improve the service quality of wet wash. After its establishment most laundrymen quietly enjoyed the fruit of the victory and left the burden of supporting Wah Kiu to the activists. Tan Yumin, manager of Wah Kiu, complained: "Our hand laundry fellows know the significance of Wah Kiu very well. They often saluted us and encouraged us. But when asked to do business with us, they were not very enthusiastic. Some promised to do it, but when we tried to materialize the promises, they changed their minds."[60]

Because Wah Kiu was unable to expand its business, although it could maintain a balance of revenue and expenditure by mid-1948, its profit was so low that it could not meet its monthly mortgage payment. Some Wah Kiu shareholders felt frustrated and angry. A few even suggested that they close Wah Kiu and forget about the fight against the power laundries.[61] Wah Kiu was supposed to be a "mass cause" against the exploitation and oppression of the Chinese power laundries, but now it seemed that a few loyal shareholders had to make personal sacrifices while the "masses" took advantage of them. Why, some shareholders asked, should they make these sacrifices for those who did nothing, for those who made no sacrifices and still benefited?

After long discussions most of the Wah Kiu shareholders decided to keep the factory open. Fang Fu'er, a veteran CHLA member in his sixties, pointed out to his fellow laundrymen: "Although we are running Wah Kiu according to usual methods of doing business, it is not a usual business. We therefore cannot see and handle its problems according to the principles of a usual business."[62] Since Wah Kiu could not attract new customers and could not expand its business to increase its income, at an all-shareholders meeting held on September 26, 1948, it was decided to adopt an extrabusiness measure to preserve the factory. A Committee to Support Wah Kiu Wet-Wash Factory was set up, and all shareholders were required to join and to pay a one-dollar "preservation fee" each week for a year. Other hand laundrymen were urged to join voluntarily and contribute. The money would be used to pay the mortgage. In addition, the shareholders who had not done business with Wah Kiu were required to do so. If they still refused, they would be punished by receiving dividends on the basis of half the value of their original shares.[63]

By the beginning of November one hundred out of the total three hundred Wah Kiu shareholders had joined the Committee to Support Wah Kiu Wet-Wash Factory.[64] Eventually, about two hundred of the shareholders took part in the crusade to save Wah Kiu.[65] An examination of the list of shareholders who joined the committee indicates that they were the most active members and the staff members of the CHLA.[66] Thus the strongest supporters of Wah Kiu were at the same time loyal members of the CHLA. Without the CHLA and its perseverance in maintaining Wah Kiu, the wet-wash factory would have been short-lived. Conversely, if Wah Kiu had failed, the CHLA would have lost much of its influence in the community.

One Wah Kiu shareholder stated in his simple language:

> I am one of the Wah Kiu Wet-Wash Factory shareholders. I also joined the Committee to Support Wah Kiu Wet-Wash Factory. Since Wah Kiu began its business, I have been its customer. No matter how many difficulties Wah Kiu had, I always stood by it. Why did I do so? Simple—I know the whole situation, and I support the mass cause. I know that if there were no Wah Kiu, my fellow hand laundrymen would be bullied by the scums. Yes, I contributed my money to the mass cause; and, yes, I had made some personal sacrifice, but look, in the past two years no Chinese power laundries dared to humiliate me, nor did they dare to bully other hand laundrymen.[67]

It was this kind of firm support that enabled Wah Kiu to survive its first two difficult years. By 1950 it had paid off its debt and was beginning to distribute dividends to its shareholders. After it accumulated some capital, it moved to Long Island and bought new equipment. In the following years, when CHLA members were harassed and persecuted by the FBI and the traditional forces in Chinatown, Wah Kiu provided job opportunities for many of them. The Wah Kiu Wet-Wash Factory still exists today.

The CHLA and the Trade Union

When the CHLA pulled its members together to build the Wah Kiu Wet-Wash Factory, it encountered the sabotage of the Chinese power laundries at every step of the way. The most peculiar means the Chinese power laundries used to undermine Wah Kiu was to ally themselves with the Laundry Workers Union to prevent the establishment of Wah Kiu. This made the situation very complicated. The episode provides a rare opportunity to analyze the relationship between the Chinese laboring class and American trade unions. Unfortunately, few relevant documents are available. Here I present a brief account of this complex aspect of Chinese American history, focusing on the issue of why New York's Chinese hand laundrymen, under the leadership of the CHLA, consistently rejected the efforts of the Laundry Workers Union to organize them.

The CHLA, as a new force led by a group of young and educated immigrants, made every effort to attack the established elite in Chinatown, to fight against racial prejudice and discrimination, to improve the image of the Chinese in the mind of the American public, and to encourage its members and other Chinese to become "Chinese Americans." Thus it had always been regarded as a "progressive" organization, an image of which it was proud. While resisting the unionization efforts, the CHLA also tried to defend its progressive image. It never denounced the white labor movement, which in general was seen as a progressive cause, but simply maintained that the Chinese hand laundry business was unique in the American economy and that uniqueness made it unnecessary for the trade to be unionized.

An examination of the CHLA's perceptions of and attitude toward the trade unions suggests that its persistent rejection of the Laundry Workers Union was influenced by the following factors: the nature of the Chinese hand laundries as small, self-employed, urban service businesses; the laundrymen's accumulated distrust of the U.S. government as well as American society—a deep scar brought about by the sufferings caused by institutional racism; and some American labor unions' racial discrimination against blacks and other "colored people" and the willingness of some union organizers to cooperate with Chinatown's elite merchants, as well as the participation of many unions in the witch hunts of the McCarthy years.

Some scholars have suggested that Chinese resistance to unions was in part determined by "traditional Chinese values."[68] A closer examination of the situation reveals that it was not traditional values but current American realities that defined the CHLA's attitude toward trade unions.

Years before the Laundry Workers Union of the Amalgamated Clothing Workers' Union (ACWU) came to organize the Chinese hand laundries, the racially discriminatory policy of some labor unions made them unwelcome in the Chinese community. In January 1933, three months before the founding of the CHLA, a trade union's racist campaign against Chinese seamen had shocked the New York Chinese community. The Seamen's International Union (SIU), which was affiliated with the American Federation of Labor (AFL), requested the Immigration and Naturalization Service to deport several hundred Chinese seamen who served on the S.S. *Lincoln*, an American vessel, because it claimed that

Chinese seamen accepted lower wages and took work away from Americans.[69] Ever since then the Chinese community had held an unfavorable opinion of labor unions. The SIU's racist practice also created strong doubts in the minds of left-wing Chinese. Because of this incident, Chinese leftists were cautious in their contacts with trade unions. They began to differentiate between two types of labor unions: the progressive ones and the "reactionary yellow" ones. As a whole, the Chinese community was very suspicious of the trade unions.

The opponents of the CHLA used the issue of trade unions to smear the alliance. In August 1941 a rumor circulated in New York's Chinatown that the CHLA had colluded with some whites in founding a "Chinese Laundry Workers International Union, Local 211 (AFL)." The CHLA immediately made public statements denouncing the rumor as an attempt "to slander the glorious reputation of this alliance,"[70] and declared that "since its founding, the CHLA has never flirted or cooperated with any white trade union. It does not mean that we have any bias against the union, it is because we do not have any actual need to join it."[71]

To answer the inquiries of the CHLA members and other hand laundrymen who were confused by the rumor, the CHLA's English Language Secretary, Tan Lian'ai, published an article in *CDN*. Entitled "The Question of the Chinese Hand Laundries and the Trade Union," it was the first document to address comprehensively the position of the CHLA on trade unions and is worth extensive quotation here:

We are not opposed to trade unions. But this is not to say that [we believe that] all unions are good. . . . What is a trade union? Whom do the trade unions serve? How does a trade union work? Let's study these first.

A trade union is an organization of workers. Its purpose is to win good working conditions for workers, such as increasing wages, reducing working hours, improving welfare, and collective bargaining. In other words, a trade union is a workers' organization; it is not an organization of both employers and employees.

In the Chinese hand laundry business, the boundary between employees and employers is not clear. The majority of the hand laundry owners are at the same times the workers. Only a few hire their relatives and friends as helping hands. As for welfare and benefits, we all know that owners and their partners share the same food and lodging. Therefore there is no need for a trade union in the Chinese hand laundries.

The CHLA is the only correct form of organization for the hand laundries. The central task of the CHLA is not to help increase wages or to sign contracts with employers; rather, it is to help its members to cope with various problems of the hand laundry business.[72]

It turned out that several KMT members were actually involved in the effort to organize "Local 211." Thomas Tang, a former CHLA secretary and editor of *CDN*, conducted an intensive investigation of the case. His series of reports exposed the identities of the "Local 211" organizers: John Lee (Li Xinzhi), the leading figure, was a member of the Standing Committee of the KMT Branch in the Eastern United States; Stanley Chen (Chen Zhilong) was a friend of John Lee and a "professional student" (who was ordered to watch other students); and Bunny Lin (Lin Zhuofeng) was a former editor of the *Chinese Nationalist Daily* and a staff member of the Chinatown Branch of the Bank of China. Their purpose, according to Tang's reports, was to organize at least half the Chinese hand laundrymen in the city into their own "trade union" and to collect membership dues of four thousand dollars a month.[73]

The attempt to organize "Local 211" ultimately failed, and it left the Chinese community with the impression that those Chinese who cooperated with trade unions were selfish people seeking personal gain at the expense of the laboring class. In 1947 this impression was reinforced by the exposure of the secret collaboration between the Chinese power laundries and some officials of the Laundry Workers Union in a plot to undermine the Wah Kiu Wet-Wash Factory.

To prevent the establishment of the CHLA's new wet-wash factory, the Chinese power laundry owners bribed several officials of the Laundry Workers Union to "organize" the Chinese hand laundries. If the hand laundries were organized into a branch of the union controlled by the power laundry owners, according to the latter's plan, these hand laundries would be required to do their wet-wash work with the power laundries, and as a result, Wah Kiu would not be able to compete with the power laundries. The CHLA found out about the plot, however, and reported it to the top leaders of the Laundry Workers Union.

The union leaders were shocked by the scandal. Fearing a lawsuit that would inevitably damage its image, the union set up a special committee to investigate the affair. The result was the dismissal of the five low-ranking officials who had accepted the bribes. The Laundry Workers Union called in representatives of all Chinese power laundries and Wah Kiu to have a meeting with the union's vice-president, treasurer, and lawyer, who told the Chinese that the union had no intention of preventing the opening of Wah Kiu and warned them not to bribe union officials, an illegal action that the union would not tolerate.[74]

Interestingly, although the Chinese power laundry owners' plot to use the union to sabotage Wah Kiu failed, the workers in their factories were nevertheless unionized by the Laundry Workers Union. To the CHLA, this did not mean that the Chinese power laundry owners now had a "progressive" outlook and were taking the lead in integrating Chinese into American society. Rather, the hand laundrymen saw it as the same old scheme of the established forces in Chinatown: to collaborate with some evil whites to control and exploit ordinary Chinese.

Two years later, therefore, in 1949, when the Chinese power laundries tried to negotiate a new contract with the union, the CHLA joined the fight against the union, which once again tried to organize the hand laundries. The CHLA's arguments, summarily expressed in a series of editorials in *CDN*, further reveal the laundrymen's perception of the trade unions as tools of either the Chinese power laundries or the white laundry companies in exploiting Chinese hand laundries. The editorials argued that the Laundry Workers Union's organizing drive was a "crisis" that threatened the survival of the Chinese laundry business. One of these editorials focused its discussion on "the root of the crisis":

> On appearance, this crisis seems to come from the trade union. In actuality, the trade union is but a puppet used by the large white laundry companies, which recently lost a lot of business. The Chinese hand laundries, however, can still maintain their business at the wartime level, because they mainly wash such items as underwear, shirts, and sheets for the customers, and thus are not affected much by the competition of the self-service launderette. The white laundry companies become jealous, and they try in every possible way to scrap the business of the Chinese hand laundries. One of their important policies is to use the trade union, in the guise of organizing workers, to increase the labor cost of the Chinese hand laundries, and to impose many restrictions on them, in order to disadvantage the Chinese hand laundries in the competition and to make up for their loss.[75]

It is important to note that the editorial linked the union's organizing drive in 1949 to the "conspiracy of the white laundry companies to destroy our Chinese hand laundries" in 1933. The same editorial asserted:

> During the Depression, white laundry companies had lobbied the city government, proposing a bill to prohibit aliens from getting laundry licenses. Its aim was to destroy our Chinese laundry business. But we Chinese united to-

gether and fought against it, and eventually killed the bill. Now that the laundry business is again suffering a recession, the white laundry companies again employed the same old trick—to destroy our Chinese laundries so as to save themselves. However, in light of the past lessons, this time they adopted a new strategy, that is, they secretly ganged up with the scums of the union and came to attack our laundry business in the guise of organizing workers.

Therefore, it is the white laundry companies that cause trouble for us; they are our real enemy. The trade union is but the tool of the white laundry companies.[76]

The editorial urged Chinese hand laundrymen to understand this relationship between the white laundry companies and the trade union and to explain it to their customers, "so as to win the sympathy of the public. We should let our customers know that we do not oppose the trade unions blindly. What we oppose is the injustice and unfair actions of the trade union."[77] Another editorial suggested that the Chinese should "study" and "prepare to refute" specious arguments and propaganda, such as "the Chinese are backward and they sabotage the American labor movement," "the cheap Chinese labor would lower the standard of American life," and "the Chinese work long hours and disrupt the American social order."[78]

To help its readers comprehend the relationship between white laundry companies and trade unions, *CDN* further exposed the "secrets" of the "yellow trade union" in another editorial.

What is the nature of the Laundry Workers Union affiliated with the Amalgamated Clothing Workers Union? Why is it willing to be the tool of the white laundry companies to make trouble for the Chinese laundry business? It's simple—the union is a reactionary yellow union. Within the yellow union, workers have no power; its so-called leaders are corrupt bureaucrats. They have deep racial prejudice and always despise us Chinese. For example, the majority of the union members are black but the blacks have no power whatsoever in the union. Everything is controlled by the few appointed whites. . . . This kind of union is completely manipulated by the union bureaucrats. When it goes out to organize workers, it does not start out with the workers but with management. Its motivation in organizing workers is to collect more fees to increase the union's revenue so that the bureaucrats can get more income. . . . This is the nature of the American yellow unions.[79]

Apparently, these conceptions of the Laundry Workers Union were developed from the CHLA's experiences in dealing with it. The most revealing example was the union's drive to organize the Chinese hand laundries in 1950. Frustrated by its failures to unionize the Chinese hand laundries in the past, the union took the opportunity in 1950 to include an article in the new contract with the Chinese power laundries, Article 33, which required the Chinese power laundries to accept wet-wash jobbers only from those Chinese hand laundries that had joined the union. This imperious measure caused tremendous concern and resentment on the part of the Chinese hand laundries. To reach its goal, the union mobilized thirty staff members to work among the Chinese power as well as hand laundries, and in January it picketed one Chinese power laundry that refused to comply with the new contract.[80]

It was the union's attempt to unionize the entire Chinese laundry business that drew the conflicting Chinese in the trade together to oppose it. When the union picketed Xing Guang Power Laundry, it sent people to identify Xing Guang's hand laundry customers by following the company's delivery trucks. The union men threatened to picket these hand laundries if they continued to do business with Xing Guang. At the same time, they offered to help find other power laundries for the hand laundries. Not surprisingly, these power laundries were the "white laundry companies."[81] The Chinese hand laundries were thus alerted, and the warning of the CHLA and *CDN* that there was a conspiracy between the union and the white laundry companies proved to be well founded and was taken seriously.

Now that the unionization drive was exposed as part of a conspiracy to destroy the Chinese laundry business, ethnic solidarity began to have a great appeal. Both the Chinese power and hand laundries believed that if they were unionized and subject to union regulations, they would lose their edge in competing with the white laundry companies and would eventually be driven out of business. To save the economic lifeline of the Chinese community, the power laundries and hand laundries united to fight Article 33.

After long negotiations failed to reach an agreement on Article 33, the union unilaterally announced on February 21, 1950, that if the Chinese power laundries still refused to sign the new contracts by February 26, the union would organize a strike the next day.[82] All Chinese power laundries, including the Wah Kiu Wet-Wash Factory, vowed to fight the union. At an emergency meeting attended by the CHLA, Wah Kiu and other Chinese power laundries, and a CCBA representative, a resolution was passed that if the union called a strike against one power laundry, all Chinese power laundries should close down in protest.[83] A *CDN* editorial described the threat to strike as "outrageous" and "imperialistic" and called on all Chinese hand laundries to support the power laundries. In case there was a showdown between the two sides, the editorial urged, the Chinese hand laundries "must not turn to the white laundry companies to do wet wash; otherwise we will just fall into the trap set by the white laundry companies and the yellow union." Moreover, the editorial asked the Chinese laundries to prepare English-language flyers "to explain the truth to the customers, and to reveal the dirty secrets of the yellow union to the public so as to win our customers' sympathy and to launch a movement to investigate the union."[84]

The CHLA's legal advisor, Julius Bezozo, fully supported the Chinese position. He negotiated with the union as the legal representative of the Wah Kiu Wet-Wash Factory and other Chinese power laundries. After the Chinese decided to fight instead of accepting the union's conditions, Bezozo reported the case to the Amalgamated Clothing Workers Union and asked it to intervene. The vice-president of the ACWU talked to the representatives of the Chinese power laundries for three hours on February 27 and eventually agreed that the union should exclude Article 33 from the new contracts and should "indefinitely postpone" its effort to unionize the Chinese hand laundries.[85]

To the Chinese, this outcome was a great victory, especially since the ACWU vice-president seemed to understand the situation of the Chinese laundry business. His remarks during the meeting were welcomed by the Chinese. According to the *CDN* reports, the ACWU vice-president, a native New Yorker, recalled that "fifty years ago all hand laundries in this city were operated by Chinese." Now people of other ethnic backgrounds also engaged in the trade; however, the vice-president said, he would try to prevent anyone "who wants to use the union to take business from or to destroy the Chinese hand laundry business." If the union attempted to organize the Chinese hand laundries, it should do so itself. It must not force others to undertake that task on its behalf. Furthermore, he admitted, the situation of the Chinese hand laundries was unique in American society. The Chinese had language difficulties and different cultural customs and were often discriminated against. The union should not mechanically apply its rules or regulations to the Chinese hand laundries, the vice-president said; otherwise it behaved just like others who discriminated against the Chinese.[86]

The vice-president's comments on the corrupt officials of the union were most meaningful to the CHLA. He revealed that he had been the man who had handled the dispute between the union and the Chinese

hand laundries in 1947, and he condemned the five "corrupt union officials" who were dismissed by the ACWU for accepting bribes and for
their improper attempts to press the Chinese hand laundries to join the
union.[87] This comment again vindicated CHLA members' argument that
the union officials were used by a few evil men and justified the alliance's
fight against them in 1947. This was important to the CHLA, since it
claimed to have a progressive outlook and to support trade unions as a
working-class cause in general. It was always concerned that its position,
to oppose only bad unions, be understood by other American pro-
gressives.

The CHLA's persistent resistance to the Laundry Workers Union reveals that the conditions of the Chinese hand laundries had not improved
much. In a struggle for survival in an urban economy, the Chinese hand
laundries met tremendous challenges from all directions. They had to
deal not only with the competition from white laundry companies, the
exploitation of the Chinese power laundries, and the manipulation of the
Chinatown establishment, but also with the demands of the white Laundry Workers Union, which ignored their specific situation and interests.

The CHLA, after so many years of promoting Chinese integration into
American society, was still confined within the limits of Chinatown politics and its economy. The alliance's perception of the Laundry Workers
Union as a "yellow union" resulted from the laundrymen's contacts and
fights with the union within the American context and not from Chinese
cultural ideas. Facing the cruel reality of the racist policies of some trade
unions, these Chinese hand laundrymen could not be convinced that they
should identify with the unions. After all, it was the labor unions, such as
the Knights of Labor, that first campaigned vigorously against the Chinese in the nineteenth century.[88] The laundrymen's suspicions of the
unions and resistance against them, therefore, should not simply be labeled "backward" or "clannish." Rather, such opposition should be seen
as a part both of the Chinese American history of struggling for survival
and of American labor history. Even if the Chinese community seemed to
hold on to the idea of ethnic solidarity longer than other ethnic groups, it
was not because the Chinese refused to integrate, but rather because they
had been rejected over and over again in their attempts to become part of
American society.[89]

Chapter Seven

Where Is the Gold Mountain?

In the turbulent years of the 1940s the CHLA underwent great changes. Acting as a spokesperson for laboring Chinese Americans, it criticized the corruption of the Chiang Kai-shek regime and won more and more support as that regime became increasingly unpopular in the Chinese American community. In its battles against KMT publicists and agents in the United States, the CHLA and its organ, the *China Daily News*, criticized the KMT regime on the basis of the democratic principles the laundrymen had learned in the United States. Their censure reflected a popular view among Chinese Americans that the KMT should engage in democratic reforms. By 1949, when the KMT was losing China to the Communist party, the CHLA, together with other progressive forces, had acquired substantial influence in the politics of the New York Chinese community.

Soon the situation began to change, however. A few months after the CHLA and other Chinese groups celebrated the downfall of the Chiang Kai-shek regime and the founding of the People's Republic of China in October 1949, the Korean War broke out. China and the United States became enemies in the first hot war of the cold war years, and Chiang Kai-shek regained support from the United States. The merchant elite in the Chinese community in America reaffirmed its loyalty to Chiang and took the opportunity to launch offensives against the CHLA and other progressive groups that had emerged after the 1930s. FBI investigation and harassment, encouraged by the Chinatown establishment, was a blow to the CHLA, whose membership declined rapidly.

While the core members of the CHLA endured these hardships in the United States, the news from China was heartbreaking. Their family members in China were labeled "relatives of overseas Chinese capital-

ists" and consequently suffered a great deal during the land reform movement. CHLA members tried but failed to understand why their relatives
should suffer under a revolutionary regime that they had sincerely supported in its struggle with Chiang Kai-shek. Many chose to stay in the
United States instead of going home, and many dropped out of the
CHLA.

This chapter tells the stories of CHLA members during this period. It
analyzes the factors that affected the attitudes of this group of Chinese
Americans toward China and toward America and describes their feelings about the rapid political and social changes of those years.

"We Are Not Stupid Arding"

In March 1945 Zhu Jiazhao, vice-president of the Chinese Hongmeng
Zhigong Party of the Americas, a Chinese community leader in Havana,
Cuba, was greatly impressed with the CHLA when he visited the New
York Chinese community. After he returned to Havana, Zhu reported
to the Cuban Chinese: "The CHLA is the number one Chinese organization in New York, having the largest membership and with greatest
strength.... Well organized and very efficient, the CHLA has made a
great contribution to the welfare of the Chinese hand laundrymen in
New York."[1]

Proud of the CHLA's achievements and its strength, a member asserted
that with the CHLA the ordinary laundrymen should no longer be regarded as "arding"—stupid folks easily manipulated by the elite and
whose only role was to donate money.[2] The CHLA was able to gain more
influence in the New York Chinese community in the 1940s because
KMT policies alienated Chinese Americans.

During the war years (1937–45) CHLA members, like all Chinese
Americans, were anxious to help China resist Japan's invasion. Chiang
Kai-shek's nonresistance policy toward Japan in the early 1930s caused
a great deal of resentment among New York's Chinese Americans. After
Chiang vowed to fight the Japanese in 1937, the CHLA, like most of the
Chinese inside and outside China, supported him as a national leader in
the cause of saving China from Japan's invasion. In the following years,
however, many Chinese Americans became disappointed by the performance of Chiang's troops in the war. They were also critical of the
KMT's dictatorial policies in China and its attempts to control overseas Chinese communities. The KMT government censored the press in

China, and its agents in the United States watched and attacked those Chinese American newspapers that independently reported on China. The extremely unfair exchange rate between the U.S. dollar and the Chinese yuan, caused by war conditions and KMT corruption, which greatly reduced the purchasing power of the money that Chinese Americans sent to their families, further alienated Chinese Americans. Gradually, the KMT lost the confidence of most Chinese Americans.

In January 1941 the New Fourth Army Incident shattered the morale of Chinese Americans and diminished their desire to make donations to the KMT government. Determined to maintain his military superiority over the Chinese Communists, Chiang Kai-shek trapped the Communist-led New Fourth Army in southern Anhui, where thousands of the Communist soldiers were slaughtered.[3] The entire Chinese American community was shocked. Except for a few KMT agents who defended Chiang's action, most Chinese Americans were greatly distressed. Believing that all Chinese should unite to fight the national enemy, Japan, the majority of Chinese Americans considered Chiang's massacre of the New Fourth Army in the face of the Japanese invasion outrageous. The letter of a CHLA member, Chen Junming, to *CDN* was representative:

> After China launched the war of resistance against Japan, the human dignity of the Chinese in the U.S. has increased 100 times. [Though] we haven't won the war, a civil war is on the verge of breaking out. How bitterly distressed I am!
>
> Before the Marco Polo Bridge Incident [of July 7, 1937], some devil kids [white children] often shouted in front of my laundry shop: "Chink! Chink! Chinaman! Japan has conquered your China!" After China began the war of resistance, no more such shouting; and people praised China for resisting the Japs. These praises made me happy and I tended to believe that now I could walk in the street with my head up, no longer worrying that people would look at me contemptuously. However, when the news of the internal conflict came, though the devil kids no longer shouted, "Chink! Chink! Chinaman!" someone began to ask: "Charlie, any news from home about fighting the Japs?"
>
> ... We ordinary folks did our best to contribute to the war effort. But I heard that some government officials made money out of the national calamity, and they had foreign bank accounts.... How detestable they are! May I ask: How can we succeed in the war? And how can we save China?
>
> Now [the government] has wiped out the New Fourth Army on the excuse that it did not obey orders. Next it will be the Eighth Route Army. We overseas Chinese are heartbroken to see this happen. Is there still any hope that China can be saved?[4]

The bloody internal conflict worried Chinese Americans. On January 15, 1941, the CHLA cabled both the Kuomintang and the Communist party, urging them "to unite together to defend the motherland" and to set the fight against the Japanese as the highest goal above anything else.[5] *CDN* was the first Chinese-language newspaper to report the New Fourth Army Incident. The paper also published letters and ran editorials commenting on the episode.

The immediate effect of the New Fourth Army Incident in Chinese American communities was a decline of Chinese Americans' enthusiasm for donating money to China. More and more Chinese Americans were disappointed by the KMT's performance in the war and felt hopeless about the political situation in China. "In the past two years," one article published in July 1942 reported, "the decline of salvation work has become a common phenomenon in the United States [Chinese American communities]. There are many reasons, but the main one was the internal conflict in China."[6]

To revive Chinese American enthusiasm for donations, a Conference of All-U.S. Chinese Anti-Japanese Fund-Raising Organizations was held in New York City in September 1943. Representatives from Chinese communities all over the United States discussed the causes of the recent decline. Many pointed to the depressing situation in China as the main reason. The corruption of the KMT government was cited as the most important element in destroying Chinese American confidence.[7]

Chinese Americans learned of the KMT's corruption in two ways. First, their families were directly affected by the KMT officials' embezzlement of their remittances. Many relatives of Chinese Americans relied entirely on these funds for subsistence, and many starved to death during the war because of delays or embezzlement of the remittances. Chinese Americans were very upset when they received letters reporting such sad stories.[8]

Second, they knew about KMT corruption through their observations of KMT officials and their relatives living in the United States. During the war years many KMT officials sent their family members to the United States, especially Washington, D.C., and New York City. "They were as numerous as the mice in a slum," one report stated. "From the top KMT officials to third-class politicians, almost no one has not sent relatives to the United States. Some even manage to get the whole family out here, having bought a house or invested in something." These people reportedly brought to the United States huge amounts of money, which was believed to have been squeezed from the Chinese people or accumulated through speculation in black-market currency. Ordinary Chinese Americans resented these people and called them "high-class refugees."[9] These wealthy newcomers looked down on Chinese American laundrymen and restaurant workers. The wife of a KMT official had reportedly called Chinese American restaurant workers "inferior people," and another official's wife was surprised to find that many Chinese Americans worked in hand laundry shops: "My God! They work in those jobs!"[10]

The extravagant lifestyle of the high-class refugees in the United States and the sufferings of the Chinese Americans' relatives in China constituted a striking contrast. Angry and sorrowful, Chinese Americans decided to stop donating their hard-earned "blood-and-sweat money" to the KMT government. As a reflection of this sentiment, the Conference of All-U.S. Chinese Anti-Japanese Fund-Raising Organizations passed a resolution to "demand that Generalissimo Chiang Kai-shek punish the 'high-class refugees' who fled abroad to escape from donating money [to the resistance war], so that we will be able to promote donations among overseas Chinese."[11] Chiang's government did little to change the situation, however, and throughout the 1940s the KMT's corruption continued to alienate overseas Chinese.

In the New York Chinese community, the CHLA became a spokesperson for laboring-class Chinese Americans in criticizing the KMT's corruption and demanding democratic reforms, and *CDN* was the essential instrument through which ordinary Chinese Americans shared information and expressed their opinions on China's politics. By the mid-1940s *CDN* had become one of the most influential Chinese-American newspapers, with distribution in all major cities in the United States and in many Latin American countries, such as Mexico, Cuba, Chile, and Venezuela.

In November 1943, to provide opportunities for its members to express their concerns about politics in China, the CHLA Executive Committee passed a resolution to hold "Sunday Discussion on Current Events" twice a month. Some of the summaries of the discussions were published in the Special CHLA Column in *CDN*. The first Sunday Discussion focused on two issues: the effects and causes of the famine in Taishan County, whence many Chinese Americans came; and whether there would be an economic recession in the United States and how it would affect the Chinese hand laundries.[12]

The Taishan famine of 1943 was catastrophic. About 100,000 people (out of a population of 860,000) died of starvation or diseases caused by malnutrition. Many of the victims relied on overseas remittances from Chinese American relatives for survival, but the remittances were cut off by the war and much of the money that did reach Taishan was embezzled by local officials.[13] Angry Chinese hand laundrymen insisted that the tragedy was caused more by human failure—the corruption and black-market speculation of government officials and unscrupulous merchants—than by natural calamity. Zhong Huitang, a member of the CHLA Executive Committee, summed up the discussions on the issue: "The corruption of the motherland's politics and the unfair exchange rate between the dollar and yuan were the root of the famine. So, if we want to save China and to save our families, we have to be concerned with reforming China's politics."[14]

Focusing on issues that concerned hand laundrymen the most, the first CHLA Sunday Discussion stimulated the interest of the members. The second Sunday Discussion was attended by more members, and they took the floor one after another. Wu Yushu, who would become president of the CHLA in 1944, suggested that his fellow members come to the discussions and "learn how to speak." Eugene Moy, editor of *CDN*, also encouraged the hand laundrymen to be more interested in Chinese politics and asked them to think of what they could do to improve the situation. Undoubtedly, the Taishan famine was mainly caused by political corruption, Moy said, but there were reasons that the corruption ran so wild. The people should stand up to build a democratic government to prevent corruption, Moy argued eloquently.[15]

The two major themes that emerged from the first two CHLA Sunday Discussions—how to eliminate the corruption in Chinese politics and how to build a democratic government in China—dominated these discussions in the years to come. The CHLA's criticisms of the KMT government bore distinctive Chinese American characteristics. The CHLA criticized the KMT regime from the perspective of laboring-class Chinese Americans, based on their deep concern for their relatives at home. Moreover, the CHLA used the democratic principles that the hand laundrymen had learned in the United States to measure the KMT's performance and to demand political reforms. From these criticisms of the KMT, interestingly, a positive identification with some basic values of American democracy developed.

In September 1943, to mitigate the increasing demand for democracy, the KMT announced that a national constitutional convention would be held within the first year after China won the war against Japan. An Association to Promote the Implement of the Constitution was set up in Chongqing (Chungking), the wartime capital of China, with a stated purpose of soliciting opinions and suggestions from Chinese at home and abroad. Some overseas Chinese organizations, including the CHLA, were excited about this move. After several months of discussion the CHLA submitted to the association a long "Letter of Opinion," which examined line by line the constitution drafted by the KMT and suggested numerous changes. It is not necessary to cite here in detail the CHLA's opinions on the proposed constitution, but it is worth noting the alliance's desire to introduce American democratic ideas to China. In the brief preface of the "Letter of Opinion," the CHLA stated: "We, the overseas Chinese in the United States, are living in a democratic and free country. What we see and hear here is the politics of the people and for the people. We not only have long admired the excellence and efficiency of the [American] political institutions, as well as the ways the government functions, but also desire that our motherland build institutions after this pattern so as to become a wealthy and powerful nation."[16]

This praise for American political institutions and their operation is one of the ironies in Chinese American history. If the statement above is juxtaposed to the CHLA's criticisms of U.S. anti-Chinese legislation expressed a few months earlier in the campaign to repeal the Chinese exclusion acts, as well as its comments on American China policy a few years later, one cannot help but feel that the CHLA's understanding of U.S. politics was full of contradictions. On the one hand, the CHLA criticized the United States for the injustices Chinese had suffered; on the other, it held up American democracy as an ideal model for China to follow.

It is precisely this kind of ambivalent attitude that characterized the true feelings of the Chinese hand laundrymen regarding the United States. The contradictions were a reflection of the contradictions in U.S. society itself and especially those in the hand laundrymen's experiences. The United States claimed to be a free and equal society, but Chinese experienced severe racial discrimination and exclusion. Nevertheless, when the Chinese stood up to fight against the injustices and to defend their interests, they appealed to American democratic principles and legal procedures. Though many times the laundrymen failed in their struggle for equality and felt disillusioned about the way in which American democracy actually worked, sometimes they won, as, for example, in the CHLA's struggle against the New York City government's discriminatory laundry ordinance in 1933. Most significantly, the repeal of the Chinese exclusion acts in 1943 provided a new atmosphere in which some Chinese Americans, such as the CHLA members, could affirm their experiences of fighting injustice within American society and identify more positively with the basic values and principles embodied in the U.S. Constitution.

This identification with basic American values has many meanings in Chinese American history. As discussed in Chapter Five, the CHLA and *CDN* in 1943 had criticized the Chinese exclusion acts from the perspective of American democratic principles. It was in its criticism of the KMT government, however, that the CHLA members applied such principles most frequently. To these Chinese hand laundrymen, the fundamental principles of democracy were simple, direct, and, even more important, applicable to China. In the 1940s many CHLA members attacked KMT corruption and discussed how to reform the Chinese political system in short articles or letters, written in their own simple language. The article quoted below is representative:

> China belongs to Chinese, and the Kuomintang must end its one-party dictatorship.
>
> To understand the essence of democracy, we don't have to talk about abstract theories. We can just take a look at some plain facts. Living in the democratic United States, it's not difficult for us to know the effectiveness of democracy through what we see and hear. For example, if there is a problem in a local community, any citizen can write to [his or her] Representatives and Senators, and in most cases, the Representatives and Senators respond quickly. Why? Because they are elected by local people. . . . They are obligated to serve the people.
>
> Now let's examine the situation in China. Does any Chinese official have to be responsible to the people? They all have a contemptuous attitude to the people. We saw much of this when we were in China. Even a petty official always strutted about in front of people. . . . Recently, every newspaper [in the New York Chinese community] has run reports on the problems in [overseas Chinese] remittances. But our protests met the deaf ear of the Bank of China. Why? Because the bank is run by the government, and its managers are officials of the ruling dictatorial party that is not responsible to the people.[17]

The CHLA members addressed these issues not for the sake of flaunting their knowledge of democracy, but because they were compelled by the sufferings of their relatives to speak out and because they believed that "Chinese politics has a direct influence on our economic conditions and our social status in the United States."[18] Also, they felt obliged to express support for the "people's zealous struggle for democracy at home."[19] Furthermore, their criticisms of the KMT government were related to their attacks on the Chinatown establishment, a subject discussed in detail in the next section. All these issues were important in the political life of Chinese Americans, but few dared to or had the chance to address them.

That is why the CHLA, as the largest occupational organization in the New York Chinese community, was able to become a spokesperson for laboring-class Chinese Americans. For example, in December 1943, when some of the Chinese relief organizations adopted compulsory measures to force Chinese Americans to donate money to China, one of the CHLA leaders openly commented: "Most of us in the United States are selling our labor to make a living. We have to support our families and donate money to save the motherland. After the United States joined the war, we are more burdened with new taxes and donations. All these are too much for us. Now, we can only voluntarily contribute what we can afford. We should not be forced to make extra donations."[20]

If an individual Chinese made such a comment, he or she might be severely punished for being unpatriotic. Because the CHLA was a large organization with a long history of contributing to China's war efforts, the voice of its representatives carried weight. Even though such comments irritated the establishment in Chinatown, it could do little about them. In the following years the CHLA not only criticized KMT policies in China and the established elite in Chinatown, but also tried to initiate some fundamental changes in the New York Chinese community.

"When Shall We Go Home?"

"When the news came that Japan had surrendered," CHLA member Li Chengzhu wrote in August 1945, "there was a common phrase among the Chinese: 'Go home!' [*Fan Tangshan*]."[21] The war had kept many Chinese Americans from returning to China for nearly a decade, and they were eager to go home immediately to see their families, their hometowns, and their country of origin.

Like other Chinese Americans, many CHLA members also talked about going home, but people had different motives. Some, especially the elderly, simply wanted to follow the old pattern of the Chinese "gold diggers"—or sojourners—of bringing their lifetime savings back to China to finish their lives in comfort. The younger bachelors wanted to find brides in their native villages and bring the women over to build families in the United States. Others dreamed of becoming rich through investing in postwar China, since they did not see good investment opportunities for themselves in the United States.

From 1945 to 1948 the idea of returning to China was discussed by CHLA members as well as other groups of Chinese in the United States. According to Paul Siu, Chinese laundrymen in Chicago clung to Chinese culture no matter how long they lived in the United States. Their ultimate goal was to make money and go back to China. The only constraint in realizing this dream was money: if one did not have enough money, one would not consider going home because that would be "losing face."[22] This observation ignores the impact of conditions in China—political, economic, and social—on the decision of the sojourners to go home.

Siu's interpretation may have applied to the experiences of certain Chinese Americans, but not to CHLA members in the 1940s. To many alliance members, going home was no longer an automatic matter but a complicated issue that involved numerous considerations. Although some members realized that postwar China "needs our capital to develop industries and to stabilize the postwar economy, and our skills for various constructions,"[23] they were reluctant to go back to China because of the chaotic situation there. In short, Chinese politics was a key factor in the home-going decision.

When Li Chengzhu discussed this issue in August 1945, he urged his fellow Chinese to remain in the United States until three conditions were met in China: the establishment of a coalition government and the elimination of corruption; the guarantee of the basic rights of citizens so that they could effectively oversee the government; and the punishment of traitors and corrupt officials. The last demand arose from Li's knowledge that the KMT government had used former Japanese collaborators as police officers and guards in the coastal cities. "Since the Chinese in the United States had been engaged in the struggle against these Japanese collaborators," Li stated, "I am afraid that once we set foot on the soil of the motherland, we will be mistreated by them."[24]

While discouraged by the unsettled situation in China, many CHLA members were indeed tortured by the idea that they could not fulfill their dreams of going home as successful Guests from the Gold Mountain (*Jing Shan Ke*, a term used in Guangdong for those who brought money home from the United States). A CHLA member who gave himself the pen name Jing Shan Ke wrote in the Special CHLA Column in *CDN*:

> I believe that like me, many have been thinking about this issue: Why can't I feel at ease about going home?
>
> ... When you get home, the problem of food will first make you lose

heart [inflation had made the cost of rice very high]. Then, if you want to do business, there is no way you can even start it: everything is controlled by the bureaucrats. You will find no investment opportunity if you are returning from overseas without any personal connections. . . . We cannot do anything in the motherland. The money we bring back will soon be used up because of the spiraling inflation; then we will starve.[25]

Those who wanted to go home also were discouraged by the news from relatives, as indicated by Cai Geng's letter to the *CDN* editor:

Everyone wants to go home to see one's family members. . . . However, I and my friends got letters from home dissuading us from returning now because the reality at home is far worse than what people anticipated. . . .

In this big chaos, we have a home to which we cannot return. If we go home now, it is not *"rong xuan"* [to return to the native village with wealth and glory],[26] but to suffer.

Who caused this chaos? The corrupt officials. They are still ruling our hometowns. As long as they have power and the motherland and our hometowns are in chaos, we cannot go home.[27]

Some did go home but soon came back to the United States after having some very unpleasant experiences, such as those of this heartbroken Chinese American:

After the war, I wanted to see my brothers and sisters so I found a job on an American ship and went to Shanghai in June. I was shocked by what I saw and by what Shanghai people told me.

I stayed in Shanghai but did not go to my hometown because the political and economic situation was very unstable. . . . The humiliating words from the American GIs and seamen were hard to take. They said, "China should not proclaim to be a strong power. Isn't it true that the United States provides you with everything?" When you look at the river [in Shanghai], it is filled with American warships and commercial vessels; American troops are stationed in metropolitan Shanghai; the great amounts of currency changing hands in the stock market are American dollars; the Custom Service claims to be autonomous but is controlled by American advisors; foreign ships sail freely along China's coast and inner rivers. . . . All these facts make it hard for me to denounce the humiliating words of the American GIs. . . . Under such conditions, I lost my enthusiasm for going back to my village. How can I return to such a hometown? So I came back to the United States on the same American ship.

What I came to know is that unless China immediately stops the civil war, carries out democratic political reforms, sweeps out corruption, and reconstructs the economy, there is no future in our beloved motherland.[28]

According to one estimate, between 50 and 70 percent of the Chinese Americans who returned home in 1947 came back to the United States in 1948.[29] Most who stayed in China were either over sixty years old or in poor health. The average length of time that these Chinese Americans stayed in the villages was six to eight months. The chaotic political, social, and economic situation destroyed their hopes of investing or living in peaceful retirement, and the high inflation rate exhausted their life savings. When interviewed by a Chinese reporter in Hong Kong, one old Chinese American sighed, "It seems that I am destined to go back to the United States to be poor laborer forever."[30]

Losing hope in China, many Chinese Americans focused more on developing their communities in the United States—a development that was already under way. Almost all members of the CHLA were first-generation Chinese males who, as individuals, continued to feel frustrated by the discussion "when shall I go home." But as an organization, the CHLA encouraged its members to focus on their settlement in the United States and began to lay the economic foundations for its own further development. In the intensifying discussions of "when shall we go home" immediately after Japan's surrender on August 15, Li Qiying (then a member of the CHLA Executive Committee) reminded his fellow CHLA members that "America is our chosen home; we will stay here, and our descendants will come to join us."[31] One *CDN* editorial urged Chinese Americans not to rush into decisions about going home. "Never forget: our economic base is in the United States," the paper advised.[32]

The CHLA's effort to strengthen itself economically started during the war years. The Chinese hand laundry business enjoyed a short prosperity in the early 1940s. In 1944 members of the CHLA, with more savings and stronger identification with their organization than before, wanted to bolster its economic basis in order to provide more services for the membership. The plans under consideration included purchasing a building as a headquarters, founding a wet-wash factory, opening a laundry-supply cooperative, and organizing "study classes" to help members learn English and "other knowledge."[33]

The plan to purchase a building was first realized in early 1946. It was mainly the effort of Quon Shar members, who initiated the drive to organize the Wah Kiu United Company (Huaqiao Lianhe Shiye Gongsi) in late 1945. Some supporters of the CHLA, such as the staff members of *CDN* and members of the Huizhou Gongshang Hui (Huizhou Association), joined the venture. In early 1946 the Wah Kiu United Company purchased the building at 191 Canal Street, which the CHLA had rented as its headquarters for many years, for thirty thousand dollars.[34] With money contributed by its members (five dollars each), the CHLA became the biggest shareholder in the Wah Kiu United Company.[35]

The CHLA decided to buy the building because the members felt that racial discrimination made it very difficult for Chinese to rent living and working space in New York City. "There are many troubles—the landlords may raise the rent or evict you without reason, or may not rent to you at all in the first place."[36] The purchase of the CHLA headquarters building was but the first step in the long-term plan of the Wah Kiu United Company: it intended to buy more buildings in "proper locations in the city" to be rented to Chinese, "so as to spare them the troubles of renting spaces from white landlords" and, of course, to increase the CHLA's revenue.[37]

The Wah Kiu United Company was not able to implement its plans in the following years. The main reason was that the planning and establishment of the Wah Kiu Wet-Wash Factory absorbed most of the CHLA members' energy and financial resources. It took more than three years for the CHLA to consolidate the wet-wash factory, a period in which the Wah Kiu United Company was unable to buy real estate because CHLA members had to devote their limited resources to strengthening the factory. After that, as we will see, the fear caused by FBI harassment of CHLA members ultimately ended the ventures of the company as well as its existence.[38]

While trying to consolidate itself economically through founding the Wah Kiu Wet-Wash Factory and the ventures of the Wah Kiu United Company, the CHLA took initiatives to improve the political conditions in Chinatown. The democratization of the Chinese community was one of its primary goals. One important move was its attempt to transform the leading power in Chinatown, the CCBA, through democratic reforms.

As described in Chapter One, the CCBA was not a democratic organization. Its president and the seven permanent members of its Standing Committee were not elected, but were chosen behind the scenes by the merchant elite. The CHLA and *CDN* had been criticizing the CCBA for years for its failure to hold democratic elections. In 1947 the CCBA planned to raise funds from all Chinese in the state of New York for building a new headquarters. To raise enough money, the CCBA took the suggestion of some Chinese Americans to revise its constitution. The CHLA and *CDN* saw this as an opportunity to push the CCBA to carry out some reforms.

In June 1947 the CHLA and *CDN* tried to press the CCBA to adopt a democratic direct-election system similar to that of the CHLA. Citing "the American motto"—"Taxation without Representation Is Tyranny"—*CDN* pointed out that the CCBA constitution ignored the basic right of its members, the right to vote. It urged the CCBA to introduce direct general elections into its system. Refuting the argument that many Chinese Americans were not well educated and therefore could not exercise these rights, the paper stated, "Many of us functioned well in casting our votes in American presidential elections and local governmental elections, why can we not vote in the Chinese community?" Given the increasing political awareness among Chinese Americans, the paper asserted, the CCBA must reform itself or lose its position as a "leading organization" in the community.[39]

The established elite ignored this appeal to democratic principles. The new CCBA bylaws, which were revised and became effective on January 1, 1948, retained the old clause specifying that the office of president would be held alternately by the candidates nominated by the two largest district associations, Ning Yang Hui Guan and Lian Cheng Gongsuo.[40]

The CHLA's and *CDN*'s effort to change the power structure in Chinatown failed. But what is significant is that such an attempt was made, reflecting a confidence in the potential of ordinary Chinese Americans to improve their conditions in America by adopting democratic ways. More explicitly, the CHLA hoped that laboring-class Chinese Americans would have more say in community affairs and that the repressive, arbitrary system through which the CCBA had ruled Chinatown for decades would be changed.

The CHLA's and *CDN*'s demand for democratic reforms in the Chinese community was not mere rhetoric. If the principles of democratic elections, such as "one person, one vote," were introduced into the elections of CCBA officials, with each organization having equal access to power (making the CCBA a genuine coalition organization instead of a merchant-dominated organ), the CHLA, with its large membership and its widespread connections with other grassroots organizations, would very likely have a powerful voice in the organization and could potentially make fundamental changes in the political life of New York's Chinatown.

The CHLA's criticisms of the KMT regime in China and the CCBA monopoly of power in Chinatown were based on the same point: they did not represent the people. Implicit in these criticisms and in seemingly sentimental statements of "we have a home but cannot return to it" was a strong desire to acquire and exercise political rights and power. Going back to China or staying in the United States, this group of Chinese Americans was determined to practice and protect its rights. Since the depressing situation in China discouraged them from returning there, the improvement of their conditions in their land of settlement became their primary concern. Therefore, the CHLA's criticisms of the KMT regime must be read alongside its criticisms of the CCBA, and vice versa. And its discussions of democracy more often reflected its view of the realities in China and Chinatown than its theoretical understanding of abstract principles.

"We Had a Hard Time"

In the 1940s, as the CHLA attained more influence in the community, the KMT's popularity among Chinese Americans declined rapidly. Except for controlling the overseas Chinese communities so as to collect more donations, the KMT government developed no policy to protect the interests or promote the welfare of overseas Chinese. Yang Gang, reporter of *Da Gong Bao* (a Chinese newspaper based in Chongqing), who lived in the United States from 1944 to 1948, made this observation:

> I may say that up to now the [KMT] government has not had a policy for the Chinese in the United States.... Earlier this year, a Chinese was beaten up without reason in a street in Philadelphia, put in jail, and died there. The Chinese government did not demand an apology and compensation, and did not even protest!
>
> On the other hand, the government spared no effort in trying to get donations from those poor Chinese, whose welfare is cared for by neither America nor China.[41]

Yang Gang went on to ridicule the KMT government officials who repeated Sun Yat-sen's famous comment—"Overseas Chinese are the mother of the revolution"—to flatter overseas Chinese in order to collect donations: "should overseas Chinese, who were elected as the mother of revolution for a while, nurse [China] forever?"[42]

Even if the KMT wanted overseas Chinese to continue to nurse it, by 1948, as it was about to lose the civil war to the Chinese Communist Party (CCP), it lost the support of a majority of Chinese Americans. Sympathizing with the Chinese Communists as the underdog in Chinese politics and as a patriotic force in the fight against the Japanese aggressors, the CHLA and *CDN* were excited by the Communist victories over the KMT. They saw the CCP as an alternative to the corrupt KMT regime.

Most Chinese Americans were fed up with KMT policies, especially the KMT regulation over the exchange rate between the dollar and the yuan. They concluded that the KMT did not represent their interests, nor could it come to their protection when they needed it. Disillusion with the KMT regime led to a curiosity about the CCP, which had demonstrated a capacity to challenge and defeat the superior KMT military forces and appeared to have a chance to set up a new government. The CCP proposal to build a coalition government to replace the KMT regime was especially attractive to the CHLA, since its main criticism of the KMT was the latter's one-party dictatorship.

While the CHLA members experienced the corruption of the KMT regime themselves and through their relatives' sufferings, they did not know much about the CCP firsthand. They gained information about it mainly through the American media. During the war years the KMT maintained rigorous news censorship. All KMT newspapers in the United States parroted KMT propaganda and reported little on the CCP. *CDN*, after its establishment in 1940, tried to break this news blockade. As part of the effort to understand the true situation in China, the paper published available information about the CCP military performance in the war against Japan. Gradually, stories of the CCP leaders and political and economic policies of the party were also reported.

Most of the information on the CCP was provided by American journalists. The CHLA and *CDN* either translated these news reports from English-language newspapers (such as *The New York Times*, *World Telegram*, and *The Washington Post*) or invited American journalists to talk to CHLA members. In 1949, for example, several journalists, including Gunther Stein, were invited to the CHLA to report to the laundrymen on the CCP.[43] These reports, which often commented favorably on the high spirit of the CCP forces in the anti-Japanese war, the party's democratic reforms in the countryside, and its uncompromising stand toward foreign imperialists, usually were juxtaposed to reports on KMT corruption and its oppression of political dissidents, thereby drawing a sharp contrast between the two political parties and projecting the CCP as a dynamic democratic force and a representative of laboring-class Chinese. These accounts aroused both curiosity about and enthusiasm for the CCP.

By late 1948 and early 1949, when the CCP's victory in the Chinese civil war was only a matter of time, the CHLA and *CDN* began to import

CCP publications from Hong Kong so the laundrymen could gain a fuller understanding of the party's theories and policies.[44] The *CDN* began to use more and more of the news provided by the CCP news agency, Xin Hua She (New China News Agency). In their discussions the CHLA members openly endorsed the CCP.[45]

At the beginning of 1949 some of the CHLA leaders seemed to expect a fundamental change in Chinese American communities after the collapse of the KMT regime in China, and they envisioned a new power structure in the coming years in which the KMT-supported CCBA would lose its dominant position while the CHLA would come to the fore. Since the relation with the home government had been one of the major sources of the CCBA's power, it was assumed that the merchant-dominated organization would lose its influence once the KMT government was overthrown by the Communists. The CHLA expected to develop a good relationship with the new government led by the CCP, which claimed to represent the interests of workers and peasants, and this relationship would strengthen the alliance's position in the New York Chinese community.

The prospects for cultivating good relations were excellent. As early as 1945 the CHLA sponsored a banquet welcoming the CCP member of the Chinese delegation to the United Nations, Dong Biwu.[46] Situ Meitang, the head of On Leong Tong and one of the leading figures in the New York Chinese community, who had been courted by both the KMT and the CCP but chose to identify with the CCP, was a friend of the CHLA.

In March 1948, when Secretary of State George Marshall presented a plan to Congress to send military aid to Chiang Kai-shek, the CHLA sent telegrams asking New York's senators and representatives to block the proposal.[47] In April 1948, when the Committee for a Democratic Far Eastern Policy, founded by a group of American academics and journalists to promote a policy of nonintervention toward China, initiated a "China Week" aimed at preventing U.S. military aid to the KMT regime, the CHLA and *CDN* warmly responded to the activity and praised it as a step toward "strengthening the traditional friendship between the American and Chinese peoples."[48] The CHLA's core, members of the Quon Shar, had supported the committee and donated four hundred dollars to it when it was founded in 1946.[49]

As everyone in the community knew that the CCP would eventually win the civil war, some leaders of the CCBA began to make moves to cultivate a good relationship with the CHLA and *CDN*. In July 1948, when *CDN* celebrated its eighth anniversary, the president of the CCBA, Lu

Guanli (Luo Kuan Lai), sent a congratulatory note to the paper.[50] This was the first sign that the CCBA recognized *CDN* as an influential newspaper. Lu's gesture was immediately attacked by KMT agents in the United States.[51] In the following months Lu was harassed by KMT supporters in a variety of ways.[52]

Lu Guanli's courting of the CHLA and *CDN* can be explained as an opportunistic act in which he sought to arrange for his protection after power changed hands in China. But the CHLA and *CDN* saw it as a chance to influence the CCBA and to change the political situation in Chinatown. On January 23, 1949, when the CHLA invited community leaders and newspaper editors to its headquarters to discuss the political situation in China, Lu Guanli was included. Lu apparently shared the view that the KMT was losing the war, as he explicitly commented, "Now that Chiang Kai-shek had overthrown himself . . . we should express ourselves freely." Nevertheless, he did not join in supporting the CCP's goal of eliminating all the KMT forces; rather, he called on Chinese Americans to draft a peace program for a compromise between the CCP and the KMT. And he suggested that the CHLA invite more people from the community to discuss the situation.[53]

Eager to see the end of the Chinese civil war, CHLA members hailed the successes of the Chinese Communists. Since Chiang Kai-shek's regime had received large amounts of American military and economic aid and was viewed as subordinate to the United States, the CCP, which appeared to be largely self-reliant, seemed to be the best hope for China's national independence. Many CHLA members argued that only a truly independent China could extend meaningful support to overseas Chinese. In their eyes, a regime like that of the KMT, which always begged support from Americans, only strengthened the discrimination against Chinese in the United States.[54] Thus, when the People's Liberation Army bombarded the British warship *Amethyst* on the Yangtze River near Nanjing in April 1949 in retaliation for alleged provocative actions, the CHLA hailed the event as marking an end to the "humiliation that the Chinese people have suffered from British imperialist aggression in China in the last 100 years" and as "an important step to elevate the status of the Chinese nation."[55] On April 25 the CHLA cabled Mao Tse-tung and Zhu De, chairman of the CCP and commander-in-chief of the People's Liberation Army, respectively, congratulating them on their success over the KMT forces and praising the attack on the *Amethyst* as a "heroic protection of China's national dignity."[56]

Impressed with the CCP's victory over the U.S.-supported KMT and its uncompromising stand against imperialism, the CHLA hoped that the new CCP government would provide political and legal protection to Chinese Americans, put pressure on the U.S. government to abolish discriminatory immigration laws, extend economic and technical aid to Chinese Americans in "strengthening and expanding our economic base in the United States," and improve the living conditions of their relatives at home.[57] These hopes reflected the traditional expectations of Chinese Americans rather than an understanding of the CCP's actual policies.

With these expectations, the CHLA became the first Chinese American organization on the East Coast to celebrate the founding of the People's Republic of China (PRC). On October 9, 1949, hundreds of CHLA members and guests from Washington, D.C., and Philadelphia attended the celebration.[58] The five-star national flag of the PRC was displayed in front of the CHLA headquarters on 191 Canal Street.[59]

The celebration was seen as a sign of Communist activity in the local Chinese community. From this moment on, the CHLA, the Chinese Youth Club, and *CDN* were placed under investigation and surveillance by the Federal Bureau of Investigation. On October 11, 1949, J. Edgar Hoover, director of the FBI, sent notes to the Central Intelligence Agency and the army and navy intelligence agencies informing them that, based on the evidence made manifest in its celebration of the founding of the PRC, the CHLA was a "Communist infiltrated" organization.[60]

After the outbreak of the Korean War, Hoover directed his New York agents to conduct a "comprehensive, thorough investigation" of the CHLA "at once"[61] and to open "individual cases for investigation on officers or members of" the CHLA, the Chinese Youth Club, and *CDN* "who might be considered as potentially dangerous to the internal security." "In addition, if possible, membership lists for the foregoing organizations should be obtained for submission to the Bureau for appropriate handling."[62] By November 1950 the CHLA was regarded as the "largest single Chinese Communist group in New York,"[63] and the FBI intensified its investigation of the laundrymen's alliance, the Chinese Youth Club, and *CDN*.

Meanwhile, KMT agents in New York City stepped up their campaign to exploit the anti-Communist atmosphere in the United States to rally support for the KMT government, which had fled to Taiwan. In July 1949 some KMT agents had come to New York and taken control of the CCBA, and the moderate president of the organization, Lu Guanli, was forced to change his conciliatory attitude toward the CHLA and *CDN*. At a meeting of the CCBA Standing Committee, telegrams were sent to the American president and vice-president, speaker of the house, and secretary of state, urging them to support the KMT regime. Telegrams were also sent to Chiang Kai-shek and Li Zhongren, then acting president of the KMT government, pledging loyalty to the regime and demanding that it continue its "suppression of the Communist rebellion."[64] Since the telegrams were political statements made in the name of the whole Chinese community in New York without the consent of many organizations, the CHLA was furious and, along with other Chinese Americans, issued a statement denouncing the CCBA's action and declaring that the telegrams did not represent the will of all New York Chinese Americans.[65]

In the same month the pro-KMT Chinese organized a League for Free and Democratic China, aimed at soliciting support for the KMT regime.[66] In subsequent days KMT newspapers in New York spread the rumor that the U.S. government was conducting an investigation of the Chinese "Communist bandits" as well as "the Chinese Americans and Chinese students who were fooled and used by the Communists," and that U.S. government agencies were going to check their immigration papers and passports. They warned Chinese Americans to keep their distance from the CHLA and *CDN*, or they would be implicated and "deported by the U.S. authorities."[67]

The KMT agents and supporters were thrilled by the U.S. decision to send troops to Korea and the Seventh Fleet to the Taiwan Strait on the outbreak of the Korean War. They hoped for a war between the United States and the PRC, which would provide an opportunity for the KMT to return to mainland China.[68] In early July 1950 KMT supporters put a note in front of the Chinese School in Chinatown, stating that "the U.S. government has ordered the arrest of the Communists for national security reasons. All Chinese who are members of the Chinese Hand Laundry Alliance and the Huizhou Association should withdraw at once so as not to be sent to concentration camps. . . . And all subscribers to the *China Daily News* and *Hsin Pao* [a New York-based Chinese-language newspaper critical of the KMT regime] should discontinue their subscriptions so as not to be implicated."[69]

The open hostility and military confrontation between the PRC and the United States in the Korean War seemed to jeopardize all Chinese Americans. Even without the KMT supporters' anti-Communist propaganda, many feared that they might suffer what Japanese Americans had experienced during the Second World War, and rumors spread quickly in Chinatown that the U.S. government was ready to put Chinese into concentration camps.[70] Under these circumstances, the CCBA in New York as well as in other cities led a campaign to pledge loyalty to the U.S. government and took advantage of the anti-Communist atmosphere to recover what it had lost in the preceding few years.

Once again politics in China and the China policy of the United States divided Chinese American communities. In New York, on December 2, 1950, a few weeks after the Chinese Army engaged U.S. troops in battle in Korea, the CCBA issued an "anti-Communist declaration" at a press conference and adopted a resolution to boycott *CDN*. The people who attended the meeting were mainly KMT members and the editors of KMT newspapers in New York City, such as *The Chinese Journal* and *The Chinese Nationalist Daily*. They told the community that a war between China and the United States would soon break out and that anyone who had relations with the CHLA and who subscribed to *CDN* would be seen as Communists or Communist sympathizers and would be sent to concentration camps. Anyone who did not want to be identified as a Communist should donate money to the CCBA and apply for an "identification card."[71]

Pro-KMT organizations in other cities soon issued similar statements. Meanwhile, the tension between the United States and the PRC increased. On December 16 the U.S. government announced an embargo of China, banning all exports and imports, and the freezing of Chinese assets in the United States. The next day the KMT embassy in Washington, D.C., issued a statement urging the American media and people to use "red China" or "Communist China" to refer to the People's Republic in the mainland, so as to differentiate it from Chiang Kai-shek's "free China" in Taiwan.[72]

While attempting to recover and consolidate their power in the community, the CCBA and KMT agents tried to isolate the CHLA and *CDN* and to use the U.S. government to destroy the CHLA and the newspaper. This tactic was effective. The CHLA's membership shrank rapidly, and many shops and firms withdrew their advertisements from *CDN*. Only the core of the CHLA, the members of the Quon Shar and the Chinese Youth Club, remained to support it and *CDN*. In response to the frightening stories circulated by the CCBA, these people pointed out that if the U.S. government were to repeat what it had done to Japanese Americans, all Chinese would suffer. "How could the CCBA guarantee any Chinese's safety if war [between China and the United States] broke out and if the U.S. government decided to round up Chinese as they [the CCBA] expected?"[73]

In their paranoia, some Chinese became informants for the FBI. But the FBI was frustrated in its effort to obtain evidence that could bring the CHLA to a criminal trial. One New York agency of the FBI reported to Hoover: "During the investigation of this case considerable difficulty was encountered in obtaining specific information from the Chinese interviewed even though they expressed themselves as violently opposed to Communism. They appear by nature to believe that their flat statements characterizing an organization or person as Communist should suffice and questions aimed to develop their reasons are generally fruitless."[74]

In January 1951 the CHLA and *CDN* were placed on the Master Search Warrant by the FBI. Through the search the agency expected to find: "(1) propaganda material of the enemy or insurgents; (2) propaganda material which fosters, encourages or promotes the policies, programs or objectives of the enemy or insurgents; and printing presses, mimeographing machines, or other reproducing media on which such propaganda aforementioned has been or is being prepared; (3) any and all records, including membership and financial records of any organization or group that has been declared subversive or may hereafter be declared subversive by the Attorney General."[75]

In the following years the remaining CHLA members were under strict FBI surveillance. Many were pursued and interrogated by FBI agents. "Many people were frightened by the FBI harassment and investigations," a CHLA member recalled. "A lot withdrew. By the early 1950s, the membership of our organization was reduced to several hundred. We used to have more than two thousand members. We had a hard time."[76]

Those who remained loyal to the CHLA believed that they had not done anything wrong and endured many years of hardship. One CHLA veteran recalled:

> The FBI harassed us for more than twenty years. They could not find anything to indict us, but they kept harassing us. In those years, every week I received two calls from FBI agents. What did they say on the phone? Nothing. They just checked whether you were there. They wanted to cause fear among our members. Also, they harassed us so much that they hoped we would lose our jobs and the organization would be dissolved.
>
> One time I got very angry at an FBI agent. At that time I was working at a wet-wash factory. This FBI guy followed me into the factory. I got angry and shouted at him: "Why do you bother me all the time? Why do you follow me wherever I go?" I did that purposely. I did that in front of the eighty workers in that factory. I wanted to show them I hadn't done anything wrong and I was not afraid of the goddamn FBI. I wanted to show that I was tough. After all, I didn't do anything illegal; I didn't commit any crime; why

should I be afraid? The FBI guy shouted back: "You are a Communist!" I stepped forward and pointed my finger at his nose: "You are a Communist!" He got frustrated. He did not have any evidence to prove that I was a Communist. So I called him a Communist without evidence—in his own way. Eventually he got soft, smiled uglily and said, "Nothing, nothing wrong, Mr. F. Take care of yourself." Then I said, "Take care of your job!" Another time an FBI agent followed me into Mott Street. Before I entered a building, I found this guy following me. I became furious and I was going to beat him up. I shouted: "Goddamn it! Why do you bother me all the time?" My fellows came out of the building and asked, "What happened?" I was going to beat the son of a bitch. He said something like "Not me, not me," and ran away.[77]

The pro-KMT Chinese joined the FBI in a fierce battle against the CHLA's mouthpiece, *CDN*. From 1950 on, the CCBA and the KMT newspapers in New York City told Chinese merchants to withdraw their advertisements from the paper and forced Chinese Americans to cancel their subscriptions. In January 1951 a group of CHLA members organized the Committee to Support the *China Daily News*. In its statement the committee denounced the KMT agents as the "lackeys of the Chiang Kai-shek regime who had suppressed and exploited the Chinese people and, after the downfall of the KMT regime, came to America to suppress and exploit Chinese Americans." Based on the principles of freedom of enterprise, speech, and publication "guaranteed by the law," the committee declared its support for *CDN*, "our own paper."[78]

Since many of the advertisements in the paper were canceled, *CDN* faced severe financial difficulties. The committee launched a donation campaign to support the paper. By July 1951 more than one thousand people had contributed money, and *CDN* received more than fourteen thousand dollars.[79]

The effort of the CCBA and the KMT to destroy *CDN* was aided by the U.S. government's legal action against the paper. In September and October 1951 agents from the Treasury Department visited *CDN* many times and demanded to see its books and records. After the treasury agents indicated their objection, *CDN* refused all advertisements from the PRC's Bank of China. When the paper protested the harassment and "asserted its legal right against further unwarranted inspection," the Treasury Department issued a subpoena. *CDN* complied and submitted its books and records which it had already voluntarily allowed the treasury officials to inspect.[80]

Then, in March 1952, Eugene Moy, editor-in-chief and manager of

CDN, was summoned to appear before the grand jury of the Southern District of New York to testify in regard to an alleged violation of Title 18, No. 371, U.S. Code, the 1917 Trading with the Enemy Act. On April 28, 1952, the grand jury handed down an indictment charging *CDN*, Eugene Moy, Huang Wenyao (former manager of *CDN*), and three CHLA members—Tan Shen, Chen Kangming, and Chen Youyun—with fifty-three counts of violation of the Foreign Assets Control Regulations under the Trading with the Enemy Act.[81] The first eight counts of the indictment concerned the receipts and transfers of credits by the paper for carrying advertisements from the Bank of China and one Hong Kong bank. Counts 9 through 30 charged the three CHLA members with making remittances to China. The rest of the counts, from 31 to 53, listed 23 remittances to China, totaling five thousand dollars, without listing the names of the senders.[82] *CDN* was held responsible for these remittances, even though the paper had no knowledge of them.

The defendants pleaded not guilty. Though their attorney argued that carrying advertisements for the Bank of China was normal business practice, that the paper had received only three hundred dollars for such ads and had no intention of committing any illegal act, and that remitting money to relatives in the home country was a tradition among all immigrants to the United States, the defendants were nevertheless found guilty. The legal battle lasted for more than three years. In 1954 the court fined *CDN* twenty-five thousand dollars, Eugene Moy was sentenced to a two-year jail term, and Chen Kangming and Chen Youyun were each sentenced to a one-year jail term. The charges against Huang Wenyao were dropped. Tan Shen was sentenced to a one-year jail term but was pardoned.[83] In 1955 the U.S. Supreme Court rejected the defendants' appeal and the district court's decision was upheld, though the jail terms for the defendants were modified—Eugene Moy's was reduced to one year, and Chen Kangming and Chen Youyun's to six months. The fine imposed on *CDN* was upheld in full.[84]

From the beginning, the case was perceived by the loyal CHLA members and *CDN* staff as a conspiracy by the KMT and the "American reactionaries" to "destroy the progressive forces in the Chinese community." Since Eugene Moy was *CDN*'s editor-in-chief and had sharply criticized KMT activities in Chinese American communities and the China policy of the U.S. government, and the three CHLA members implicated were important figures in the CHLA-owned Wah Kiu Wet-Wash Factory, the charges against them were seen as aimed at crushing the laundry alliance and its paper.[85] When *CDN*'s appeal for an extension on the payment of the fine was rejected by the court, the paper once again turned to Chinese Americans for support.[86] On November 30, 1955, the paper carried an emergency appeal to the Chinese American community asking for donations.[87] If *CDN* failed to pay the fine by December 16, 1955, it would be closed by court order.

The response from Chinese Americans all over the United States was tremendous. From the very beginning, *CDN* had reported the details of the case, and the Chinese translation of the court documents was printed in the paper to keep the readers informed. Many readers became financial supporters of the paper. Within ten days *CDN* had received more than twenty thousand dollars. On December 15, one day before the deadline on the payment of the fine, the total donation reached twenty-eight thousand dollars, three thousand more than was necessary.[88] The donations came not only from cities where there were large Chinese communities such as New York, San Francisco, Los Angeles, Philadelphia, and Washington, D.C., but also from individual Chinese living in Illinois, Maryland, Massachusetts, Michigan, Missouri, New Jersey, Ohio, Oregon, Virginia, Washington State, and Wisconsin. The amount of the donations varied, ranging from one dollar to seven hundred dollars, and they were contributed by laundrymen, restaurant workers, housewives, merchants, and students. Chinese in Canada, Mexico, Cuba, Venezuela, and El Salvador also sent donations.[89] The warning of the KMT newspaper *Meizhou Ribao* (*The Chinese Journal*) that it was dangerous to donate to *CDN*[90] was apparently ignored by many in the Chinese community.

Many readers wrote to *CDN* to extend their support for the paper and Eugene Moy as well as the two CHLA members and to express their indignation against the political persecution. One reader wrote to Moy from California: "You and *China Daily News* have done a lot for the justice, for the welfare of overseas Chinese in America, and for all people who love democracy and peace. . . . So it is your glory to go to jail; it is not a shame."[91] A group of Canadian Chinese praised Moy as "a brave soldier defending the interests of overseas Chinese."[92] A schoolgirl said in her letter: "My family decided to donate to your paper. My dad contributed $50, my mom $10, my older brother $15, and myself $5. The total is $80. My family entrusted me to write to you. So I am sending you this letter."[93] Some Chinese students also sent donations along with supporting letters.[94]

Many readers stated in their letters that they supported *CDN* because they believed it was part of the "overseas Chinese progressive forces." One reader asserted that "the cause of justice will ultimately succeed."[95]

One self-named "democratic person" said in his letter: "I do not agree completely with your paper's stand. . . . But I hate the KMT agents who oppress overseas Chinese and persecute you. So I am sending two hundred dollars to express my support to your paper. I hope you will continue to fight the KMT agents."[96]

Despite the overwhelming support from Chinese Americans, this case did not arouse much attention in the American public at large. At the beginning of the case, *The New York Times* and other English-language newspapers in New York City reported the sensational charges against *CDN*. But when *CDN* was found guilty in 1955, the American press mentioned the case only in passing. A small group of white Americans organized a "Committee of the Friends of Eugene Moy" to express sympathy and support for *CDN*, but there is little record of it, except for a *CDN* report that the committee held a banquet for Moy on the night of December 13, three days before he began his jail term, and that the next day six members of the committee came to the office of *CDN* "urging the staff of the paper to continue to work for world peace and the long-term friendship between the Chinese and American peoples."[97]

It is interesting to note that Eugene Moy himself, many supporters of *CDN*, and CHLA members I interviewed saw the case as part of their struggle against KMT forces. Before he went to serve his jail term, Moy told his supporters in his *CDN* column that "this paper has been fighting the residual KMT forces for years" and had now "lost one round to them" because of "difficult and dangerous circumstances." But he claimed, "I firmly believe that the progressive forces will overcome the evil forces in the future."[98] This belief was echoed by many readers' letters to the paper in December 1955.

When I asked Chen Youyun to reflect on his experience, he said:

> Let me tell you, I don't want to talk about my experiences in the political persecution too much. It all happened in the past. Although the case was settled in the American court, the thing was much more complicated. You know at that time China was backward, poor, being exploited by imperialists. Why so? Because China had a bad feudal system. To make China rich and powerful, you got to get rid of the feudal system. At that time, Chiang Kai-shek represented the feudal system. So if you wanted to get rid of the feudal system, you had to overthrow Chiang Kai-shek. That's what Mao Tse-tung did. But the United States, at that time, wanted to control East Asia and it supported Chiang Kai-shek. Mao Tse-tung won and both the United States and Chiang lost. But in the United States there were some Chinese who supported Chiang Kai-shek, even after he fled to Taiwan. That's what happened. They wanted to support Chiang Kai-shek, what can you do? Ac-

tually, our case was complicated by the supporters of Chiang Kai-shek and the Kuomintang. They made trouble for us behind the scenes. Now I don't want to talk about it. It happened in the past. I just want to forget it.[99]

Where Is the Gold Mountain?

On August 2, 1954, the FBI installed "technical surveillance" on the telephone at the CHLA headquarters at 191 Canal Street, an action authorized by Hoover.[100] Believing that CHLA officials and members "will converse freely in the Chinese language without fear of being detected," the FBI sought to find out about the CHLA's "pro-Communist activity" and "its activity in relations to the *China Daily News*" through the surveillance, whose length was to be "indefinite."[101] The resulting two reels of recording tape were handled by the FBI's Philadelphia office, and the English translations of the recorded conversations were provided to Hoover and the FBI's New York office.[102]

The FBI investigation and harassment caused many members of the CHLA, as well as the Chinese community, to live in fear. Tan Yumin, the dedicated manager of the Wah Kiu Wet-Wash Factory, became a victim of FBI harassment. One of his friends recalled: "After Eugene Moy went to jail [in December 1955], Tan Yumin could no longer bear the FBI harassments. At that time he was about sixty years old and not in a very good shape. The FBI asked him why he read *China Daily News*, and they asked him the same question again and again. Eventually he broke down. He jumped off the Brooklyn Bridge. His body got stuck in the mud under the river for many days before it finally surfaced."[103]

Only the most loyal members remained in support of the CHLA. In the early 1950s the Quon Shar was dissolved.[104] The Chinese Youth Club, which had been supported by CHLA members and was designated as "affiliated with the CHLA" by the FBI, held a membership meeting on May 27, 1956, and adopted a resolution to dissolve itself.[105]

Some CHLA leaders, members, and supporters went back to China. A few were deported by the U.S. authorities. Zhang Manli, the former business manager of *CDN*, was deported by the Immigration and Naturalization Service in 1956.[106] Chen Ke (Chan Fo), who had joined the CHLA when it was founded in 1933 and served on its Executive Committee several times, recalled his experience:

First the U.S. Immigration Service sent agents to my laundry shop to check my papers. But since I had lived in America for more than seven years and was entitled to permanent residency, they couldn't find anything wrong with my status. So they accused me of reading *China Daily News*. But that's not a crime. . . . Later they charged me with smuggling opium, but they had no evidence. After they failed in all these false accusations, they employed dirty means.

In November 1952, two FBI agents, without giving any reason, asked me to pack and leave with them within three minutes. I phoned my relatives to take care of my laundry shop. They [the FBI agents] brought me to Ellis Island, charged me with illegal entry [into the U.S.]. But when they interrogated me, they always asked me political questions, such as "Do you know what kind of organization is the CHLA?" "What kind of newspaper is the *China Daily News*? . . . Do you know that it propagandizes for the Communist Party?" I gave them simple answers. Later they asked me directly: "Which one is better, in your opinion, the Kuomintang or the Communist Party?" I replied: "Of course the Communist Party is better! I don't know what's good about the KMT! I only know that in new China there is no opium, no gambling, and everyone has a job."

. . . One year later I was released, but had to report to Ellis Island every week, and any time they called me I had to go. Only a few months later the FBI arrested me again. I hired a lawyer and paid him $120, but he was silent in the court. I became helpless. In May 1954, FBI agents escorted me to San Francisco, put me on a ship sailing for Hong Kong. One month later I arrived in Hong Kong, and was sent to Shenzhen immediately. I was penniless at that moment, and my laundry shop in America sold for only $400.[107]

Some CHLA members returned to China voluntarily either to take part in building a new China or to avoid potential problems in the United States after the outbreak of the Korean War. Two former CHLA leaders found positions in the central government of the PRC. Tang Mingzhao (Thomas Tang), former CHLA English Secretary and manager of *CDN* from 1940 to 1950, when he secretly returned to China, became a deputy director of the Liaison Department of the Committee for Resisting the U.S.A. and Aiding Korea in October 1950. Later he was elected a deputy for overseas Chinese to the first National People's Congress in 1954, and in the 1970s he was a member of China's mission to the United Nations and served as undersecretary-general of the UN from 1972 to 1979.[108] His daughter, Nancy Tang, born in Brooklyn,[109] became an English interpreter for Mao Tse-tung and served in that capacity when Richard Nixon visited China in 1972. Lin Tang, who once served on the CHLA Executive Committee, returned to China in 1949 and became a member of the Overseas Chinese Affairs Commission of the central government.[110] Several CHLA leaders and active members went back to Taishan, the home county of many Chinese Americans, and served in the local government. Chen Houfu, the CHLA's man of ideas in the late 1940s, returned to China in 1951 and became a deputy magistrate in Taishan County's government.[111] Tan Wei and Tan Guangpan, both of whom had served on the CHLA Executive Committee in the 1940s, became members of the Taishan Returned Overseas Chinese Association after they went back to China in the early 1950s.[112] Others chose to live in Guangzhou, as did Lei Zhuofeng, one of the founders of the CHLA, and Fang Fu'er, who made significant contributions to the success of the Wah Kiu Wet-Wash Factory.[113]

Some returned CHLA members helped to cultivate a positive image of the new CCP regime among Chinese Americans through refuting rumors spread by KMT agents. In their propaganda campaign against the CCP government, some KMT newspapers either exaggerated or distorted facts. For example, the KMT newspapers in New York once reported that the city of Guangzhou was "occupied by 100,000 Russians." Lei Zhuofeng, who went back to China in 1953 and attended a meeting of Returned Overseas Chinese in Guangzhou, made a special reference to this piece of propaganda in a letter to his friends in New York: "I haven't seen a single Russian or any other foreigner in the last two months since I came back to Guangzhou."[114] In addition, these returned Chinese Americans reported that gambling, opium smoking, and prostitution— the traditional vices of the overseas Chinese communities in Taishan and other counties— had been eliminated by the new government.

During the Resisting the U.S.A. and Aiding Korea campaign (1950– 53) the new government used the returned CHLA members in its effort to root out the "imperialist American influence" in the overseas Chinese communities in Guangdong. On arriving in Taishan in early 1951, Chen Houfu was invited by the local government to give talks to the relatives of overseas Chinese about Chinese life in America. At a time when Chinese and Americans were fighting each other in an undeclared war in Korea, Chen "exposed the brutal nature of American imperialism by citing vivid cases of Chinese Americans being abused by American imperialists" and by "describing his personal experiences." In two months Chen spoke to audiences of more than thirty-five thousand, and these talks were printed in the Taishan local newspapers and *Nanfang Ribao*, a provincial CCP organ. It was reported that Chen's speeches were "greatly welcomed" and "many relatives of overseas Chinese began to change their American-philic and American-phobic attitudes."[115] Along the same lines, Situ Meitang, who had lived in the United States for seventy years and served as a leader of the On Leong Tong and the Zhigongtang, two powerful Chinese American organizations, and who returned to China in 1949 to become a member of the central government's Overseas Chinese Affairs Commission, published a series of articles in *Guangmin Ribao* (a national newspaper based in Beijing), describing his painful personal experiences in the United States and all the injustices that Chinese Americans suffered. These articles later were published as a book entitled *I Bitterly Hate Imperialist America.*[116]

Only a small proportion of the CHLA members returned to China. Most stayed in the United States and dropped out of the CHLA in the early 1950s. The membership of the CHLA shrank from about two thousand to about three hundred in the early 1950s.[117] From 1949 on, the CHLA became one of the strongest supporters of the People's Republic of China in the United States. But if these laundrymen supported the PRC as wholeheartedly as they claimed and had suffered so much in the United States, why did so few of them go back to China? One possible answer is the harsh policy of the CCP toward the overseas Chinese during the land reform movement (1950–52), which alienated many Chinese Americans, including former CHLA members who had once sincerely supported the CCP.

The CCP's land reform of the early 1950s was an attempt to eliminate the parasitic gentry-landlord class and to increase agricultural productivity. Originally, the CCP adopted a moderate policy, but the Korean War radicalized the movement. From 1951 on, while the Korean War was going on, land reform was often carried out in a harsh manner and landlords were physically abused or summarily executed. In Guangdong many relatives of overseas Chinese were classified as "overseas Chinese landlords," and their land and other properties were confiscated.

The radical land reform frustrated the remaining CHLA members as well as other supporters of the CCP government and provided perfect ammunition for the new regime's enemies. In the KMT agents' campaign to attack the CCP's land reform, a 1952 pamphlet that provided detailed, though exaggerated, descriptions of the sufferings of the relatives of overseas Chinese in Taishan County after the CCP took power was especially useful. The pamphlet was edited by someone who was apparently pro-KMT and gave himself the pen name Hei Yan (Black Swallow). It described in detail "the crimes that the Communist bandits committed in Taishan": the "brutal slaughter of a large number of people loyal to the KMT," "the detention of merchants," "the brain wash campaign," "extortion," "imposition of heavy taxes and numerous forced donations," and various forms of torture. It also depicted horrifying scenes of "mass class struggle meetings" in which landlords and local despots were summarily executed; the means that the CCP cadres employed to exploit the relatives of overseas Chinese or returned overseas Chinese in the name of reforming their "parasitic lifestyle"; and the ways the Communists "destroyed traditional [Chinese] culture and ethical principles." To add to its authenticity, the pamphlet provided a long list of the names of the people who had been killed, fined, tortured, detained, persecuted, or had their properties confiscated or had committed suicide.[118] This kind of pamphlet, along with KMT newspaper propaganda in the United States, information passed on by those who escaped from China, and family letters received by many Chinese Americans which reported the confiscation of their land and other properties, helped to create a negative opinion of the CCP government in the Chinese American community.

In fact, many Chinese American families did suffer during the land reform movement in Guangdong Province in 1952. The CCP made gross mistakes in dealing with the overseas Chinese. One contributing factor was the CCP Central Committee's persistent reliance on cadres who came from the north to direct the land reform. These northern cadres had no knowledge of the local history nor did they speak the local dialect. They ruthlessly labeled the overseas Chinese families "landlords" or "exploiting elements" just because these families had a piece of land or a western-style building. These northern cadres failed, or at least made no effort, to understand that the land or buildings had been purchased with the lifetime savings of laundrymen who had worked more than sixteen hours a day in the United States for thirty or forty years, and that after the catastrophic famine of 1943, many Chinese Americans purposely bought a piece of land in hopes of sparing their families starvation in the future.[119] Some CCP officials forced the relatives of overseas Chinese to ask their fathers or sons to send money home in order to avoid severe punishments. Some native Guangdong officials, such as Fang Fang, understood the situation better and tried to protect the interests of ordinary overseas Chinese, but they were dismissed from office as "rightists" who were "soft on the landlords." The narrow-minded northern cadres also tended to suspect anyone who had overseas connections during a time when China's national security seemed to be threatened by American intervention in the Korean War. To root out any potential internal disturbances that might intensify the national security crisis, they preferred a quick finish to the earlier, gradualist policy. The result was an indiscriminate, harsh policy toward anyone who owned property, which hurt many overseas Chinese families and caused tremendous resentment. Even in the 1970s and 1980s the CCP continued to take measures to remedy the damage, physical and mental.[120]

The Korean War, the FBI harassments, the pressure from the CCBA and other conservative forces, as well as the radical land reform in China, combined to create a situation that led many members to drop out of the CHLA. Some may have left the organization for fear of being persecuted by American authorities, for resentment against China's radical land reform policy, or for both reasons. Although many Chinese Americans seemed to be sympathetic toward the CHLA and *CDN*, as indicated by their donations to *CDN* in 1955, only a few were willing to keep their affiliation with the CHLA. Those who chose to remain vowed to continue their fight for equality, dignity, and justice.

What about the injustice that their relatives suffered during the land reform campaign in China? Why should the relatives of laboring overseas Chinese be classified as "revolutionary targets" and "class enemies"? An examination of these loyal CHLA members' discussions of the subject published in *CDN* suggests that they accepted the CCP argument that it was historically necessary to have such a social revolution in the countryside to liberate the peasants, the majority of the Chinese population. They believed that without such a social revolution it would be difficult for China to industrialize its economy; and without industrialization, China would have no real national independence.[121] In 1951 *CDN* printed a series of reports by Situ Meitang on his inspections of the land reform in those communities in Guangdong populated largely by families of overseas Chinese. These inspections were arranged by the PRC central government and personally approved by Mao Tse-tung. In his reports Situ emphasized that poor peasants needed and supported the land reform; he cited many cases of the exploitation and bullying of poor peasants by landlords, including the relatives of overseas Chinese; and he concluded that land reform was absolutely needed and that the CCP had accomplished the revolutionary goal of "land to the tiller" first set by Sun Yat-sen.[122] But as Situ Meitang's personal secretary recalled thirty-five years later, Situ had actually agonized over the complaints his overseas Chinese friends had made against the radical land reform and the "correct line" that he believed he should follow. Unable to modify the radical land reform policy and protect the interests of his fellow Chinese Americans, Situ Meitang comforted himself privately by saying that in a great revolutionary movement, mistakes and personal sacrifices were inevitable; if the movement benefited the majority of the people and served the purpose of building a strong and independent country, "I will support it."[123] The loyal CHLA members seemed to share this logic and mentality. As one of them stated, "How exciting to see that tens of thousand people became happy over a few landlords' sorrow."[124] This attitude may help explain how they were able to endure the personal sacrifices and hardships they and their families suffered during the radical land reform movement and other political campaigns launched by the CCP.

To those who chose to stick with the CHLA in the 1950s, the political persecution that they suffered in the United States, which led to their isolation not only in American society at large but also in the Chinese American community, may have helped to strengthen their loyalty to the PRC. In a world that was rapidly polarizing between the socialist and capitalist camps during the cold war years, the CHLA chose to support the PRC. In time the organization became ideologically rigid and completely changed its opinion about American democracy, which its members no longer considered an appropriate model for China. During the 1952 national elections *CDN* issued editorials attacking American democracy. "The American election system is actually not democratic. Elections are completely manipulated by the Democratic Party and the Republican Party, the two political parties of the monopoly capitalists. . . . Under the capitalist system, the American people are actually deprived of all rights and freedom to vote," the paper asserted.[125]

Meanwhile, the remaining CHLA members supported the PRC uncritically. The PRC became a symbol of Chinese nationalism and national independence, of ordinary people's power, though it did not extend any substantial aid to this group of loyal supporters. The irony here is that once the PRC became an abstract symbol of all the principles for which the laundrymen had fought, these CHLA members lost the critical spirit that some of them had demonstrated in their condemnation of the KMT regime in the 1940s. They accepted the PRC so unconditionally that they even tried to defend those CCP policies that harmed their relatives and their former allies. They dismissed all criticisms of the PRC as "propaganda" and "slander," as one article published in *CDN* claimed: "Numerous facts of the past demonstrated a truth that all the rumors and slanders spread by imperialists and the KMT-supporters were contrary to the facts. Anything that they say is black, it must be white; anything they say is bad must be good."[126] A blind faith in and passionate defense of the new regime replaced any meaningful discussion of how to build a political system that represented the interests of the people.

Conclusion

Two important CHLA members committed suicide in the 1950s. Tan Yumin, the manager of the Wah Kiu Wet-Wash Factory, killed himself jumping off the Brooklyn Bridge because he could no longer endure the constant FBI harassment. Tan Lian'ai, who served as the English Secretary of the CHLA for more than ten years in the 1940s, returned to China after the founding of the People's Republic and became a professor at Zhongshan University. During the 1957 antirightist campaign, after being labeled a "rightist and anti-party element," he chose to end his life rather than live in humiliation.[1]

These two tragic suicides reflected a sad aspect of the CHLA's experiences. Tan Yumin's death was triggered by the witch-hunting hysteria in the McCarthy years in the United States, and it symbolized a disillusion with American democracy. The death of Tan Lian'ai was caused by the witch-hunting hysteria of the antirightist campaign in China. He perhaps died confused. He went back to China to avoid possible political persecution in the United States, but he did not fit into the new Chinese society as he had expected to. "His outspoken style brought him political trouble, and his experiences of living overseas [in the United States] made him a target of suspicions. His life became so miserable. The 'rightist' label was but the last straw."[2]

In the 1950s the CHLA lost not only a large portion of its membership but also the political influence it had enjoyed earlier. Conservatives reaffirmed their domination of the Chinese community.[3] The FBI surveillance of the CHLA was not lifted until the late 1970s (its files were declassified in 1986), and the alliance was forced to refrain from expressing political opinions on many issues concerning China and U.S.-China relations. Its newspaper, CDN, even abolished its editorial column, reprinting instead

Kung Fu stories from Hong Kong newspapers and other nonpolitical entertainment. Yet the organization continued to exist, and its core members still upheld the principles they had fought for in the 1930s and 1940s. The CHLA participated in the civil rights movement of the 1960s and 1970s and continued to take active part in the Chinese American struggle for equality. Overcoming many political and financial difficulties, the alliance managed to continue publishing *CDN*, and it maintained the Wah Kiu Wet-Wash Factory to support its members. As an independent organization, the CHLA served as a symbol for forces contending against the traditional merchant elite in the New York Chinese community. Nevertheless, by and large, the CHLA was once again reduced to the level of mere survival. Even within the Chinese community, it was on the periphery.

The CHLA experiences, when examined in broad historical context, point to some new ways to think about the meaning of the Chinese American experience. The material contributions of the Chinese to the agricultural development in the West and to the building of the transcontinental railroad have been documented;[4] their exclusion and isolation have been analyzed.[5] But a systematic examination of the opinions of Chinese Americans in regard to their position in American society is needed to understand how Chinese American experiences fit into the larger picture. John Higham has argued that the different experiences of ethnic groups in the United States suggest a process of "pluralistic integration." Despite their diversity, all these immigrant groups, especially their American-born children, had a common culture in the United States.[6]

The fundamental difference between the Chinese and other ethnic groups was that only the Chinese were excluded explicitly by name from the United States from 1882 to 1943. Every aspect of Chinese life in the United States was influenced by the exclusion acts. Any comparative study must give serious consideration to this fact. Compared with the "alienation" felt by other ethnic groups in the migratory process, as defined by Oscar Handlin,[7] the sufferings of Chinese were not only multiple but also involuntary. From the very beginning, however, Chinese protested the exclusionary policies and persistently demanded equal treatment.[8] As one Chinese American wrote in 1885:

Sir:

A paper was presented to me yesterday for inspection, and I found it to be specially drawn up for subscription among my countrymen toward the Pedestal Fund of the Bartholdi Statue of Liberty. Seeing that the heading is an appeal to American citizens, to their love of country and liberty, I feel that my countrymen and myself are honored in being thus appealed to as citizens in the cause of liberty. But the word liberty makes me think of the fact that this country is the land of liberty for men of all nations except the Chinese. I consider it an insult to us Chinese to call on us to contribute toward building in this land a pedestal for a statue of liberty. That statue represents liberty holding a torch which lights the passage of those of all nations who come into this country. But are the Chinese allowed to come? As for the Chinese who are here, are they allowed to enjoy liberty as men of all other nationalities enjoy it? Are they allowed to go about everywhere free from the insults, abuses, assaults, wrongs, and injuries from which men of other nationalities are free?[9]

The CHLA carried on this tradition of protesting against exclusionary and discriminatory policies and demanding equal treatment. A basic pattern of the CHLA's response to Chinese exclusion and isolation was to hold American society up to the democratic values and principles embodied in the Declaration of Independence and the U.S. Constitution. Eugene Moy, editor-in-chief of *CDN*, once characterized the nature of the Chinese American struggle in the United States in one phrase: "I am a human being too."[10] The CHLA's and *CDN*'s call for repeal of the Chinese exclusion acts summarily expressed a deep desire to be treated as equal members in American society, a fundamental right to which these Chinese Americans believed they were entitled, premised on their understanding of basic democratic values.

If one accepts John Higham's notion of pluralistic integration, in which all ethnic groups have a common culture of which democratic values are a part, then one may say that the CHLA's identification with basic democratic values is a significant expression of its members' integration. In that sense, protesting against exclusion and discrimination was in fact the beginning of their integration into American society.

It was necessity that forced them to protest, rather than quietly assimilate, for the historical reality is that, while the CHLA—whether philosophically and ideologically or for the sake of political expediency— chose to identify positively with the basic democratic values generally upheld in American society, its members were physically, politically, socially, and economically kept at the periphery of that society. Before 1943 the legal system denied them the right to be naturalized, and the social and political conditions in the larger society rendered their demands for equal rights isolated voices. The Chinese laundrymen's marginal position limited the scope of their efforts and accomplishments. Their voices were ignored in the past, just as the voices of black slaves were ignored; nevertheless, their testimony can make a constructive and instructive contribution to a more sophisticated understanding of American democracy. In short, Chinese American history is part of the American past.

The CHLA's identification with democracy was reflected not only in its rhetoric, but also in its efforts to follow democratic principles within the organization and to promote democratic reforms in the New York Chinese community in the 1940s. Thus, the CHLA's vigorous effort to change the power structure in the Chinese immigrant community, though a failure, poses a question, for recent theoretical and methodological approaches tend to emphasize the persistence of Old World traditions among ethnic groups and contend that immigrant institutions helped reduce the newcomers' sense of alienation. By paying attention to the heritage of different ethnic groups, the new social historians have found that it played a positive role in maintaining their ethnic identities.[11] But one must be cautious in applying this explanation to the Chinese immigrant experience. The U.S. government-sanctioned exclusionary policies made the isolation of the Chinese community fundamentally different from the relative autonomy of other ethnic groups.[12] While the latter found positive meanings in their communities' autonomy, few Chinese had reason to cherish their isolation. As the discussions in this book show, in a situation of forced isolation the functions of the Chinese immigrant institutions varied—some provided assistance to the laborers, while others mainly served the interests of the elite and abused the common people. The CHLA was founded in 1933 because the New York Chinese laundrymen felt that neither the bona fide mutual-aid organization (gongsi fang) nor the elite-dominated CCBA adequately protected their interests. Once organized, these humble Chinese laborers, who had been passive and silent in the past, as described in many books, consistently challenged the authority of the CCBA. They saw the elite-dominated association as a corrupt organization—which had inherited the "feudal traditions" from China and whose power was enhanced by American institutionalized racism—that stood in the way of the Chinese struggle for equality in American society. Therefore, from the perspective of the CHLA's members, an immigrant institution such as the CCBA that symbolized Old World traditions could provide no solution to their problems but was itself a problem. Only a democratic reform of the power structure in the Chinese community in America, as the CHLA proposed in the 1940s, could be the solution, the laundrymen argued.

As a new type of immigrant institution that vowed to protect the interests of its members, the CHLA never claimed to preserve Old World traditions. Rather, the organization was eager to change the way in which power was distributed in Chinatown according to traditional Chinese values, and it actively promoted in the Chinese American community the democratic and progressive ideals that the Chinese laundrymen had learned in America. Ironically, the CHLA's efforts were largely ignored by the larger society except for a few white leftists, while the conditions in the larger society helped to perpetuate the traditional power structure in the Chinese American community. A cruel fact here is that the larger society did not nurture the nascent democracy in the Chinese community, and those Chinese Americans who wished to live in a democratic way were forced to put up with the traditional institutions they criticized. The exclusionary policies and this forced isolation constituted a double rejection of these Chinese Americans' demands for a decent life.

Therefore, the general hostility to or neglect of the Chinese in the host society largely determined how far the CHLA and similar organizations could carry out their plan to create a new mode of life according to democratic values.[13] Lacking the resources to change its environment substantially, the CHLA often fell back on the idea of ethnic solidarity. But as the discussion in Chapter Six suggests, using the language of ethnic solidarity to defend the interests of its members was only a strategy that the CHLA employed in opposing the dominant merchants. It should not be misconstrued as a manifestation of the persistent influence of traditional Chinese culture. As the CHLA members' own arguments indicate, their struggle against the CCBA and the Chinese power laundry owners was partially inspired by their understanding of democratic values.

We also learn from the CHLA stories that another motivating force driving the CHLA to identify with basic democratic values and principles was its faith in their applicability to China. As I pointed out in Chapter Five, the CHLA's criticism of the KMT government represented a new form of overseas Chinese nationalism, characterized by an awareness of the basic rights of the people and a new way to judge the homeland government according to democratic values.[14] These Chinese laundrymen not only donated money to help China resist Japan's invasion, but also raised questions about why China was poor, weak, humiliated by foreign powers, and, as a result, unable to protect the interests of overseas Chinese. They pointed to "feudalism" and an undemocratic government as the causes. Even their decision about whether or not to return home, a long-held Chinese immigrant dream, was influenced by this desire for democracy in China. Although concern for the homeland is not a phenomenon unique to Chinese Americans,[15] the CHLA's history suggests that the laundrymen's experiences in the United States influenced their perceptions of their relationship to their native country.

Persecution by the U.S. authorities in the 1950s produced a profound disillusion about as well as a cynicism toward American democracy among the CHLA's members, in one of the cruelest ironies in American history. These Chinese laundrymen do not reject democracy—even now old CHLA members love to praise the organization as "the most democratic organization in the Chinese community."[16] But they regard the persecution they suffered as proof of the hypocrisy of Americans. Out of their experiences they developed an accumulated distrust of the U.S. government and the meaning of American democracy. We may compare this sociopsychological phenomenon to black separatism, for both are the result of the discriminatory policies of the larger society. The Chinese laundrymen's experiences suggest that to live as an equal of white Americans is an uphill battle for minorities. Democracy is not something ready-made for everyone to enjoy. One has to fight for one's rights. And sometimes, even when one fights, one may not win.

It is understandable why those CHLA members who had to deal with FBI interrogations once or twice a month for more than twenty years became cynical about American democracy. With this cynicism came an unquestioned acceptance of their homeland, a blind faith in the People's Republic of China. Instead of judging the new regime under the Chinese Communist Party according to democratic values, the CHLA, as well as *CDN*, swallowed the party's propaganda and tried to justify its actions. In the beginning, however, some Chinese Americans did express skepticism about the nature of the PRC government. One reader by the name of Liang Chengkang wrote this letter to *CDN*:

> To the editor:
> [Now] newspapers often carry the slogan "Long Live Chairman Mao." But the phrase "long live" came from the feudal times during which emperors hoped to live forever so they demanded that people wish them long lives. Since Chairman Mao is a great leader of the people, is it proper to wish him "long live?"[17]

The editor of *CDN* answered in this apologetic manner:

> The phrase "long live" was monopolized by emperors only after the Han Dynasty. Like the land, it originally belonged to the people but was grabbed by the feudal class. . . . Now everything has been returned to the people, and

it is not strange that the phrase ["long live"] used for celebration has been returned to the people.

In the past a few people were forced to shout "long live the emperor"; now it is the liberated people who freely and happily hail "Long Live Chairman Mao" to express their sincere respect and love of their leader.[18]

In subsequent years the *CDN* staff and the CHLA both followed this kind of logic in discussing the PRC. The CHLA found comfort in its emotional ties with the homeland, which, after the founding of the PRC in 1949, was supposedly a country of the people. *CDN* did not change its stand of supporting the Chinese government until April 1989, when the prodemocracy movement broke out in Beijing. The new manager of the newspaper, a young man from Hong Kong, chose to sympathize with the students and condemned the government's brutal suppression of a peaceful protest movement. But the CHLA adopted a different position. It issued a statement denouncing the manager's action as "slandering the motherland" and "deviating from the original purpose of *China Daily News*."[19] Obviously, the CHLA chose to identify with the current regime in China. What an irony! The Chinese laundrymen's experiences and reflections could have been very inspiring to the Chinese students fighting for basic democratic rights, but the painful memory of their own futile struggle for those rights in American society led these Chinese Americans to embrace their homeland uncritically, oblivious to the younger generation's desire for democracy in China. History is certainly full of ironies and contradictions. But perhaps its contradictory nature makes the study of the past all the more instructive.

Notes

Introduction

1. See James B. Gardner and George Rollie Adams, eds., *Ordinary People and Everyday Life: Perspectives on the New Social History* (Nashville, Tenn.: American Association for State and Local History, 1983).

2. Many recent studies in immigrant/ethnic history have explored the immigrant press. See, for example, Robert Mirak, *Torn between Two Lands: Armenians in America, 1890 to World War I* (Cambridge, Mass.: Harvard University Press, 1983).

3. Ronald Takaki, *Strangers from a Different Shore: A History of Asian Americans* (Boston: Little, Brown, 1989), p. 8.

4. In recent years some authors have made an effort to change the trend. See, for example, Diane Mei Lin Mark and Ginger Chih, *A Place Called Chinese America* (Dubuque, Iowa: Kendall/Hull, 1982); Ruthanne Lum McCunn, *Chinese American Portraits: Personal Histories, 1828–1988* (San Francisco: Chronicle Books, 1988).

5. Paul C. P. Siu, *The Chinese Laundryman: A Study of Social Isolation* (New York: New York University Press, 1987).

6. Paul C. P. Siu, "The Sojourner," *American Journal of Sociology* 58 (July 1952): 34–44. The quotation is from p. 34.

7. John K. W. Tchen, "Editor's Introduction," in Siu, *Chinese Laundryman*, p. xxxii. Franklin Ng has discussed the applicability of Siu's sojourner concept and surveyed similar experiences of other ethnic groups in his essay "The Sojourner, Return Migration, and Immigration History," in *Chinese America: History and Perspectives 1987* (San Francisco: Chinese Historical Society of America, 1987), pp. 53–71.

8. Rose Hum Lee, *The Chinese in the United States* (Hong Kong: Hong Kong University Press, 1960).

9. See, for example, ibid., p. 140. Other scholars who are influenced by Lee's interpretative approach also pass judgment on the impact of Chinese culture on Chinese Americans without the support of careful empirical research. For example, Betty Lee Sung explains the low status of Chinese laundrymen in American society in terms of their cultural "inertia" or "indifference" in her *Mountain of Gold: The Story of the Chinese in America* (New York: Macmillan, 1967), p.

196. Works of this school include Shien Woo Kung, *Chinese in American Life: Some Aspects of Their History, Status, Problems, and Contributions* (Seattle: University of Washington Press, 1962); Mely Giok-lan Tan, *The Chinese in the United States: Social Mobility and Assimilation*, Asian Folklore and Social Life Monographs, vol. 21 (Taipei: Orient Cultural Service, 1971); and Melford S. Weiss, *Valley City: A Chinese Community in America* (Cambridge, Mass.: Schenkman, 1974). Stanford Lyman, in his *Chinese Americans* (New York: Random House, 1974), questions the adequacy of the assimilationist approach, but his discussions of Chinese Americans are also based more on sociological theoretical models than on historical empirical studies, and he relies mainly on secondary sources in English.

10. Peter Kwong, *Chinatown, New York: Labor and Politics, 1930–1950* (New York: Monthly Review Press, 1979).

11. Ibid., p. 148.

12. Other works dealing with the Chinese community of New York share these limitations. See, for example, Chia-ling Kuo, *Social and Political Change in New York's Chinatown: The Role of Voluntary Associations* (New York: Praeger, 1977), and Bernard Wong, *Patronage, Brokerage, Entrepreneurship and the Chinese Community of New York* (New York: AMS Press, 1988).

13. The Chinese exclusion laws include a series of acts passed by the United States Congress: Act of May 4, 1882, 22 United States Statutes at Large 60, which suspended the immigration of Chinese laborers to the United States for ten years and prohibited the naturalization of Chinese in this country; Act of July 5, 1884, 23 United States Statutes at Large 116, an amendment to the 1882 act; Act of September 13, 1888, 25 United States Statutes at Large 476, which prohibited a Chinese laborer from reentering the country unless he had "a lawful wife, child, or parent in the United States or property therein of the value of one thousand dollars, or debts of like amount due him and pending settlement"; Act of October 1, 1888, 25 United States Statutes at Large 504, also called the Scott Act, which was more restrictive in prohibiting the reentry of any Chinese laborers who had departed from the United States; Act of May 5, 1892, 27 United States Statutes at Large 25, also called the Geary Act; Amendatory Act of November 3, 1893, 28 United States at Large 7, also called the McCreary Amendment to the Geary Act; Act of April 9, 1902, 32 United States Statutes at Large 176; Act of April 27, 1904, 33 United States Statutes at Large 394, which extended all laws "regulating, suspending, or prohibiting the coming of Chinese" then in force indefinitely. All these Chinese exclusion acts were repealed by the Act of December 13, 1943, 57 United States Statutes at Large 600. For analyses of these laws' impact on the Chinese community as well as the Chinese reactions to them, see Sucheng Chan, ed., *Entry Denied: Exclusion and the Chinese Community in America, 1882–1943* (Philadelphia: Temple University Press, 1991), and Shih-shan Henry Tsai, *China and the Overseas Chinese in the United States, 1868–1911* (Fayetteville: University of Arkansas Press, 1983).

Chapter One

1. The best discussion of the subject is John K. W. Tchen, "New York Chinese: The Nineteenth-Century Pre-Chinatown Settlement," in *Chinese America: History and Perspectives 1990* (San Francisco: Chinese Historical Society of America and Asian American Studies, San Francisco State University, 1990), pp. 157–92.

2. Louis J. Beck, *New York's Chinatown: An Historical Presentation of Its People and Places* (New York: Bohemia Publishers, 1898), p. 57.

3. Wong Chin Foo, "The Chinese in New York," *Cosmopolitan* (New York: Cosmopolitan Magazine Co.) 5 (March–October 1888): 297–311. The quotation is from p. 297. In another article Wong made the same estimate that there were ten thousand Chinese in the city of New York, and he stated that over 90 percent of them were in the hand laundry business. See Wong, "The Chinese in the United States," *The Chautauquan* 9 (October 1888–July 1889): 215–17.

4. U.S. Department of Commerce, Bureau of the Census, *Thirteenth Census of the United States Taken in the Year 1910*, Population (Washington, D.C.: Government Printing Office, 1914), Volume 1: General Report and Analysis, pp. 210, 226; Volume 4: Occupation Statistics, pp. 433, 497.

5. For various reasons, there have been great differences between the number of Chinese listed in the United States census and the estimates given by contemporary observers and the Chinese themselves. Usually, the Chinese estimate was larger than the number given in the census. That is especially true in the case of New York, a port of entry and departure. As early as 1897, an observer of New York Chinatown noticed this problem: "The Chinese population of New York is a matter of conjecture. It is well known that it is next to impossible to obtain a correct census of these people, since their ignorance of our customs and doings makes them extremely suspicious and uncommunicative. The United States census in 1890 placed the number at 2,048. But a few months later a private canvass of the laundries and of the stores of Chinatown—not including the buildings there used as residences, and which shelter many hundreds—showed a population of upward of 6,000. The Chinese themselves estimate it at from 8,000 to 10,000. When the certificates of residence were issued in 1894, over 6,000 Chinese registered from one district alone. At the Morning Star Mission, every Sunday for three years past, we have distributed in an hour from 2,000 to 4,000 copies of the 'Chinese News' and that only in Chinatown. There has been nothing to cause either a great accession or diminution in the Chinese colony during the last five years, and hence it seems to me only a matter of justice to estimate this population at the exceedingly reasonable figure of 5,000." Helen F. Clark, "The Chinese of New York," *The Century* (New York: Century Co.) 53 (November 1896–April 1897): 104–15. The quotation is from the note on p. 111. Louis J. Beck recorded 8,000 Chinese laundrymen in the New York area in his study, *New York's Chinatown*, p. 58. As late as 1933 a report of the New York City

Department of Licenses indicated that even that department did not have an accurate number of the Chinese laundrymen in the city. The report estimated that there were 15,000 laundries in the city, of which 6,000 to 7,500 were owned by Chinese, a figure based on the estimate of "representatives of Chinese trade organizations." See City Department of Licenses, *Report for June 30, 1933*, Box 633, Collection of John O'Brien, 1922–33, Municipal Archives, New York.

6. Thomas Chinn, Him Mark Lai, and Philip Choy, eds., *A History of the Chinese in California* (San Francisco: Chinese Historical Society of America, 1971), p. 63; Paul Siu, *The Chinese Laundryman: A Study of Social Isolation* (New York: New York University Press, 1987), pp. 45–46.

7. *Newark Sunday Call*, October 9, 1932.

8. Ted Brush, "Chinese Labor in North Jersey," *North Jersey Highlander* (North Jersey Highlander Historical Society) (Spring 1973): 19–20. Brush stated that "Harvey brought in a total of one hundred and sixty Chinese. In 1873 there were only seventy-five left" (p. 20).

9. *Newark Sunday Call*, October 9, 1932.

10. Wong, "Chinese in New York," p. 297.

11. Fred DeArmond, *The Laundry Industry* (New York: Harper & Brothers, 1950), p. 208.

12. Wong, "Chinese in New York," p. 298.

13. Ibid.

14. DeArmond, *Laundry Industry*, p. 16.

15. Siu, *Chinese Laundryman*, p. 92.

16. Wong, "Chinese in New York," p. 298. For a detailed discussion of the function of "whey" (*hui*; spelled "*Woi*" in Siu's book) in Chicago's Chinese community in the twentieth century, see Siu, *Chinese Laundryman*, pp. 92–96.

17. Fang Fu'er and Zhang Manli, "Niuyue Huaqiao xiyiguan de bianqian" [Changes in New York's Chinese hand laundries], recorded by Luo Jirui, *Guangzhou wenshi ziliao (xuanji)* [Selections of cultural historical materials, Guangzhou] (Guangzhou: Guangdong Renmin Chubanshe), no. 23, 1981, pp. 186–203.

18. Beck, *New York's Chinatown*, p. 62. For a detailed description of and insights into partnerships in the Chinese hand laundry business, see Siu, *Chinese Laundryman*, pp. 77–85.

19. Beck, *New York's Chinatown*, p. 59.

20. Clark, "Chinese of New York," p. 110.

21. Beck, *New York's Chinatown*, p. 62.

22. Wong, "Chinese in New York," p. 300; also see Beck, *New York's Chinatown*, pp. 57–58.

23. Clark, "Chinese of New York," p. 106.

24. Quoted in Tchen, "New York Chinese," p. 174.

25. Ibid., pp. 174–75.

26. Fang and Zhang, "Niuyue Huaqiao xiyiguan," pp. 193–94.

27. Interview with Mr. Yang, Brooklyn, New York, March 28, 1988.

28. Y. K. Chu, *Meiguo Huaqiao gaishi* [History of the Chinese people in America] (New York: China Times, 1975), p. 116.

29. Liu Pei Chi, *Meiguo Huaqiao shi* [A history of the Chinese in the United States of America] (Taipei: Limin Wenhua Shiye Gongsi, 1976), p. 224; the spellings of the names of these organizations are from *Chinese Commercial Directory of United States, Eastern Section, 1925–26* (New York: Chinese General Information Bureau, 1925).

30. See Stanford M. Lyman, *Chinese Americans* (New York: Random House, 1974), pp. 31–32.

31. Ho Ping-ti, *Zhongguo huiguan shilun* [A historical survey of landsmannschaften in China] (Taipei: Xuesheng Shuju, 1966), p. 11.

32. Dou Jiliang, *Tongxiang zhuzhi zhi yanjiu* [A study of the district association] (Shanghai: n.p., 1943), p. 71; Ho, *Zhongguo huiguan shilun*, p. 11.

33. Dou, *Tongxiang zhuzhi zhi yanjiu*, pp. 67–87.

34. Liu, *Meiguo Huaqiao shi*, p. 150; William Hoy, *The Chinese Six Companies* (San Francisco: Chinese Consolidated Benevolent Association, 1942), p. 2.

35. Liu, *Meiguo Huaqiao shi*, p. 204.

36. Rose Hum Lee, *The Chinese in the United States of America* (Hong Kong: Hong Kong University Press, 1960), p. 147; Charles C. Dobie, *San Francisco's Chinatown* (New York: Appleton-Century, 1936), p. 124; Yuk Ow, Him Mark Lai, and Philip Choy, *Lu Mei San-i Tsung Hui Kuan Chien Shih* [A history of the Sam Yup Benevolent Association in the U.S., 1850–1974] (San Francisco: Sam Yup Benevolent Association, 1975), pp. 126, 129.

37. As early as 1936 a Chinese American journalist, Leong Gor Yun, called the Chinese Consolidated Benevolent Association (CCBA) "an American product." Leong, *Chinatown Inside Out* (New York: Barrows Mussey, 1936), p. 52.

38. Hoy, *The Chinese Six Companies*, p. 21.

39. Him Mark Lai, "Historical Development of the Chinese Consolidated Benevolent Association/Huiguan System," in *Chinese America: History and Perspectives 1987* (San Francisco: Chinese Historical Society of America, 1987), pp. 13–51.

40. Liu, *Meiguo Huaqiao shi*, p. 182. In 1890 the organization registered with the New York State government under the name of The Chinese Consolidated Benevolent Association of the City of New York. From 1894 to 1963 it was located at 16 Mott Street; in 1963 it moved to its current location, 62 Mott Street. Ibid., p. 191.

41. For the story of the San Francisco CCBA's fight against anti-Chinese legislation, see Liu, *Meiguo Huaqiao shi*, pp. 196–201, 542, 584–86; Shih-shan Henry Tsai, *China and the Overseas Chinese in the United States, 1868–1911* (Fayetteville: University of Arkansas Press, 1983), pp. 83, 97.

42. Gunther Barth, *Bitter Strength: A History of the Chinese in the United States, 1850–1870* (Cambridge, Mass.: Harvard University Press, 1971), p. 100.

43. CCBA bylaws, Article 7, section (a) and (b). Liu Pei Chi, *Meiguo Huaqiao shi, xubian* [A history of the Chinese in the United States of America, II] (Taipei: Limin Wenhua Shiye Gongsi, 1981), p. 185.

44. Ibid., pp. 184, 186.

45. Warner Van Norden, *Who's Who of the Chinese in New York* (New York: n.p., 1918), p. 84.

46. For criticisms of the inefficiency of the CCBA, see Liang Qichao, *Xindalu youji* [Diary of traveling in the New World] (Japan: Xinminchongbao, 1904; rpt. Changsha: Hunan Renmin Chubanshe, 1981).

47. Liu, *Meiguo Huaqiao shi, xubian*, p. 189.

48. Ibid., p. 188.

49. Ibid., p. 189; Leong, *Chinatown Inside Out*, pp. 35–37.

50. *California Senate Journal* (1852), p. 15. Quoted in Chinn et al., *Chinese in California*, p. 23.

51. Tchen, "New York Chinese," p. 178.

52. Clark, "Chinese of New York," p. 111.

53. For details, see Chinn et al., *Chinese in California*, p. 24.

54. For the full text of the act, see *United States Statutes, 1881–83*, vol. 22, (Washington, D.C.: Government Printing Office, 1883), pp. 58–61; or Cheng-Tsu Wu, *"Chink!" A Documentary History of Anti-Chinese Prejudice in America* (New York: World Publishing Co., 1972), pp. 70–75. For analyses of these exclusion acts and their impact on Chinese Americans, see Benjamin B. Ringer, *"We the People" and Others: Duality and America's Treatment of Its Racial Minorities* (New York: Tavistock Publications, 1983), pp. 629–80; Lyman, *Chinese Americans*, pp. 63–69; and Shih-shan Henry Tsai, *The Chinese Experience in America* (Bloomington: Indiana University Press, 1986), pp. 62–67.

55. Sucheng Chan, "The Exclusion of Chinese Women, 1870–1943," in *Entry Denied: Exclusion and the Chinese Community in America, 1882–1943*, ed. Sucheng Chan (Philadelphia: Temple University Press, 1991), pp. 94–146; the discussion on the two decisions is on p. 112.

56. Shepard Schwartz, "Mate-Selection among New York City's Chinese Males, 1931–38," *American Journal of Sociology* 56 (May 1951): 562–68; for the numbers, see p. 564.

57. Ibid., p. 565.

58. Fowler V. Harper and Jerome H. Skolnick, *Problems of the Family*, rev. ed. (New York: Bobbs-Merrill, 1962), pp. 96–99.

59. Schwartz, "Mate-Selection," p. 564.

60. Chan, "Exclusion," p. 128.

61. Lyman, *Chinese Americans*, pp. 89–90.

62. See Stuart C. Miller, *The Unwelcome Immigrant: The American Image of the Chinese, 1785–1882* (Berkeley and Los Angeles: University of California Press, 1969).

63. William Tung, *Chinese in America, 1820–1973: A Chronology and Fact Book* (Dobbs Ferry, N.Y.: Oceana Publications, 1974), p. 21.

64. Him Mark Lai, "Chinese," in *Harvard Encyclopedia of American Ethnic Groups*, ed. Stephan Thernstrom (Cambridge, Mass.: Belknap Press, 1980), p. 223.

65. See Siu, *Chinese Laundryman*, pp. 195–200.

66. Chen Ke, "Fangwen lu Mei Huaqiao Chen Ke xiansheng" [An interview with Mr. Chen Ke, a Chinese returned from America], in *Huaqiao shi lunwen ji* [Essays on overseas Chinese history] (Guangzhou: Ji'nan Daxue Huaqiao Yanjiu-suo), vol. 2, 1981, pp. 340–41.

67. Ibid., pp. 341–43.

68. Fang and Zhang, "Niuyue Huaqiao xiyiguan," pp. 197–98.

69. DeArmond, *Laundry Industry*, p. 208.

70. Interview with Mr. Yang, owner of Moy's Hand Laundry, Brooklyn, New York, January 29, 1988.

71. Fang and Zhang, "Niuyue Huaqiao xiyiguan," pp. 191–92.

72. Siu, *Chinese Laundryman*, p. 138.

73. Clark, "Chinese of New York," p. 110.

74. Interview with Mr. Yang, owner of Moy's Hand Laundry, Brooklyn, New York, January 29, 1988.

75. Chen, "Fangwen lu Mei Huaqiao Chen Ke," p. 345.

76. Huang Shun, "Wo zai Meiguo congshi xiyiye de jingguo" [My experience working in the laundry business in the U.S.], in *Huaqiao shi lunwen ji* [Essays on overseas Chinese history] (Guangzhou: Ji'nan Daxue Huaqiao Yanjiusuo), vol. 2, 1981, p. 317.

77. Fang and Zhang, "Niuyue Huaqiao xiyiguan," p. 190.

78. Interview with Mr. C., the Wah Kiu Wet-Wash, Inc., Long Island City, New York, March 29, 1988. Chen Ke also complained that he could not sleep well because of bug bites. See Chen, "Fangwen lu Mei Huaqiao Chen Ke," p. 345.

79. Fang and Zhang, "Niuyue Huaqiao xiyiguan," p. 193.

80. Leong, *Chinatown Inside Out*, p. 23.

81. Wong, "Chinese in New York," p. 299.

82. Siu, *Chinese Laundryman*, pp. 139, 148.

83. One laundryman believed that only 40 percent of the Chinese laundrymen could save money and return to China, while the other 60 percent were stuck and died in the United States. Siu, *Chinese Laundryman*, p. 242.

84. For the term *yishangguan*, see Siu, *Chinese Laundryman*, p. 179. Siu spells *yishangguan* according to the pronunciation of the Taishan dialect (*yee-shing-kuon*), and he translates it as "a clothing house." In 1979 I participated in a project jointly sponsored by UCLA and Zhongshan University to investigate the influence of overseas Chinese on a Chinese community in Guangdong and spent three months in Taishan. The observations came from several dozens of oral history interviews with the relatives of Chinese Americans.

85. Interview with Mr. L., Chinatown, New York, February 28, 1988.

86. Siu, *Chinese Laundryman*, p. 116.

87. Interview with Mr. Z., the Wah Kiu Wet-Wash, Inc., Long Island City, New York, March 29, 1988.

Chapter Two

1. Louis Beck, *New York's Chinatown: An Historical Presentation of Its People and Places* (New York: Bohemia Publishers, 1898), pp. 59–61.
2. Leong Gor Yun, *Chinatown Inside Out* (New York: Barrows Mussey, 1936), p. 86.
3. Ibid., p. 87. Because of the protest of the Chinese consul general in New York City and the cooperation of the police department, most of the insulting cartoons later were removed.
4. *Minqi Ribao* (*The Chinese Nationalist Daily*, New York City), April 10, 1933, p. 1.
5. Leong, *Chinatown Inside Out*, p. 88; *The Chinese Nationalist Daily*, April 10, 1933, p. 1.
6. *The Chinese Nationalist Daily*, April 18, 1933, p. 3; Leong, *Chinatown Inside Out*, p. 91.
7. Leong, *Chinatown Inside Out*, p. 91.
8. *The Chinese Nationalist Daily*, April 17, 18, 1933, p. 1.
9. *The Chinese Vanguard*, April 27, 1933.
10. *The Chinese Nationalist Daily*, April 27, 1933, p. 3.
11. Ibid., April 25, 1933, p. 3; Leong's *Chinatown Inside Out* stated that more than six hundred attended. (p. 92).
12. *The Chinese Nationalist Daily*, April 25, 1933, p. 3.
13. Ibid., April 24, 1933, p. 1.
14. For the early activities of the Chinese left in the United States, see Him Mark Lai, "A Historical Survey of the Chinese Left in America," in *Counterpoint: Perspectives on Asian America*, ed. Emma Gee (Los Angeles: University of California, Asian American Studies Center, 1976), pp. 63–80.
15. The political situation in the Chinese American communities after 1927 was extremely complex and confusing. For details, see Him Mark Lai, "The Kuomintang in Chinese American Communities before World War II," in *Entry Denied: Exclusion and the Chinese Community in America, 1882–1943*, ed. Sucheng Chan (Philadelphia: Temple University Press, 1991), pp. 170–212; and Liu Pei Chi, *Meiguo Huaqiao shi, xubian* [A history of the Chinese in the United States of America, II] (Taiwan: Limin Wenhua Shiye Gongsi, 1981), pp. 485–90.
16. Lai, "Historical Survey," p. 67.
17. *The Chinese Vanguard*, April 15, 1934, supplementary, p. 1.
18. For a more detailed account and analysis of the Chinese Anti-Imperialist Alliance, see Peter Kwong, *Chinatown, New York: Labor and Politics, 1930–1950* (New York: Monthly Review Press, 1979), pp. 50–61.
19. "Lu Mei guiqiao, qian Meizhou Huaqiao Ribao she yewuzhuren Zhang

Manli xiansheng fangwen lu" [Record of an interview of a Chinese returned from America: Mr. Zhang Manli, former business manager of the *China Daily News* of New York], in *Huaqiao shi lunwen ji* [Essays on overseas Chinese history], (Guangzhou: Ji'nan Daxue Huaqiao Yanjiusuo), vol. 2, 1981, pp. 322–32.

20. Ibid., p. 327.

21. Liu Xiaoyun, "Chongjian Taishan zhi jihua" [The plan to rebuild Taishan], *Xinning Zazhi* [Xinning Magazine] (Taishan) 12 (1912). Also see Renqiu Yu, "Chinese American Contributions to the Educational Development of Toisan, 1910–1940," *Amerasia Journal* 10:1 (1983): 49–72.

22. See the paper's call for support, *The Chinese Vanguard*, July 15, 1933, p. 1; October 1, 1933, p. 1.

23. The paper's office and the CAIA's headquarters used the same building as the CPUSA's organ, *The Daily Worker*, on East 13th Street. *The Chinese Vanguard*, March 1, 1933.

24. *The Chinese Vanguard*, March 1, 1933, p. 1.

25. He was given a pseudonym, "Louis Wing," in Leong Gor Yun's *Chinatown Inside Out.*

26. Lei Zhuofeng, "Niuyue Huaqiao Xiyiguan Lianhehui chengli jingguo" [The founding of the Chinese Hand Laundry Alliance of New York], in *Guangzhou wenshi ziliao (xuanji)* [Selections of cultural historical materials, Guangzhou] (Guangzhou: Guangdong Renmin Chubanshe), no. 22 (4), 1984, pp. 216–17, 219.

27. The Constitution of the Chinese Hand Laundry Alliance of New York (New York: CHLA, 1936), p. 1.

28. Leong, *Chinatown Inside Out*, p. 93.

29. *The Chinese Nationalist Daily*, May 8, 1933, p. 3; Leong, *Chinatown Inside Out*, p. 93.

30. Leong, *Chinatown Inside Out*, pp. 102, 94.

31. For a complete list of the CHLA's first elected committee members, see *The Chinese Nationalist Daily*, May 9, 1933, p. 3; for the list of the signatories of the declaration, see April 24, 1933, p. 3.

32. *The Chinese Nationalist Daily*, May 9, 1933, p. 3; Lei, "Niuyue Huaqiao," p. 220.

33. Lei, "Niuyue Huaqiao," p. 220.

34. Leong, *Chinatown Inside Out*, p. 94.

35. Fang Fu'er and Zhang Manli, "Niuyue Huaqiao xiyiguan de bianqian" [Changes in the Chinese hand laundries in New York City], in *Guangzhou wenshi ziliao (xuanji)*, [Selections of cultural historical materials, Guangzhou] (Guangzhou: Guangdong Renmin Chubanshe), no. 23, June 1981, pp. 197–98.

36. Lei, "Niuyue Huaqiao," pp. 221–22; Leong, *Chinatown Inside Out*, pp. 95–96. For a brief biographical sketch of William M. Chadbourne, see John W. Leonard, *Who's Who in Jurisprudence: A Biographical Dictionary of Contemporary Lawyers and Jurists, 1925* (New York: John W. Leonard Corporation, 1925), p. 249.

37. Lei, "Niuyue Huaqiao," p. 222.

38. *The Chinese Nationalist Daily*, April 27, 1933, p. 3.

39. *The Chinese Vanguard*, June 15, 1933, p. 2.

40. *The Chinese Nationalist Daily*, June 28, 1933, p. 10.

41. See the editorial of *The Chinese Vanguard*, August 1, 1933, which warned the CHLA that it "should maintain organizational independence, never involve in the crazy dog-eat-dog fight between the reactionary forces . . . and resist any attempt of the feudal forces to seduce this newly built organization into their internal conflicts." Also see August 15, 1933, p. 1.

42. *The Chinese Vanguard*, June 15, 1933, p. 2.

43. Leong, *Chinatown Inside Out*, pp. 154–55.

44. Ibid., p. 150.

45. *The Chinese Vanguard*, June 15, 1933, p. 2.

46. Ibid.

47. Leong, *Chinatown Inside Out*, pp. 99–100.

48. *The Chinese Vanguard*, August 15, 1933, p. 3.

49. Ibid.

50. Ibid., September 1, 1933, p. 3.

51. Ibid., August 15, 1933, p. 1.

52. Ibid., p. 3; September 1, 1933, p. 3.

53. Ibid., October 15, 1933, p. 3.

54. Ibid., July 1, 1933, p. 1.

55. Ibid., p. 3.

56. Ibid.

57. Ibid., July 15, 1933, p. 1.

58. Ibid., p. 3.

59. Ibid., July 1, 1933, p. 3.

60. Ibid., July 15, 1933, p. 3.

61. Ibid.

62. Lei Zhuofeng, "1933-nian Niuyue Huaren Xiyiguan Lianhehui chengli qian-hou" [Before and after the establishment of the Chinese Hand Laundry Alliance of New York in 1933], in *Huaqiao shi lunwen ji* [Essays on overseas Chinese history] (Guangzhou: Ji'nan Daxue Huaqiao Yanjiusuo), vol. 2, 1981, pp. 333–39.

63. Leong, *Chinatown Inside Out*, p. 99. Leong Gor Yun is Zhu Xia's pen name.

Chapter Three

1. Leong Gor Yun, *Chinatown Inside Out* (New York: Barrows Mussey, 1936), p. 95.

2. See *China Daily News* (*CDN*), December 6, 1940, p. 7; January 15, 1941, p. 7; November 15, 1941, p. 7; Leong, *Chinatown Inside Out*, pp. 96–97.

3. *Yilian wuzhounian tekan* [The CHLA fifth anniversary special bulletin] (New York: The CHLA, 1938), p. 32.

4. Interview with Mr. C., Chinatown, New York, March 20, 1988.

5. This observation is based on a reading of CHLA publications and *CDN*, 1940–55.

6. *Yilian wuzhounian tekan*, p. 45.

7. *CDN*, April 18, 1943, p. 6.

8. Interview with Mr. C., Chinatown, New York, March 20, 1988.

9. *The Chinese Vanguard*, February 1, 1934, p. 1.

10. Ibid., March 1, 1934, p. 3.

11. Ibid.

12. Ibid.

13. Ibid., March 15, 1934, p. 3.

14. Ibid., April 1, 1934, p. 3.

15. Ibid.

16. Ibid., May 15, 1934, p. 1.

17. Ibid., July 15, 1934, p. 3.

18. Ibid., August 1, 1934, p. 3.

19. Leong, *Chinatown Inside Out*, p. 103.

20. *The Chinese Vanguard*, June 15, 1934, p. 3.

21. Ibid.

22. Ibid., December 15, 1934, p. 1; December 22, 1934, p. 1; and the leaflet "All Overseas Chinese in New York City, Rise to Resist the Tong war!" by the Su Zhaozheng Branch of the International Labor Defense, November 24, 1934.

23. *Qinghua daxue shigao* [A history of Qinghua University] (Beijing: Zhonghua Shuju, 1981), p. 78; Shiji, "Shihuang," in *Qinghua xiaoshi congshu* [A collection on history of Qinghua School] (Beijing: Qinghua University Press, 1983), Renwuzhi [Biographies], vol. 1, p. 74.

24. *The Chinese Vanguard*, February 15, 1933, p. 4.

25. Ibid.

26. Ibid., March 1, 1933, p. 4.

27. Interview with Mr. F., Chinatown, New York, February 7, 1988.

28. *The Chinese Vanguard*, October 1, 1933, p. 1.

29. Ibid.

30. Ibid., April 15, 1933, p. 3.

31. Ibid., February 15, 1933, p. 4.

32. Ibid., April 15, 1934, p. 1.

33. Ibid.

34. Ibid., October 14, 1934, p. 3.

35. Ibid.

36. Ibid., October 20, 1934, pp. 1, 3.

37. Ibid., November 10, 1934, p. 1.

38. Ibid., October 20, 1934, p. 3.

39. Ibid., October 27, 1934, p. 1.

40. Ibid., November 10, 1934, p. 3.

41. Ibid., November 3, 1934, p. 3.

42. Ibid., November 10, 1934, p. 1.

43. Ibid.

44. Ibid., p. 3.

45. Ibid., November 17, 1934, p. 3.

46. *The Chinese Nationalist Daily*, May 22, 1935, p. 9.

47. *The Chinese Vanguard*, April 13, 1935, p. 1.

48. Ibid.

49. Ibid., February 29, 1936, p. 3.

50. Ibid., March 7, 1936, p. 1.

51. Ibid.

52. Ibid.

53. Ibid., March 14, 1936, p. 1.

54. Ibid., March 26, 1936, p. 1.

55. Ibid., March 21, 1936, p. 1.

56. Ibid.

57. Ibid., March 26, 1936, pp. 1, 3.

58. Ibid., April 4, 1936, p. 1.

59. Ibid., May 2, 1936, p. 1.

60. Ibid., July 4, 1936, p. 3.

61. *The New York Times*, April 26, 1937, p. 38; for the Chinese translation of the court verdict, see *The Chinese Vanguard*, May 22, 1937, p. 4.

62. *The New York Times*, April 26, 1937, p. 38.

63. CDN, April 14, 1941, p. 6.

64. *The Chinese Vanguard*, April 15, 1934, p. 3; July 15, 1934, p. 3.

65. Peter Kwong, *Chinatown, New York: Labor and Politics, 1930–1950* (New York: Monthly Review Press, 1979), p. 80.

66. For an account of this complicated division of opinions within the CHLA, see *The Chinese Vanguard*, June 15, 1935, p. 3; June 29, 1935, p. 1.

67. Minutes of the Quon Shar meeting on March 12, 1937; FBI file 100-365097-140, p. 32.

68. Minutes of the Quon Shar meeting on March 28, 1937; FBI file 100-365097-140, p. 35.

69. FBI file 100-365097-140, pp. 1–68.

70. Minutes of the Quon Shar meeting on April 17, 1937; FBI file 100-365097-140, pp. 37–38.

71. Interview with Mr. C., Chinatown, New York, April 9, 1988.

72. See the CHLA letter to the Chinese community in *The Chinese Vanguard*, February 24, 1937, p. 3.

73. Interview with Mr. C., Chinatown, New York, February 21, 1988.

74. Minutes of the Quon Shar meeting on November 9, 1940; FBI file 100-365097-140, p. 52; see also pp. 32–34, 42, 47.

75. Jinjian, "Fuwu jingshen yu zhandou jingshen" [The spirit of serving and the spirit of fighting], *CDN*, December 21–22, 1943, p. 6.

76. Quoted in Virginia Heyer, "Pattern of Social Organization in New York City's Chinatown" (Ph.D. dissertation, Columbia University, 1953), p. 92.

77. *CDN*, June 26, 1944, p. 6.

78. This observation is based on a reading of *Yilian wuzhounian tekan* and *CDN*, 1940–50.

79. Interview with Mr. S., Chinatown, New York, March 26, 1988.

80. *CDN*, June 25, 1943, p. 6.

81. Ibid.

82. Leong, *Chinatown Inside Out*, pp. 98–99.

83. To find information about the laundry alliances in other cities, I checked three Chinese-language newspapers published in New York City: *The Chinese Vanguard*, 1933–38; *The Chinese Nationalist Daily*, 1933–39; and *China Daily News*, 1940–55. All three covered the Chinese communities on the East Coast in detail. If any of the laundry alliances established in other cities had been as active as the CHLA was in New York City, these newspapers would have carried reports on them. No such evidence was found.

Chapter Four

1. *Yilian wuzhounian tekan* [The CHLA fifth anniversary special bulletin] (New York: CHLA, 1938), p. 2.

2. Leong Gor Yun, *Chinatown Inside Out* (New York: Barrows Mussey, 1936), p. 143.

3. Ibid., pp. 144–45.

4. Dorothy Borg, *The United States and the Far Eastern Crisis* (Cambridge, Mass.: Harvard University Press, 1964), p. 197.

5. Huang Jingwan, *Huaqiao dui zuguo de gongxian* [Overseas Chinese contributions to the motherland] (Shanghai: Tangli Chubanshe, 1940), pp. 268–69.

6. Douglas W. Lee, "The Overseas Chinese Affairs Commission and the Politics of Patriotism in Chinese America in the Nanking Era, 1928–1945," *Annals of the Chinese Historical Society of the Pacific Northwest* (Bellingham, Wash.: Chinese Historical Society of the Pacific Northwest) (1984): 198–231; quotations from pp. 216–17.

7. *The Chinese Vanguard*, October 1, 1932, p. 1; March 1, 1933, p. 1; January 5, 1934, p. 1; April 15, 1934, p. 2.

8. Leong, *Chinatown Inside Out*, p. 147.

9. *The Chinese Vanguard*, September 15, 1932, p. 3.

10. Ibid., October 1, 1933, p. 2.

11. Ibid., May 2, 1936, p. 3; October 10, 1936, p. 3. For information about the Blue Shirts, see Lloyd E. Eastman, *The Abortive Revolution: China under Nationalist Rule, 1927–1937* (Cambridge, Mass.: Harvard University Press, 1974).

12. Borg, *Far Eastern Crisis*, pp. v–vi; Michael Schaller, *The U.S. Crusade in China, 1938–1945* (New York: Columbia University Press, 1979), pp. 5–7.

13. In October 1937 President Roosevelt stated in a speech given in Chicago that just as health officials must "quarantine" disease carriers "in order to protect the health of the community against the spread of disease," the United States should sponsor some form of international quarantine against aggressor nations spreading the disease of war.

14. Quoted in Michael Schaller, *The United States and China in the Twentieth Century* (New York: Oxford University Press, 1979), p. 41.

15. See Liu Zhongxun, *Huaqiao aiguo zidong juanxian* [Overseas Chinese patriotic and voluntary donations to China] (Taiwan: Qiaowu Weiyuanhui Qiaowu Yanjiushi, 1969).

16. Y. K. Chu, *Meiguo Huaqiao gaishi* [History of the Chinese people in America] (New York: China Times, 1975), p. 121.

17. Ibid.

18. Situ Meitang, *Zuguo yu Huaqiao* [The motherland and overseas Chinese] (Hong Kong: Wenhui Bao Chubanshe, 1956), vol. 1, p. 90.

19. Cai Tingkai, *Cai Tingkai zizhuan* [Autobiography of Cai Tingkai] (Harbin, Helongjiang: Helongjiang Renmin Chubanshe, 1982), pp. 338–45; *The Chinese Vanguard*, September 1, 1934, pp. 1–3. When Cai first published his autobiography in 1946 in Hong Kong, he replaced Chiang Kai-shek's name with that of Wang Jingwei (another KMT leader, who surrendered to the Japanese in 1939 and died in 1944) because of political considerations. The contemporary Chinese-language newspaper accounts indicate that Cai actually attacked Chiang during his American trip.

20. *The Chinese Vanguard*, September 1, 1934, pp. 1–3.

21. Situ Meitang, *Zuguo yu Huaqiao*, vol. 1, pp. 90–91.

22. *The Chinese Vanguard*, September 1, 1934, p. 3.

23. *China Daily News* (*CDN*), August 7, 1941, p. 7. The surnames Tan and Tan have the same Anglicized spelling, but have two different Chinese characters.

24. Ibid., August 27, 1941, p. 7.

25. *The Chinese Vanguard*, October 5, 1935, p. 3.

26. Ibid., November 2, 1935, p. 3; November 23, 1935, pp. 1–3.

27. Ibid., December 14, 1935, p. 1; December 21, 1935, p. 1; December 28, 1935, p. 1.

28. Ibid., December 21, 1935, p. 1; December 28, 1935, p. 1.

29. Ibid., February 1, 1936, p. 1.

30. Ibid., January 4, 1936, p. 1; February 1, 1936, p. 1.

31. Ibid., January 4, 1936, p. 1.

32. Ibid., February 1, 1936, p. 1.

33. *The Chinese Nationalist Daily*, February 5, 1936, p. 1.

34. *The Chinese Vanguard*, February 8, 1936, p. 1.

35. Ibid., March 14, 1936, p. 3.

36. Ibid., February 15, 1936, p. 1.

37. Ibid., March 14, 1936, p. 1.

38. Ibid.

39. Ibid., May 2, 1936, p. 1.

40. Ibid., June 6, 1936, p. 3.

41. Ibid., August 4, 1936, p. 1.

42. Ibid.

43. Ibid., September 19, 1936, p. 1.

44. Ibid., November 11, 1937, p. 1.

45. Ibid., August 26, 1937, p. 1. The OCASGC was formally founded on November 7, 1937, but its preparation dated back to August 1937. In August its name was Niuyue Quanti Huaqiao Kangri Jiuguo Couxiang Ju (New York Chinese Anti-Japanese Salvation Bureau for Military Funds). The nineteen organizations kept their seats on the executive committee even after the group adopted the name OCASGC in November.

46. *The Chinese Vanguard*, August 26, 1937, p. 1.

47. Ibid., August 12, 1937, p. 1.

48. *Yilian wuzhounian tekan*, p. 53.

49. *The Chinese Vanguard*, August 26, 1937, p. 1.

50. Ibid., p. 2.

51. Ibid.

52. Ibid., September 30, 1937, p. 2

53. Ibid.

54. CDN, May 5, 1944, p. 6.

55. *The Chinese Vanguard*, July 28, 1938, p. 1.

56. Ibid., July 14, 1938, p. 1; interview with Mr. C., Chinatown, New York, March 6, 1988.

57. CDN, January 1, 1941, p. 2; August 25, 1941, p. 2.

58. Ibid., July 8, 1940, p. 1.

59. Ibid., July 31, 1940, p. 2.

60. A leading scholar in Chinese American history, Him Mark Lai, comments that "this is the opinion rarely heard in the Chinese communities in that time period." See Lai, *Meiguo Huaren jianshi* [A brief history of the Chinese in the United States], in *Shi Dai Bao* [*San Francisco Journal*], December 30, 1981, p. 2. Further research may benefit from a comprehensive comparison of CDN's opinion with that of others.

61. CDN, July 8, 1940, p. 1.

62. Ibid., November 3, 1942, p. 2.

63. Ibid., November 1, 1942, p. 2.

64. Ibid., October 24, 1942, p. 7.

65. Ibid., November 2, 1942, p. 2.

66. Interview with Mr. C., Chinatown, New York, February 14, 1988. There is little information about Tang before 1937. He began to be active in the New

York Chinese community after 1937, as his name frequently appeared in the local Chinese-language newspapers. See *The Chinese Vanguard*, November 11, 1937, p. 3; July 14, 1938, p. 3.

67. "The *China Daily News* Case," a pamphlet compiled by the Committee to Support the *China Daily News* (New York, n.d. [ca. 1951]), p. 4.

68. Interview with Ms. W., editor of *CDN*, Chinatown, New York, October 15, 1987.

69. This observation is based on a reading of the CHLA Special Column in *CDN* from 1940 to 1948.

70. *CDN*, July 10, 1943, p. 2.

71. Ibid., October 30, 1944, p. 6.

Chapter Five

1. Interview with Mr. S., Chinatown, New York, January 10, 1988.

2. *The Chinese Vanguard*, October 28, 1937, p. 2.

3. *Yilian wuzhounian tekan* [The CHLA fifth anniversary special bulletin] (New York: CHLA, 1938), p. 47.

4. *The Chinese Vanguard*, August 19, 1937, p. 1.

5. Ibid., October 28, 1937, p. 2.

6. Interview with Mr. Y., Brooklyn, New York, November 20, 1987. Also see Chapter One.

7. *The Chinese Vanguard*, October 28, 1937, p. 2.

8. Ibid., February 3, 1938, p. 2; *Yilian wuzhounian tekan*, p. 53.

9. Edgar Snow, *The Battle for Asia* (New York: Random House, 1941), p. 281.

10. *The Chinese Vanguard*, February 3, 1938, p. 2. According to Richard P. Traina, *American Diplomacy and the Spanish Civil War* (Westport, Conn.: Greenwood Press, 1980), p. 206, the Medical Bureau and North American Committee to Aid Spanish Democracy was one of the most influential organizations supporting the loyalists in the Spanish Civil War.

11. *The Chinese Vanguard*, February 3, 1938, p. 2.

12. Ibid., February 24, 1938, p. 1; March 3, 1938, p. 1.

13. Ibid., March 3, 1938, p. 1.

14. Ibid.

15. *Yilian wuzhounian tekan*, p. 53.

16. Tan wrote essays and translated related materials to introduce the American Youth Congress to the Chinese community. See Tan, "Meiguo Qingnian Yihui" [The American Youth Congress], in *Huaqiao qingnian* [Overseas Chinese youth] (New York: Chinese Youth Club), special issue, no. 3 (1940): 21–26; and Tan's translation of the Declaration of the Seventh National Meeting of the American Youth Congress, *China Daily News* (*CDN*), August 4, 1941, p. 6.

17. *CDN*, January 5, 1942, p. 7.

18. *The Chinese Vanguard*, March 3, 1938, p. 1; *Yilian wuzhounian tekan*, p. 53. Scott was elected to the 74th and 75th Congress (January 1935–January 1939). He held an internationalist stand in American foreign relations. See U.S. Congress, *Biographical Directory of the American Congress 1774–1971* (Washington, D.C.: U.S. Government Printing Office, 1971), p. 1667; *The New York Times*, April 19, 1938, p. 1; May 21, 1938, p. 7.

19. *The New York Times*, April 23, 1938, p. 7. All Chinese sources indicate that the CHLA purchased only four ambulances. *The New York Times* reported that the "five ambulances" "cost $10,000."

20. *CDN*, July 8, 1940, p. 4.

21. Michael Schaller, *The U.S. Crusade in China, 1938–1945* (New York: Columbia University Press, 1979), p. 17.

22. For example, A. T. Steele, *The American People and China* (New York: McGraw-Hill, 1966), a book that deals with American public opinion on China, gives no space to Chinese Americans.

23. Schaller, *U.S. Crusade*, p. 37.

24. Ibid., pp. 61–62.

25. See Barbara Tuchman, *Stilwell and the American Experience in China, 1911–1945* (New York: Macmillan, 1972), passim.

26. *The New York Times*, January 15, 1942, p. 8.

27. Ibid.

28. Other organizations were the Chinese Women's Relief Association, Chinese Chamber of Commerce, Chinese-American Restaurant Association, Chinese Free Masons, Chinese Industrial Cooperatives, Kim Lan Association, and Chinese International Laundry Institute (founded by the CCBA; ceased to exist in 1943). See *The New York Times*, January 15, 1942, p. 8.

29. The names of the sixteen organizations were translated from English into Chinese and published in *CDN*, January 17, 1942, p. 2.

30. Chen Ruzhou, *Meiguo Huaqiao nianjian* [Handbook of Chinese in America] (New York: Zhongguo Guomin Waijian Xiehui zhu Mei banshichu, 1946), pp. 406–7; "Guomin Waijian Xiehui Niuyue Fenhui gongzuo gangyao" [Outline of the work of the New York Branch of the People's Foreign Relations Association of China], *CDN*, August 15–16, 1940, p. 7.

31. *CDN*, August 14, 1940, p. 6. This branch was reorganized in August, 1942 probably as a result of internal conflicts caused by the widespread nepotism within the KMT government. See Chen, *Meiguo Huaqiao nianjian*, p. 406.

32. *CDN*, January 17–27, 1942, p. 2.

33. Ibid., January 20, 1942, p. 7.

34. Ibid.

35. Ibid., January 26, 1942, p. 7.

36. *The New York Times*, January 15, 1942, p. 8.

37. For example, see *CDN*, January 28, 1942, p. 2; February 4, 1942, p. 2; February 10, 1942, p. 2.

38. *CDN*, January 27, 1942, p. 8. For more information about the Chinese

Workers' Mutual Aid Association in San Francisco, see Him Mark Lai, "A Historical Survey of the Chinese Left in America," in *Counterpoint: Perspectives on Asian America*, ed. Emma Gee (Los Angeles: University of California, Asian American Studies Center, 1976), pp. 68–69.

39. *CDN*, February 5, 1942, p. 7.

40. Ibid., February 13, 1942, p. 7.

41. Ibid., June 22, 1942, p. 6.

42. Ibid., June 26, 1944, p. 6.

43. Ibid., December 9, 1941, p. 2. *CDN* first spread the news of Japan's attack on Pearl Harbor in New York's Chinatown through posting "special notes" in the streets. There were many Chinese in Chinatown that day (Sunday, December 7), and the crowd was reported to be "very excited," "both angered at the Japanese ferocious action and pleased that Japan would be defeated by a strong United States soon." Ibid., p. 7. Soon the Chinese embassy in Washington sent "emergency notices" to all the Chinese organizations in the United States, urging them "not to hold any celebration [of the entry of the United States into the war because of the Japanese attack] so as to avoid any misunderstanding on the part of the U.S. government and American people." Ibid., December 20, 1941, p. 7.

44. *CDN*, November 20, 1941, p. 7. There is no record of the size of the CHLA membership for the years 1938–40.

45. Ibid., March 31, 1943, p. 7. On March 28, 1943, a CHLA report stated that "more than one hundred new members joined this Alliance last month" and expected more to join.

46. Ibid., February 15, 1941, p. 2.

47. Ibid., September 17, 1942, p. 2.

48. Ibid., May 23, 1942, p. 7.

49. Ibid., June 22, 1943, p. 2.

50. Ibid., June 25–26, 1943, p. 2.

51. Interview with Mr. C., Queens, New York, March 29, 1988.

52. *CDN*, July 1, 1943, p. 2; Lee Finkle, *Forum for Protest: The Black Press during World War II* (Cranbury, N.J.: Associated University Presses, 1975), p. 205n. Liu's last name is misspelled as "Lin" in Finkle's book.

53. *CDN*, July 1, 1943, p. 2.

54. Ibid.

55. For example, see *CDN*, January 1, 1944, p. 8; April 7, 1944, p. 2.

56. Interview with the president of the CHLA, Chinatown, New York, May 29, 1988.

57. Finkle, *Forum for Protest*, p. 205n.

58. Li Guhong, "Sannian lai de Qingjiu" [The Youth Club in the last three years], *CDN*, May 26, 1941, p. 6.

59. *Huaqiao qingnian* 3 (1940): 2; *CDN*, June 2, 1943.

60. *CDN*, May 26, 1941, p. 6.

61. Guhong, "Tan 'qiaoju' qingnian yu 'tusheng' qingnian" [On China-born youth and native-born youth], *CDN*, November 24, 1941, p. 6.

62. *Huaqiao qingnian* 3 (1940): 9.

63. Ibid.

64. Frank B. Leung, "Our Future in America," *Huaqiao qingnian* 3 (1940): 41. This article was published in English.

65. Ibid., p. 38.

66. Interview with Mr. C., Chinatown, New York, July 10, 1988.

67. Leung, "Our Future," p. 37.

68. *CDN*, October 30, 1944, p. 6.

69. Interview with Mr. C., Chinatown, New York, July 24, 1988.

70. Chen Houfu, "Yanlun wei shishi zhi mu" [Words are the mother of deeds], *CDN*, April 24, 1944, p. 6.

71. *Yilian wuzhounian tekan*, p. 78.

72. *CDN*, October 30, 1944, p. 6.

73. Ibid., June 26, 1944, p. 6.

74. For details, see Fred W. Riggs, *Pressures on Congress: A Study of the Repeal of Chinese Exclusion* (New York: Columbia University King's Crown Press, 1950).

75. Ibid., p. 129.

76. Ibid., p. 113.

77. *CDN*, February 4, 1943, p. 7.

78. Ibid.

79. Riggs, *Pressures on Congress*, p. 104.

80. Ibid., pp. 208–9.

81. *CDN*, March 15, 1943, p. 2.

82. Ibid., March 19, 1943, p. 7.

83. Ibid., May 24, 1943, p. 7.

84. For a sample, see *CDN*, May 19, 1943, p. 7.

85. Ibid., May 4, 1943, p. 2.

86. Ibid., May 6–7, 1943, p. 7.

87. Ibid., May 20, 1943, p. 7.

88. Ibid., May 21, 1943, p. 2. Dr. Arthur Hummel's testimony was published in the paper on May 21, 1943, p. 2; Pearl Buck's, on May 24, 1943, p. 3.

89. *CDN*, June 7, 1943, p. 2.

90. Ibid.

91. Riggs, *Pressures on Congress*, pp. 114–16.

92. *CDN*, May 7, 1943, p. 2; the quotation is from Mary Hornaday's report, "Asiatic Exclusion Hearings Due Soon ..." in *The Christian Science Monitor* (Boston), May 5, 1943, sec. 2, p. 11.

93. *CDN*, July 1, 1943, p. 2.

94. Riggs, *Pressures on Congress*, pp. 114–15.

95. Ibid., p. 117. In April 1924, while a proposed immigration bill that included a Japanese exclusion clause was pending in the Senate, Japanese Ambassador Masanao Hanihara, at the suggestion of Charles Evans Hughes, secretary of state, sent a letter to the State Department in which he stated that the exclusion

clause aimed at Japanese would have "grave consequences" for relations between Japan and the United States. The letter was forwarded to Congress and the phrase "grave consequences" was interpreted as a veiled threat to the United States. The senators then claimed that they felt compelled by the threat to vote in favor of the exclusion clause. For details, see Roger Daniels, *The Politics of Prejudice: The Anti-Japanese Movement in California and the Struggle for Japanese Exclusion* (New York: Atheneum, 1977), pp. 98–104.

96. *CDN*, May 4, 1943, p. 2.

97. Ibid., July 5, 1943, p. 2.

98. Ibid., October 23, 1943, p. 2.

Chapter Six

1. Chi Nu, "Jintian de xiyiguan shengyi" [Today's hand laundry business], *China Daily News (CDN)*, December 20, 1946, p. 6.

2. *The New York Times*, December 9, 1946, p. 28.

3. For the evolution of the laundry industry, see Fred DeArmond, *The Laundry Industry* (New York: Harper & Brothers, 1950), pp. 220–22.

4. *CDN*, December 3, 1946, p. 7.

5. Ibid., p. 2.

6. Ibid., December 7, 1946, p. 7.

7. Ibid., December 3, 1946, p. 7; *The New York Times*, December 9, 1946, p. 28.

8. *CDN*, December 3, 1946, p. 7; *The New York Times*, December 12, 1946, p. 21.

9. *CDN*, December 19, 1946, p. 6; interview with Mr. C., Chinatown, New York, March 20, 1988.

10. *CDN*, December 19, 1946, p. 2.

11. Ibid., December 29, 1946, p. 2.

12. Ibid.

13. Ibid.; interview with Mr. T., Chinatown, New York, March 27, 1988. Mr. T., a hand laundryman for more than forty years and a veteran CHLA member, told me that most of the Chinese hand laundries in New York in the 1940s were located in lower-middle- and lower-class neighborhoods.

14. *CDN*, December 13, 1946, p. 2.

15. Ibid., May 5, 1941, p. 2; March 19, 1941, p. 2.

16. Ibid., December 9, 1946, p. 6.

17. *The Chinese Vanguard*, March 3, 1938, pp. 1–2; March 10, 1938, p. 1; March 17, 1938, p. 4; March 24, 1938, p. 4.

18. *CDN*, July 20, 1942, p. 7; July 31, 1942, p. 2; August 1, 1942, p. 2; August 3, 1942, p. 7; August 5, 1942, p. 2.

19. Ibid., August 4, 1942, p. 2.

20. Ibid., November 29, 1946, p. 2.

21. A Chinese legend has it that in the third-century Wei Kingdom, two Cao (Ts'ao) brothers competed for the throne. The elder wanted to kill the younger so there would be no obstacle in his way. He ordered the younger to compose a poem within seven footsteps or be killed. The younger brother composed the famous "Poem in Seven Steps":

Beans are boiling to make soup,

. . .

Beanstalks burn beneath the pot;
Beans weep inside the pot.
Both grew from the same root;
Why hurry to burn each other up?

The poem so moved the elder brother that he spared the younger brother's life. English translation of the poem is from George W. Kent, *Worlds of Dust and Jade: 47 Poems and Ballads of the Third Century Chinese Poet Ts'ao Chih* (New York: Philosophical Library, 1969), p. 61.

22. In Chinese legend, Huang Di is believed to be the ancestor of all Chinese.

23. *CDN*, December 3, 1946, p. 2.

24. Ibid., December 7, 1946, p. 2.

25. Ibid., December 12, 1946, p. 2.

26. Ibid.

27. Ibid., November 29, 1946, p. 7.

28. Ibid., December 14, 1946, p. 7; December 16, 1946, p. 7.

29. Ibid., December 19, 1946, p. 7.

30. Ibid., January 4, 1947, p. 7; February 11, 1947, p. 6.

31. Ibid., February 11, 1947, p. 6.

32. Ibid., January 17, 1947, p. 7.

33. Ibid., December 10, 1946, p. 2.

34. Ibid., December 13, 1946, p. 2; December 14, 1946, p. 2; December 31, 1946, p. 2.

35. Ibid., December 18, 1946, p. 2.

36. Ibid., January 21, 1947, p. 7; February 4, 1947, p. 7.

37. Ibid.

38. Ibid., February 6, 1947, p. 2.

39. Ibid., February 4, 1947, p. 7.

40. "Huaqiao Xiyiijie zhaogu guanggao" [The advertisement for the capital raising for Wah Kiu Wet-Wash], *CDN*, November 11, 1948, p. 7.

41. *CDN*, February 6, 1947, p. 2; February 20, 1947, p. 2; the number of the Wah Kiu shareholders was reported in *CDN*, November 11, 1948, p. 7.

42. Ibid., March 12, 1947, p. 7.

43. Ibid., March 31, 1947, p. 7.

44. Ibid., March 19, 1947, p. 7.

45. Letters by hand laundrymen to *CDN*, February 6, 1947, p. 2; February 11, 1947, p. 6; February 17, 1947, p. 2.

46. *CDN*, February 20, 1947, p. 2.

47. Ibid.

48. For the negotiations and fight between the CHLA and the Chinese power laundries and the CHLA's plan to found a wet-wash factory in 1938, see *The Chinese Vanguard*, March 3, 1938, pp. 1–2; March 10, 1938, p. 1; March 17, 1938, p. 4; March 24, 1938, p. 4.

49. *CDN*, July 31 to September 22, 1942.

50. Ibid., May 8, 1947, p. 2.

51. Ibid., June 23, 1947, p. 2.

52. Ibid., May 20, 1947, p. 2.

53. "Dongshihui xiang gudong dahui baogao zhaiyao" [The excerpts of the report of Wah Kiu Wet-Wash Board of Directors], *CDN*, December 3, 1947, p. 3.

54. Ibid.

55. *CDN*, May 17, 1947, p. 7.

56. Ibid., December 3, 1947, p. 3.

57. Ibid.

58. Ibid., December 4, 1947, p. 3.

59. Ibid., October 21, 1947, p. 7.

60. Ibid., September 28, 1948, p. 7.

61. Ibid., October 4, 1948, p. 2.

62. Ibid.

63. Ibid., September 28, 1948, p. 7; September 30, 1948, p. 7; November 2, 1948, p. 7.

64. Ibid., November 11, 1948, p. 7.

65. Houfu, "Xiezhai yijie gudong xucan lianhuan huo" [Some thoughts after the dinner party], *CDN*, January 20, 1949, p. 7.

66. For the list of the names, see *CDN*, September 30, 1948, p. 7; November 11, 1948, p. 7.

67. Chen Shengcai, "Yonghu Huaqiao yiji shengchi Meizhou Ribao" [Supporting Wah Kiu Wet-Wash], *CDN*, April 6, 1949, p. 2.

68. Peter Kwong, *Chinatown, New York: Labor and Politics, 1930–1950* (New York: Monthly Review Press, 1979), p. 85.

69. *The Chinese Vanguard*, February 1, 1933, p. 1; also Kwong, *Chinatown*, p. 119.

70. *CDN*, August 5, 1941, p. 7.

71. Ibid., August 6, 1941, p. 7.

72. Ibid., August 7, 1941, p. 7.

73. Tang Mingzhao, (Thomas Tang) "Yiye zhonggonghui zhi neimu" [The secrets of the Chinese Laundry Workers International Union Local 211], *CDN*, September 12, 15, 16, 17, 22, 23, 1941, all p. 2.

74. *CDN*, May 20, 1947, p. 7; April 6, 1949, p. 7.

75. Ibid., December 23, 1949, p. 2.

76. Ibid.

77. Ibid.
78. Ibid., December 26, 1949, p. 2.
79. Ibid., December 24, 1949, p. 2.
80. Ibid., December 20, 1949, p. 7; January 11, 1950, p. 2.
81. Ibid., January 11, 1950, p. 2.
82. Ibid., February 22, 1950, p. 7.
83. Ibid., February 23, 1950, p. 7.
84. Ibid., February 25, 1950, p. 7.
85. Ibid., February 28, 1950, p. 7.
86. Ibid., March 1, 1950, p. 7.
87. Ibid.
88. See Alexander Saxton, *The Indispensable Enemy: Labor and the Anti-Chinese Movement in California* (Berkeley and Los Angeles: University of California Press, 1971).
89. The conflict between the trade unions and the Chinese American working class continues to this day and many issues discussed in this chapter are still relevant. See Peter Kwong, *The New Chinatown* (New York: Hill & Wang, 1987), chapter 8; Peter Kwong and JoAnn Lum, "How the Other Half Lives Now," *Nation*, June 18, 1988; the letter of Randy Wei, Alice Ip, and May Ying Chen to *Nation*, October 10, 1988; and Wing Lam's letter to *Nation*, December 5, 1988.

Chapter Seven

1. *Kaiming gongbao* (Havana, Cuba), April 21, 1945; quoted in *China Daily News* (CDN), May 21, 1945, p. 2.
2. *CDN*, August 22, 1945, p. 2. Those Chinese officials who came to the United States to collect money from overseas Chinese contemptuously called the Chinese Americans *Jingshan Arding*—literally, "stupid folks of the Gold Mountain"—since they could be so easily persuaded to give their money to the "representatives from the motherland." See Situ Meitang, *Zuguo yu Huaqiao* [The motherland and Overseas Chinese] (Hong Kong: Wenhui Bao, 1956), p. 105; also see *CDN*, January 29, 1951, p. 3.
3. John K. Fairbank, *The United States and China*, 4th ed. (Cambridge, Mass.: Harvard University Press, 1983), p. 297.
4. *CDN*, February 28, 1941, p. 2.
5. Ibid., January 15, 1941, p. 2.
6. Tianlai, "Huaqiao yu kangzhan jianguo" [Overseas Chinese and the war of resistance, and building China], *CDN*, July 7, 1942, p. 8.
7. *CDN*, September 9, 1943, p. 2.
8. Some letters were published in *CDN*. For a sample, see "Xielei jiashu baogao Taishan jihuang canxiang" [A blood-and-tears letter from home reporting Taishan famine], *CDN*, October 16, 1942, p. 2.

9. Lu Ming, "Gaodeng nanmin zai Meiguo suozuo heshi?" [What are the high-class refugees doing in the U.S.?], *CDN*, December 4, 1944, p. 3. Earlier reports on the high-class refugees include one *CDN* editorial, "Zhenzhi shang de tanwu bixu gengjue" [Political corruption must end], *CDN*, October 27, 1942, p. 2.

10. *CDN*, August 14, 1945, p. 6.

11. Ibid., September 11, 1943, p. 7.

12. Ibid., November 17, 1943, p. 7.

13. *Taishan Xianzhi* [The Taishan Gazetteer] (comp. Taishan Archives, Taishan, Guangdong, 1985), pp. 76–90. During the 1943 Taishan famine many appalling things happened, including cannibalism. These stories were reported in the United States, deeply distressing many Chinese Americans. *CDN*, July 31, 1944, p. 6.

14. *CDN*, November 11, 1943, p. 7.

15. Ibid., December 8–9, 1943, p. 7.

16. Ibid., April 3, 1944, pp. 2–3.

17. Li Yan, "Cong zhengzhi xieshanghui suoqi" [Comments on the Political Consultative Conference], CHLA Special Column, *CDN*, January 29, 1946, p. 6. Interestingly, one CHLA member, Shao, even discussed "the main reason that we came abroad to make a living":

> Why do we have to leave our country, work so hard in a foreign land to earn a little "blood-and-sweat" money to support ourselves and our families? We have to think about this issue.
>
> Some people believe that an "adventurous spirit" made us overcome various difficulties to go overseas. In fact, this view is quite superficial, reflecting the effects rather than the causes. Then why [did we go overseas]? The reason is simple: We were forced by the lack of means of livelihood.
>
> However, our motherland is a big country with vast territory and abundant resources and good climate, a country that is richly endowed by nature. Moreover, there are numerous people in our country, and they are absolutely not stupid in comparison with any other races. With so many advantages, then, why does China remain poor, and why do we have to go overseas due to the lack of means of livelihood? We ought to think more about this question.
>
> . . . It is the lack of democracy that leads to the lack of means of livelihood. In China, not to mention the past, even after the overthrow of the Manchu dynasty, we never carried out democracy. Because of the lack of political democracy, the people, the masters of the country, became powerless. Since the people had no power, corrupt officials colluded with local despots and evil gentry in abusing the people. Under their rule, agriculture, industry, and commerce were destroyed, and the vitality of the country undermined. This situation provided an opportunity for foreign imperialists to invade China with their economic power or military might; the result is that

China became poor and weak and the Chinese people have no means of livelihood. Therefore, the basic cause that pushed us to find means of livelihood overseas is evidently the lack of democracy, not at all the so-called "adventurous spirit."

If the motherland had practiced democracy, made good use of the various advantages in our country which is richly endowed by nature, and provided jobs for everyone, I am sure that many of us would never undertake such adventures—separating from our families, without enjoyment of family life, living in a foreign land lonely, and leaving as a young man but returning home with gray hair.

Now, with Japan's surrender, we have a great opportunity to build a democratic country. We hope the national leaders will make efforts to use this opportunity and build a democratic China.

Shao, "Zhengzhi bu minzhu wei zouwaiyang de zhuyin" [No political democracy is the main reason for going overseas], CHLA Special Column, *CDN*, October 27, 1945, p. 6. It is interesting to note that some scholars did suggest that an "independent, adventurous and unbending spirit" was what led Chinese from Guangdong (Kwangtung) and Fujian (Fookien) to emigrate overseas and that this "spirit" differentiated them from European immigrants to the United States. See Pyau Ling, "Causes of Chinese Emigration," *Annals of the American Academy of Political and Social Sciences* 39 (January 1912): 74–82.

18. Hanli, "Wo zai xinnian zhong dui qiaobao de xiwang" [My expectations of my fellow countrymen in this year], *CDN*, January 1, 1944, p. 8.

19. Wu Yushu, "Jiuzhi zhici" [Inaugural address], *CDN*, December 30, 1944, p. 6.

20. Houfu, "Tantan zuotanhui" [On the discussions], *CDN*, December 20, 1943, p. 6.

21. Li Chengzhu, "Guanyu 'fan Tangshan' " [On 'Go Home'], *CDN*, August 31, 1945, p. 6.

22. Paul Siu, *The Chinese Laundryman: A Study of Social Isolation* (New York: New York University Press, 1987), pp. 298–301.

23. Li, "Guanyu 'fan Tangshan,' " p. 6.

24. Ibid.

25. *CDN*, August 3, 1946, p. 6.

26. This was a traditional Chinese idea: after one established oneself in society, one should go back to one's native village with wealth and distinction. Another version of *rong xuan* is *fugui er gui guxiang*. See Siu, *Chinese Laundryman*, p. 176.

27. Cai Geng, letter to the editor, *CDN*, June 20, 1946, p. 2.

28. Su Ping, letter to the editor, *CDN*, August 2, 1946, p. 2.

29. *CDN*, April 12, 1948, p. 7; January 1, 1948, p. 8. Also see Y. K. Chu, *Meiguo Huaqiao gaishi* [History of the Chinese People in America] (New York: China Times, 1975), pp. 138–41.

30. *CDN*, April 12, 1948, p. 7.

31. *CDN*, August 22, 1945, p. 2.

32. Ibid., August 27, 1945, p. 2.

33. Houfu, "Yanlun wei shishi zhi mu" [Opinion is the mother of the deeds], *CDN*, April 24, 1944, p. 6; Houfu, "Yijie yu louye" [Wet-wash factory and the building], *CDN*, September 29, 1945, p. 6. Houfu indicated that many discussions on the plans were printed in the *Yilian Huikan* (the CHLA newsletter) in 1944 and 1945. I was not able to obtain these newsletters.

34. Interview with Mr. C., Chinatown, New York, July 23, 1988.

35. Ou Chanlian, "Wo dui Huaqiao Lianhe Shiye Gongshi de ganxiang" [My opinion about the Wah Kiu United Company], *CDN*, March 30, 1946, p. 6.

36. Ibid.

37. Ibid.

38. Little information exists about the Wah Kiu United Company. The only other document available about the company is a report of its first membership meeting, which lists the board of directors. See *CDN*, April 11, 1946, p. 7.

39. "Tuijin Huaqiao Shehui de Minzhu" [Promoting the democratization of overseas Chinese community], *CDN*, June 23, 1947, p. 2.

40. Liu Pei Chi, *Meiguo Huaqiao shi, xubian* [A history of the Chinese in the United States of America, II] (Taipei: Limin Wenhua Shiye Gongsi, 1981), p. 185.

41. Yang Gang, *Meiguo zhaji* [Notes on America] (Changsha: Hunan Renmin Chubanshe, 1983), p. 78. For a brief biographical sketch of Yang Gang, see R. David Arkush and Leo O. Lee, eds., *Land without Ghosts: Chinese Impressions of America from the Nineteenth Century to the Present* (Berkeley and Los Angeles: University of California Press, 1989), p. 193.

42. Yang, *Meiguo zhaji*, p. 78.

43. *CDN*, April 27, 1949, p. 7.

44. For example, see *CDN*, August 2, 1949, p. 2. These books included works of Mao Tse-tung and Liu Shaoqi, leaders of the CCP; books on building a new culture in China and on Chinese women's emancipation; and works of fiction.

45. *CDN*, January 25, 26, 27, 1949, all p. 7.

46. Fang Fu'er, "Niuyue Yilianhui huanying Dong Biwu tongzhi de jingguo" [The welcoming of Comrade Dong Biwu (on his visit) to the Chinese Hand Laundry Alliance of New York], in *Guangzhou wenshi ziliao (xuanji)* [Selections of cultural historical materials, Guangzhou] (Guangzhou: Guangdong Renmin Chubanshe), no. 17, 1979, pp. 156–59. Also see *CDN*, November 7, 1945, p. 7.

47. *CDN*, March 4, 1948.

48. Ibid., April 5, 1948, p. 2.

49. Ibid., May 14, 1946, p. 7.

50. Ibid., July 20, 1948, p. 2.

51. Ibid.

52. Ibid., November 1, 1948, p. 7.

53. Ibid., January 25, 1949, p. 7; January 26, 1949, p. 7. Lu Guanli attended

another CHLA discussion on April 10, 1949, and he was invited to the celebration of the CHLA's sixteenth anniversary on April 24, 1949, but there are no records of what he said on the two occasions. *CDN*, April 14, 1949, p. 7; April 26, 1949, p. 7.

54. *CDN*, July 11, 1949, p. 2.

55. Ibid., April 26, 1949, p. 7; see Jonathan D. Spence, *The Search for Modern China* (New York: Norton, 1990), p. 511. A few days after the news of the bombardment of the *Amethyst* arrived in New York, the CHLA held its sixteenth anniversary celebration, at which more than seventy-five members of the alliance "voluntarily donated money" to send to "salute" the People's Liberation Army soldiers who attacked the British warship. See *CDN*, May 21, 1949, p. 7.

56. *CDN*, April 29, 1949, p. 7.

57. Ibid., January 26, 1949, p. 7.

58. Ibid., October 12, 1949, p. 7.

59. *World Telegram* (New York), October 11, 1949.

60. FBI file 100-365097-1.

61. FBI file 100-365097-4, Hoover to New York FBI agency, dated August 4, 1950.

62. Ibid.

63. FBI file 100-365097-5, Hoover to New York FBI agency, dated November 6, 1950.

64. *CDN*, July 11, 1949, p. 2.

65. Ibid., July 19, 1949, p. 7.

66. *The New York Times*, July 18, 1949.

67. *The Chinese Nationalist Daily*, July 29, 1949, p. 2.

68. See Nancy B. Tucker, *Patterns in the Dust: Chinese-American Relations and the Recognition Controversy, 1949–1950* (New York: Columbia University Press, 1983), pp. 198–99.

69. *CDN*, July 4, 1950, p. 7.

70. Liu, *Meiguo Huaqiao shi, xubian*, p. 536.

71. *CDN*, December 8, 1950, p. 7.

72. Liu, *Meiguo Huaqiao shi, xubian*, pp. 536–37.

73. *CDN*, December 8, 1950, p. 7. U.S. immigration authorities arrested eighty-three members of the Qiongya Association in January 1951 and detained them on Ellis Island. Twenty of them had signed the anti-Communist statement issued by the CCBA but were not treated differently by the immigration officials. See *CDN*, February 5, 1951, pp. 3, 7.

74. FBI file 100-365097-6; dated November 22, 1950.

75. FBI file 100-365097-13.

76. Interview with Mr. G., Chinatown, New York, February 21, 1988.

77. Interview with Mr. C., Chinatown, New York, February 28, 1988.

78. *CDN*, January 18, 1951, p. 7; for a list of the members of the committee, see *CDN*, January 22, 1951, p. 3.

79. *CDN*, July 7, 1951, p. 2.

80. Committee to Support the *China Daily News*, *The China Daily News Case* (New York: n.d. [ca. 1952]); *The Facts behind the China Daily News Case* (New York: n.d. [ca 1952]); for a sample of the advertisement of the Bank of China's Overseas Chinese Service in Hong Kong, see *CDN*, August 16, 1951, p. 3.

81. *Facts behind the China Daily News Case*, pp. 13–14.

82. *CDN*, May 5, 6, 1952, both p. 2.

83. Ibid., June 21, 1954, p. 5.

84. Ibid., November 17, 1955, p. 5.

85. This observation is based on a reading of the editorials, columns, and letters in *CDN* from 1952 to 1955. For a representative article, see Eugene Moy, "Shui zai chuanmou zuo'e?" [Whose conspiracy?], *CDN*, July 1, 1954, p. 4.

86. *CDN*, November 29, 1955, p. 5.

87. Ibid., December 1, 1955, p. 5.

88. Ibid., December 15, 1955, p. 5.

89. Ibid., November 30–December 30, 1955.

90. *Meizhuo Ribao* [*The Chinese Journal*], December 3, 1955, p. 2.

91. *CDN*, December 5, 1955, p. 2.

92. Ibid., December 8, 1955, p. 5.

93. Ibid.

94. Ibid., December 10, 12, 1955, both p. 5.

95. Ibid., December 15, 1955, p. 5.

96. Ibid., December 9, 1955, p. 5.

97. Ibid., December 7, 17, 1955, p. 5.

98. Ibid., December 2, 1955, p. 4.

99. Interview with Chen Youyun, associate manager of the Wah Kiu Wet-Wash, Inc., Long Island, New York, March 29, 1988.

100. FBI file 100-365097-59, dated June 29, 1954; and 100-365097-66, enclosure, pp. 1–4.

101. FBI file 100-365097-88, dated December 29, 1954.

102. Ibid. Many of the conversations went like the following:

CHLA (A): What of it?

Caller (C): They said I was a Communist.

A: You're crazy. It all depends upon whether or not you are one.

C: They copied the name on my papers and took it away with them. They had a photograph of the Alliance displaying the flag.

A: Oh, that's all right, let them. What happened next?

C: They left after they had copied down the date I applied for naturalization.

A: What kind of people were they?

C: From the Immigration Department.

A: You didn't have to tell them your name. Next time don't do it.

C: I already gave it to them and they copied it down and took it away with them.

A: Well it can't be helped since you already gave it to them but just remember you don't have to do that the next time.

C: They said that I had not been naturalized very long, but I have been a citizen since I applied for my license. Is there any harm?

A: No. How can there be? You know that as well as I.

C: They asked whether I have been elected to work here and to protect this area and I answered no. This is the second time that they have questioned me.

A: They just wish to intimidate you.

C: The first time they questioned me I did not give them my papers but this time they asked for it.

A: What difference does it make whether you are a member [of the CHLA]. It is a legal organization.

C: They asked me if I read the *China Daily News*. I replied that I did not read it. They asked if I contributed money to help Mao Tse-tung and I replied that I had not contributed any money.

A: They are just trying to intimidate you. Look at all the people in the Chinese Hand Laundry Alliance.

C: I know. Look at all the people who attend its banquets; there are wives and lots of other people.

A: The Chinese Hand Laundry Alliance takes care of a lot of matters. They can always investigate. I don't think you should be too concerned over it, but the next time they come you just refuse to answer them.

C: I was worried that this investigation may have originated from something in Hong Kong.

A: No. Those are your private affairs.

C: Someone must have informed on me otherwise how would they have known?

A: You don't think that they take everything the party worms [literal translation referring to the people in the KMT] say, do you?

C: Someone must have informed on me otherwise they would not have known.

A: Yes, but do you think it is a pleasant thing to be an informer?

C: They asked me if I had been a member and a District Manager and many other questions. I replied that it was not so.

A: (interrupting) There is nothing wrong, just don't be duped by others.

C: Suppose they summon me for questioning?

A: Let them question you, so what? What does it matter whether or not you are a member?

C: It doesn't matter if I am not a member. I only applied for my license there because I don't know how to go about it myself. I have always applied for my license there.

A: Yes.

C: They asked me if I read the *China Daily News* and I replied that I did not.

A: It doesn't matter whether you read it or not. The paper reports all laundry affairs. Other newspapers report also the same thing.

C: They had a clipping showing the five-star flag displayed by the office on Canal Street. They had cut it out and kept it in their wallets.

A: So let them keep it. Let those "bastards" go to "hell."

C: O.K. That's all.

A: Don't be afraid.

FBI file 100-365097-88, enclosure, pp. 2–5. The English translation is original.

103. Interview with Mr. C., Chinatown, New York, February 28, 1988.

104. Interview with Mr. C., Chinatown, New York, May 28, 1988.

105. Ibid.; FBI file 100-365097-151, appendix, p. 17.

106. "Lu Mei guiqiao, qian Meizhou Huaqiao Ribao she yewuzhuren Zhang Manli xiansheng fangwen lu" [Record of an interview of a Chinese returned from America: Mr. Zhang Manli, former business manager of the *China Daily News*], in *Huaqiao shi lunwen ji* [Essays on overseas Chinese history] (Guangzhou: Ji'nan Daxue Huaqiao Yanjiusuo), vol. 2, 1981, pp. 331–32.

107. Chen Ke, "Fangwen lu Mei Huaqiao Chen Ke xiansheng" [An interview with Mr. Chen Ke, a Chinese returned from America], in *Huaqiao shi lunwen ji* [Essays on overseas Chinese history] (Guangzhou: Ji'nan Daxue Huaqiao Yanjiusuo), vol. 2, 1981, pp. 341–49.

108. See Wolfgang Barke, *Who's Who in the People's Republic of China*, 2d ed. (Munchen, N.Y.: K. G. Saur, 1987), p. 437.

109. Interview with Mr. C., Chinatown, New York, February 28, 1988.

110. *CDN*, October 27, 1949, p. 1.

111. Ibid., February 10, 1951, p. 7.

112. Ibid., June 11, 1951, p. 3; and my field notes, October 1979, Taishan, Guangdong.

113. Fang Fu'er and Zhang Manli, "Jianku fendou de Meizhou Huaqiao Ribao" [The *China Daily News*'s struggle against adversity and difficulties], in *Guangzhou wenshi ziliao (xuanji)* [Selections of cultural historical materials, Guangzhou] (Guangzhou: Guangdong Renmin Chubanshe), no. 17, December 1979, pp. 176–80.

114. *CDN*, October 31, 1953, p. 5. This letter caught the attention of Hoover, who ordered the FBI's New York office to find more information on how many CHLA members returned to China. FBI file 100-365097-47.

115. *Kang Mei yuan Cao kuaibao* [Resist America Aid Korea Express], Taishan, Guangdong, May 6, 1951.

116. Situ Meitang, *Wo tonghen Meidi: Qiao Mei qishi nian shenghuo huiyilu*

[I bitterly hate imperialist America: Reminiscences of a seventy-year sojourn in the United States], recorded by Situ Binghe (Beijing: Guangmin Ribao Zongguan-lichu, 1951).

117. Interview with Mr. C., Chinatown, New York, February 28, 1988.

118. Hei Yan, ed., *Taishan qiaoxiang xuelei shi* [A blood-and-tear history of the Taishan overseas Chinese community], 2 vols. (Hong Kong [?]: n.p., n.d. [ca. 1952]).

119. My field notes, October 1979, Taishan, Guangdong.

120. See Situ Binghe, "Sanshiwu nian qian yiduan shangxin shi" [A heart-broken episode of thirty-five years ago], *CDN*, November 7–10, 1986, p. 31.

121. *CDN*, February 28, 1951; March 2, 1951, both p. 2.

122. Ibid., March 24–April 30, 1952, all p. 6.

123. Situ Binghe, "Sanshiwu nian"; *CDN*, 1951–54, especially November 22, 23, 1951, p. 6. This mentality was shared by many of that generation. Many local CCP officials in Taishan were children of overseas Chinese themselves (see *CDN*, May 17, 1950, p. 2), and they were not necessarily less radical than the northern officials. They carried out the local land reform radically either because they were under tremendous pressure or, more likely, because they believed that such drastic social measures were absolutely necessary, and thus they put the national goal above any family or personal interests. Yue Daiyun with Carolyn Wakeman, *To the Storm: The Odyssey of a Revolutionary Woman* (Berkeley and Los Angeles: University of California Press, 1985), and Yuan-tsung Chen, *The Dragon's Village: An Autobiographical Novel of Revolutionary China* (New York: Penguin, 1986), also shed light on this mentality.

124. *CDN*, November 22, 1951, p. 6.

125. Ibid., August 8, 1952, p. 2.

126. Ibid., November 28, 1951, p. 6.

Conclusion

1. Interview with Mr. C., Chinatown, New York, May 15, 1988.

2. Ibid.

3. See Peter Kwong, *Chinatown, New York: Labor and Politics, 1930–1950* (New York: Monthly Review Press, 1979), pp. 143–47.

4. Sucheng Chan, *This Bittersweet Soil: The Chinese in California Agriculture, 1860–1910* (Berkeley and Los Angeles: University of California Press, 1986); Jack Chen, *The Chinese of America* (San Francisco: Harper & Row, 1980).

5. Stuart C. Miller, *The Unwelcome Immigrant: The American Image of the Chinese, 1785–1882* (Berkeley and Los Angeles: University of California Press, 1969); Alexander Saxton, *The Indispensable Enemy: Labor and the Anti-Chinese Movement in California* (Berkeley and Los Angeles: University of Cali-

fornia Press, 1971); Paul Siu, *The Chinese Laundryman: A Study of Social Isolation* (New York: New York University Press, 1987).

6. John Higham, *Send These to Me: Jews and Other Immigrants in Urban America* (New York: Atheneum, 1975), pp. 237, 241–42.

7. Oscar Handlin, *The Uprooted: The Epic Story of the Great Migration that Made the American People*, 2d ed., enlarged (Boston: Little, Brown, 1973).

8. See Alexander McLeod, *Pigtails and Gold Dust* (Caldwell, Idaho: Caxton Press, 1947), pp. 220–21; Liu Pei Chi, *Meiguo Huaqiao shi* [A history of the Chinese in the United States of America], pp. 575–86.

9. This letter was written by Saum Song Bo, published in the October 1885 issue of *American Missionary*, reprinted in *East/West Chinese American Journal*, San Francisco, June 26, 1986.

10. *China Daily News* (*CDN*), September 18, 1955.

11. Howard N. Rabinowitz, "Race, Ethnicity, and Cultural Pluralism in American History," in *Ordinary People and Everyday Life: Perspectives on the New Social History*, ed. James B. Gardner and George Rollie Adams (Nashville, Tenn.: American Association for State and Local History, 1983), pp. 23–49.

12. Ibid., p. 39.

13. For information about other Chinese organizations similar to the CHLA, see Him Mark Lai, "A Historical Survey of the Chinese Left in America," in *Counterpoint: Perspectives on Asian America*, ed. Emma Gee (Los Angeles: University of California, Asian American Studies Center, 1976), pp. 63–80.

14. For a different type of overseas Chinese nationalism that revived Confucianism to strengthen Chinese identity in the Dutch East Indies, see Lea E. Williams, *Overseas Chinese Nationalism: The Genesis of the Pan-Chinese Movement in Indonesia, 1900–1916* (Glencoe, Ill.: Free Press, 1960).

15. See, for example, Peter Kivisto, "Finnish Americans and the Homeland, 1918–1958," *Journal of American Ethnic History* 7(1) (Fall 1987): 7–28.

16. See the articles in the CHLA column in *CDN* in the 1940s. CHLA members were fond of quoting an obscure description of the alliance as the "largest democratic organization in New York's Chinese community" from "a major English-language newspaper." I failed to trace this quotation in New York's English-language newspapers of the 1930s.

17. *CDN*, December 22, 1949, p. 2.

18. Ibid.

19. *Zhong Bao* [*Centre Daily News*] (New York), July 11, 1989, p. 2.

Bibliography

Note on the Primary Sources in the Chinese Language

Many of the Chinese-language primary sources used in this book had not previously been tapped by researchers. CHLA documents, copies of *Huaqiao qingnian*, and newspaper clippings of "Yilian Zhengkan" (a special CHLA column that appeared biweekly in the *China Daily News*, 1942–1949) are available at the CHLA headquarters, 149 Canal Street, New York City. A complete set of the *China Daily News*, 1940–1989, is available in the office of *Qiao Bao* [the *China Express*], 15 Mercer Street, New York City. The pamphlets published by the Committee to Support the *China Daily News* in the early 1950s are available at the Asian American Studies Library, University of California, Berkeley. The microfilm of *Xianfeng Bao* [*The Chinese Vanguard*] (1930–1937) is available in the New York Chinatown History Museum (which was the New York Chinatown History Project before 1990), 70 Mulberry Street, New York City. The museum also has 1940s copies of *Meizhou Ribao* [*The Chinese Journal*], and the two-volume *Huaqiao shi lunwen ji* [Essays on overseas Chinese history] (Guangzhou: Ji'nan Daxue Huaqiao Yanjiusuo), abbreviated here as HSLJ, which contains interviews of former CHLA members. *Guangzhou wenshi ziliao (xuanji)* [Selections of cultural and historical materials, Guangzhou], (Guangzhou: Guangdong Renmin Chubanshe), abbreviated here as GZWSZL, which contains reminiscences of former CHLA members, can be found at Columbia University's C. V. Starr East Asian Library.

I. Chinese

A. Primary sources

1. CHLA Documents/Pamphlets/Memoirs

The Constitution of the Chinese Hand Laundry Alliance of New York. New York: CHLA, 1936.

Huaqiao qingnian [Overseas Chinese youth]. New York: Chinese Youth Club, special issue, no. 3 (1940).

Yilian wuzhounian tekan [The CHLA fifth anniversary special bulletin]. New York: CHLA, 1938.

Chen, Houfu. "Niuyue Xiyiguan Lianhehui de zuzhi he huodong" [The organization of the Chinese Hand Laundry Alliance of New York and its activities]. In GZWSZL, no. 12, 1962, pp. 38–49.

Chen, Ke. "Fangwen lu Mei Huaqiao Chen Ke xiansheng" [An interview with Mr. Chen Ke, a Chinese returned from America]. In HSLJ, vol. 2, 1981, pp. 340–54.

————. "Sanci fu Mei he qiao Mei er'shiwu nian de qinli" [My three journeys to the U.S. and personal experiences of twenty-five years in the U.S.]. In GZWSZL, no. 12, 1962, pp. 78–95.

Fang, Fu'er. "Niuyue Yilianhui huanying Dong Biwu tongzhi de jingguo" [The welcoming of Comrade Dong Biwu (on his visit) to the Chinese Hand Laundry Alliance of New York]. In GZWSZL, no. 17, 1979, pp. 156–59.

Fang, Fu'er, and Zhang, Manli. "Jianku fendou de Meizhou Huaqiao Ribao" [The *China Daily News*'s struggle against adversity and difficulties]. In GZWSZL, no. 17, 1979, pp. 176–80.

————. "Niuyue Huaqiao xiyiguan de bianqian" [Changes of the Chinese hand laundries in New York City]. In GZWSZL, no. 23, 1981, pp. 186–203.

Huang, Shun. "Wo zai Meiguo congshi xiyiye de jingguo" [My experience working in the laundry business in the U.S.]. In HSLJ, vol. 2, 1981, pp. 315–22.

Lei, Zhuofeng. "1933-nian Niuyue Huaren Xiyiguan Lianhehui chengli qianhou" [Before and after the establishment of the Chinese Hand Laundry Alliance of New York in 1933]. In HSLJ, vol. 2, 1981, pp. 333–39.

————. "Niuyue Huaqiao Xiyiguan Lianhehui chengli jingguo" [The founding of the Chinese Hand Laundry Alliance of New York]. In GZWSZL, no. 22 (4), 1984, pp. 216–29.

Li, Xingchuan. "Niuyue Tangrenjie ji Huashengdun Huaqiao Kangri Jiuguo Hui" [New York Chinatown and the Resist Japan National Salvation Association of Washington, D.C.]. In GZWSZL, no. 13, 1962, pp. 78–92.

Liang, Qichao. *Xindalu youji* [Diary of traveling in the New World]. Japan: Xinminchongbao, 1904; rpt. Changsha: Hunan Renmin Chubanshe, 1981.

"Lu Mei guiqiao, qian Meizhou Huaqiao Ribao she yewuzhuren Zhang Manli xiansheng fangwen lu" [Record of an interview of a Chinese returned from America: Mr. Zhang Manli, former business manager of the *China Daily News* of New York]. In HSLJ, vol. 2, 1981, pp. 322–32.

Situ, Binghe. "Sanshiwu nian qian yiduan Shangxin shi" [A heartbroken episode of thirty-five years ago], *China Daily News*, November 7–10, 1986, p. 31.

Situ, Meitang. *Wo tonghen Meidi: Qiao Mei qishi nian shenghuo huiyilu* [I bitterly hate imperialist America: Reminiscences of a seventy-year sojourn in the U.S.], recorded by Situ Binghe. Beijing: Guangmin Ribao Zongguanlichu, 1951.

_____. *Zuguo yu Huaqiao* [The motherland and overseas Chinese], 2 vols. Hong Kong: Wenhui Bao Chubanshe, 1956.

2. *Chinese-Language Newspapers/Periodicals/Pamphlets*

Meizhou Huaqiao Ribao [*China Daily News*], New York City, 1940–1989
Kang Mei yuan Cao Kuaibao [*Resist America Aid Korea Express*], Taishan, Guangdong, 1951
Jiuguo Shibao [*The China Salvation Times*], New York City, 1938–39
Meizhou Ribao [*The Chinese Journal*], New York City, 1945–57
Minqi Ribao [*The Chinese Nationalist Daily*], New York City, 1929–48
Xianfeng Bao [*The Chinese Vanguard*], New York City, 1930–37

B. Secondary sources

1. *Bibliographies/Handbooks/Directories*

Chen, Ruzhou. *Meiguo Huaqiao nianjian* [Handbook of Chinese in America]. New York: Zhongguo Guomin Waijiao Xuehui zhu Mei banshichu, 1946.
Chinese Commercial Directory of United States, Eastern Section, 1925–26. New York: Chinese General Information Bureau, 1925.
Lai, Him Mark. *A History Reclaimed: An Annotated Bibliography of Chinese-Language Materials on the Chinese of America.* Los Angeles: University of California, Asian American Studies Center, 1986.
Huaqiao shi lunwen ziliao suoyin [A reference guide to the overseas Chinese history]. Guangzhou: Zhongshan University, 1981.
Zheng, Min, et al., eds. *Huaqiao Huaren shi shukan mulu* [List of publications of history of overseas Chinese]. Beijing: Zhongguo Zhanwang Chubanshe, 1981.
Huaqiao wenti youguan ziliao suoyin [Bibliography of materials on overseas Chinese issues]. Taipei: Qiaowu Weiyuanhui Qiaowu Yanjiushi, 1965.

2. *Articles/Books/Monographs*

Cai, Tingkai. *Cai Tingkai zizhuan* [Autobiography of Cai Tingkai]. Harbin, Helongjiang: Helongjiang Renmin Chubanshe, 1982.
Chu, Y. K. *Meiguo Huaqiao gaishi* [History of the Chinese people in America]. New York: China Times, 1975.
Dou, Jiliang. *Tongxiang zhuzhi zhi yanjiu* [A study of the district association]. Shanghai: n.p., 1943.
Hei, Yan, ed. *Taishan qiaoxiang xuelei shi* [A blood-and-tear history of the Taishan overseas Chinese community]. 2 vols. Hong Kong: n.p., n.d. [ca. 1952].
Ho, Ping-ti. *Zhongguo Huiguan shilun* [A historical survey of landsmannschaften in China]. Taipei: Xuesheng Shuju, 1966.
Huang, Jingwan. *Huaqiao dui zuguo de gongxian* [Overseas Chinese contributions to the motherland]. Shanghai: Tangli Chubanshe, 1940.

Jiang furen you Mei jiniance [Madame Chiang Kai-shek's trip through the United States and Canada]. San Francisco: Chinese Nationalist Daily, 1944.

Lai, Him Mark. *Meiguo Huaren jianshi* [A brief history of the Chinese in the United States]. In *Shi Dai Bao* [*San Francisco Journal*, Chinese edition], 1981–85.

Liu, Danian. *Meiguo qinhua jianshi* [A brief history of American aggression against China]. Beijing: Xinhua Book Company, 1951.

Liu, Pei Chi. *Meiguo Huaqiao shi* [A history of the Chinese in the United States of America, 1848–1911]. Taipei: Limin Wenhua Shiye Gongsi, 1976.

———. *Meiguo Huaqiao shi, xubian* [A history of the Chinese in the United States of America, II]. Taipei: Limin Wenhua Shiye Gongsi, 1981.

———. "Meiguo Huaqiao hangkong jiuguo de shiji" [The American Chinese participation in national salvation through aviation]. *Guangdong wenxian jikan* (Taipei) 10:2, 3 (1980).

———. "Zhu Mei Taishan Ningyang zonghuiguan shilue" [A brief sketch of the Ningyang Benevolent Association of America]. *Guangdong wenxian jikan*, (Taipei) 10:4 (1980).

Liu, Xiaoyun. "Chongjian Taishan zhi jihua" [The plan to rebuild Taishan]. *Xinning Zazhi* [Xinning Magazine] (Taishan, Guangdong) 12 (1912).

Liu, Zhongxun. *Huaqiao aiguo zidong juanxian* [Overseas Chinese patriotic and voluntary donations to China]. Taiwan: Qiaowu Weiyuanhui Qiaowu Yanjiushi, 1969.

Niuyue quanti huaqiao kangri jiuguo chouxiang zonghui zhengxinlu [Record of contributions and disbursements of the General Relief Fund Committee of the Chinese Consolidated Benevolent Association of New York]. New York: General Relief Fund Committee of the Chinese Consolidated Benevolent Association, 1939.

Niuyue yixieshe tekan [Special bulletin of the New York Chinese Laundry Social Athletic Club]. New York: New York Chinese Laundry Social Athletic Club, Inc., 1972.

Ow, Yuk, Him Mark Lai, and Philip Choy. *Lu Mei San-i Tsung Hui Kuan Chien Shih* [A history of the Sam Yup Benevolent Association in the U.S., 1850–1974]. San Francisco: Sam Yup Benevolent Association, 1975.

Qinghua daxue shigao [A history of Qinghua University]. Beijing: Zhonghua Shuju, 1981.

Qinghua xiaoshi congshu [A collection on history of Qinghua School]. Beijing: Qinghua University Press, 1983.

Shen, Yiyao (I-yao). *Haiwai pai hua bainian shi* [A century of Chinese exclusion abroad]. Hong Kong: Wanyou tushu gongsi, 1970.

Taishan Huaqiao Zazhi [The Toyshan Wah Kiu Magazine]. A semimonthly magazine published in Taishan, Guangdong, 1932–43.

Taishan Xianzhi [The Taishan Gazetteer]. Comp. Taishan Archives, Taishan, Guangdong, 1985.

Yang, Gang, *Meiguo zhaji* [Notes on America]. Shanghai: Shijie Zhishishe, 1951; rpt. Changsha: Hunan Renmin Chubanshe, 1983.

II. *English*

A. Newspapers

The New York Times, 1930–55
World Telegram, 1948–49
Newark Sunday Call, October 9, 1932
Christian Science Monitor, May 1943

B. Documents/Pamphlets/Directories

Barke, Wolfgang. *Who's Who in the People's Republic of China*. 2d ed. Munchen, N.Y.: K. G. Saur, 1987.

Chen, Henin. *Official Chinatown Guide Book*. New York: Henin & Company, 1939.

Committee to Support the *China Daily News*. *The China Daily News Case*. New York: n.d. [ca. 1952].

_____. *The Facts behind the China Daily News Case*. New York: n.d. [ca. 1952].

FBI file, The Chinese Hand Laundry Alliance case, #100-365097.

U.S. Congress. *Biographical Directory of the American Congress, 1774–1971*. Washington, D.C.: U.S. Government Printing Office, 1971.

Van Norden, Warner. *Who's Who of the Chinese in New York*. New York: n.p., 1918.

C. Articles/Books/Monographs

Barth, Gunther. *Bitter Strength: A History of the Chinese in the United States, 1850–1870*. Cambridge, Mass.: Harvard University Press, 1971.

Beck, Louis. *New York's Chinatown: An Historical Presentation of Its People and Places*. New York: Bohemia Publishers, 1898.

Borg, Dorothy. *The United States and the Far Eastern Crisis*. Cambridge, Mass.: Harvard University Press, 1964.

Brush, Ted. "Chinese Labor in North Jersey." *North Jersey Highlander* (North Jersey Highlander Historical Society) (Spring 1973): 13–21.

Chan, Sucheng. *Asian Americans: An Interpretive History*. Boston: Twayne Publishers, 1991.

_____. *This Bittersweet Soil: The Chinese in California Agriculture, 1860–1910*. Berkeley and Los Angeles: University of California Press, 1986.

_____, ed. *Entry Denied: Exclusion and the Chinese Community in America, 1882–1943*. Philadelphia: Temple University Press, 1991.

Chen, Jack. *The Chinese of America*. San Francisco: Harper & Row, 1980.

Chen, Julia I. Hsuan. "The Chinese Community in New York: A Study in Their Cultural Adjustment, 1920–1940." Ph.D. dissertation, American University, 1941.

Chinn, Thomas W., H. Mark Lai, and Philip P. Choy, eds. *A History of the Chinese in California*. San Francisco: Chinese Historical Society of America, 1971.

Clark, Helen F. "The Chinese of New York." *The Century* (New York) 53 (November 1896–April 1897): 104–15.

Daniels, Roger. *The Politics of Prejudice: The Anti-Japanese Movement in California and the Struggle for Japanese Exclusion*. New York: Atheneum, 1977.

DeArmond, Fred. *The Laundry Industry*. New York: Harper & Brothers, 1950.

Dobie, Charles C. *San Francisco's Chinatown*. New York: Appleton-Century, 1936.

Fairbank, John K. *The United States and China*. 4th ed. Cambridge, Mass.: Harvard University Press, 1983.

Finkle, Lee. *Forum for Protest: The Black Press during World War II*. Cranbury, N.J.: Associated University Presses, 1975.

Fitzgerald, Stephen. *China and the Overseas Chinese: A Study of Peking's Changing Policy, 1949–1970*. London: Cambridge University Press, 1972.

Gardner, James B., and Adams, George Rollie, eds. *Ordinary People and Everyday Life: Perspectives on the New Social History*. Nashville, Tenn.: American Association for State and Local History, 1983.

Heyer, Virginia. "Pattern of Social Organization in New York City's Chinatown." Ph.D. dissertation, Columbia University, 1953.

Handlin, Oscar. *The Uprooted: The Epic Story of the Great Migration that Made the American People*. 2d ed., enlarged. Boston: Little, Brown, 1973.

Higham, John. *Send These to Me: Jews and Other Immigrants in Urban America*. New York: Atheneum, 1975.

Hoy, William. *The Chinese Six Companies*. San Francisco: Chinese Consolidated Benevolent Association, 1942.

Kivisto, Peter. "Finnish Americans and the Homeland, 1918–1958." *Journal of American Ethnic History* 7 (1) (Fall 1987): 7–28.

Kung, Shien Woo. *Chinese in American Life: Some Aspects of Their History, Status, Problems, and Contributions*. Seattle: University of Washington Press, 1962.

Koen, Ross Y. *The China Lobby in American Politics*. New York: Harper & Row, 1974.

Kuo, Chia-ling. *Social and Political Change in New York's Chinatown: The Role of Voluntary Associations*. New York: Praeger, 1977.

Kwong, Peter. *Chinatown, New York: Labor and Politics, 1930–1950*. New York: Monthly Review Press, 1979.

———. *The New Chinatown*. New York: Hill & Wang, 1987.

Lai, Him Mark. "China Politics and the U.S. Chinese Communities." In *Counter-*

point: Perspectives on Asian America, ed. Emma Gee. Los Angeles: University of California, Asian American Studies Center, 1976, pp. 152–59.

_____. "Chinese." In *Harvard Encyclopedia of American Ethnic Groups*, ed. Stephan Thernstrom. Cambridge, Mass.: Belknap Press, 1980.

_____. "Historical Development of the Chinese Consolidated Benevolent Association/Huiguan System." In *Chinese America: History and Perspectives 1987*. San Francisco: Chinese Historical Society of America, 1987, pp. 13–51.

_____. "A Historical Survey of the Chinese Left in America." In *Counterpoint: Perspectives on Asian America*, ed. Emma Gee. Los Angeles: University of California, Asian American Studies Center, 1976, pp. 63–80.

Lee, Douglas W. "The Overseas Chinese Affairs Commission and the Politics of Patriotism in Chinese America in the Nanking Era, 1928–1945." *Annals of the Chinese Historical Society of the Pacific Northwest* (Bellingham, Wash.) (1984): 198–231.

Lee, Rose Hum. *The Chinese in the United States of America*. Hong Kong: Hong Kong University Press, 1960.

Leong, Gor Yun. *Chinatown Inside Out*. New York: Barrows Mussey, 1936.

Lyman, Stanford M. *The Asian in North America*. Santa Barbara, Calif.: ABC-Clio, 1977.

_____. *Chinese Americans*. New York: Random House, 1974.

Mark, Diane Mei Lin, and Chih, Ginger. *A Place Called Chinese America*. Dubuque, Iowa: Kendall/Hull, 1982.

McCunn, Ruthanne Lum. *Chinese American Portraits: Personal Histories, 1828–1988*. San Francisco: Chronicle Books, 1988.

McLeod, Alexander, *Pigtails and Gold Dust*. Caldwell, Idaho: Caxton Press, 1947.

Miller, Stuart C. *The Unwelcome Immigrant: The American Image of the Chinese, 1785–1882*. Berkeley and Los Angeles: University of California Press, 1969.

Mirak, Robert. *Torn between Two Lands: Armenians in America, 1890 to World War I*. Cambridge, Mass.: Harvard University Press, 1983.

Ng, Franklin. "The Sojourner, Return Migration, and Immigration History." In *Chinese America: History and Perspectives 1987*. San Francisco: Chinese Historical Society of America, 1987, pp. 53–71.

Riggs, Fred W. *Pressures on Congress: A Study of the Repeal of Chinese Exclusion*. New York: Columbia University, King's Crown Press, 1950.

Ringer, Benjamin B. *"We the People" and Others: Duality and America's Treatment of Its Racial Minorities*. New York: Tavistock Publications, 1983.

Saxton, Alexander. *The Indispensable Enemy: Labor and the Anti-Chinese Movement in California*. Berkeley and Los Angeles: University of California Press, 1971.

Schaller, Michael. *The United States and China in the Twentieth Century*. New York: Oxford University Press, 1979.

————. *The U.S. Crusade in China, 1938–1945*. New York: Columbia University Press, 1979.

Schwartz, Shepard. "Mate-Selection among New York City's Chinese Males, 1931–38." *American Journal of Sociology* 56 (May 1951): 562–68.

Siu, Paul C. P. *The Chinese Laundryman: A Study of Social Isolation*. New York: New York University Press, 1987.

————. "The Sojourner." *American Journal of Sociology* 58 (July 1952): 34–44.

Snow, Edgar. *The Battle for Asia*. New York: Random House, 1941.

Spence, Jonathan D. *The Search for Modern China*. New York: Norton, 1990.

Steele, A. T. *The American People and China*. New York: McGraw-Hill, 1966.

Sung, Betty Lee. *Mountain of Gold: The Story of the Chinese in America*. New York: Macmillan, 1967.

Takaki, Ronald. *Strangers from a Different Shore: A History of Asian Americans*. Boston: Little, Brown, 1989.

Tchen, John K. W. "New York Chinese: The Nineteenth-Century Pre-Chinatown Settlement." in *Chinese America: History and Perspectives 1990*. San Francisco: Chinese Historical Society of America and Asian American Studies, San Francisco State University, 1990, pp. 157–92.

Traina, Richard P. *American Diplomacy and the Spanish Civil War*. Westport, Conn.: Greenwood Press, 1980.

Tsai, Shih-shan Henry. *China and the Overseas Chinese in the United States, 1868–1911*. Fayetteville: University of Arkansas Press, 1983.

————. *The Chinese Experience in America*. Bloomington: Indiana University Press, 1986.

Tuchman, Barbara. *Stilwell and the American Experience in China, 1911–1945*. New York: Macmillan, 1972.

Tucker, Nancy B. *Patterns in the Dust: Chinese-American Relations and the Recognition Controversy, 1949–1950*. New York: Columbia University Press, 1983.

Tung, William. *Chinese in America, 1820–1973: A Chronology and the Fact Book*. Dobbs Ferry, N.Y.: Oceana Publications, 1974.

Wei Min She Labor Committee. *Chinese Working People in America: A Pictorial History*. San Francisco: United Front Press, 1974.

Williams, Lea E. *Overseas Chinese Nationalism: The Genesis of the Pan-Chinese Movement in Indonesia, 1900–1916*. Glencoe, Ill.: Free Press, 1960.

Wong, Bernard P. *Chinatown: Economic Adaptation and Ethnic Identity of the Chinese*. New York: Holt, Rinehart & Winston, 1982.

————. *Patronage, Brokerage, Entrepreneurship and the Chinese Community of New York*. New York: AMS Press, 1988.

Wong, Chin Foo. "The Chinese in New York." *Cosmopolitan* 5 (March–October 1888): 297–311.

————. "The Chinese in the United States." *The Chautauquan* 9 (October 1888–July 1889): 215–17.

Wu, Cheng-Tsu. *"Chink!" A Documentary History of Anti-Chinese Prejudice in America*. New York: World Publishing Co., 1972.

Yu, Renqiu. "Chinese American Contributions to the Educational Development of Toisan 1910–1940." *Amerasia Journal* 10 (1) (1983): 49–72.

Index